Advance Praise for

The Principles of Product Development Flow

"If you are implementing lean or iterative product development, this will be the most often referenced volume on your bookshelf. (Mine has quickly become more dog-eared than *Managing the Design Factory*.) Unlike some other popular books, this work doesn't stop with the high-level theory; it provides explicit, real-life examples showing how to achieve it. It has guided my efforts to instill a lean philosophy in our NPD group, and the methods have already provided significant improvements to our decision-making and ultimately our throughput."

—Tim Spang, Executive Director, Radiology NPD, MEDRAD, Inc.

"At Accuer, our business depends on helping successful product developers become even better. We need to provide real results, quickly, in lots of different areas. Because we need to stay at the leading edge, I've studied and read almost every book on lean product development; this one is better than the rest of them combined! Why? It's a unique combination of practical methods and clear explanations of the science that makes them work. If you've enjoyed Don's previous books as much as I have, you're guaranteed to like this one."

—David Paulson, President, Accuer, Inc.

"The principles described in this book are relevant to every product developer and, perhaps most importantly, to every product development executive. Rather than giving dogmatic rules, Reinertsen provides insightful and pragmatic principles that can be tailored to the economic factors unique to each enterprise. These principles will improve your everyday decision-making. This book is a worthy follow-on to *Managing the Design Factory* and belongs on every product manager's bookshelf."

—Glenn Paulley, Director of Engineering, Sybase iAnywhere

"Biotechnology process development is a relatively new field, and key issues such as variability, biological system complexity, balance between process robustness and time-to-market still remain challenging. Don's new book offers insightful new concepts that can be of paramount practical importance to the biotechnology professional."

> **—Konstantin Konstantinov, VP Technology Development,**
> **Genzyme Corp.**

"This book provides a banquet table of techniques for advancing the effectiveness and efficiency of product development management. We've already used some of the small batch methods, with strong results, in software development. Now we are starting to expand them into firmware and hardware development. Don's book makes it easy to sort out and think through the specific steps needed to improve product development economics."

> **—Paul C Aspinwall, IPD Process Architect,**
> **IBM**

"The tools in this book go further than anything I've seen in my 15 years of trying to improve product development. They will change the way you think about the problem. Instead of spending time and energy trying to remove variability, you will learn to use it to your advantage. You'll get both a deep theoretical understanding and the practical tools needed to make real changes."

> **—Mikael Lundgren,**
> **Citerus AB**

"Reinertsen continues to stay ahead of the game on how lean applies in new product and process development. The book is highly readable and easily searchable, being organized into clear "bite-sized chunks" which each cover an important concept in a way that readers can grasp and apply to their project management challenges."

> **—Bernard North, Chief Engineer,**
> **Kennametal Inc.**

The Principles of Product Development Flow

Second Generation
Lean Product Development

Donald G. Reinertsen

CELERITAS PUBLISHING
Redondo Beach, California

Celeritas Publishing
Redondo Beach, CA 90277
www.CeleritasPublishing.com

For information on discounts for bulk purchases, contact Celeritas Publishing at:

SpecialSales@CeleritasPublishing.com

Printed in the United States of America

10   9   8   7   6   5   4   3   2   1

Library of Congress Control Number: 2008911906

Publisher's Cataloging-in-Publication Data

Reinertsen, Donald G., 1950–
     The principles of product development flow: second generation
     lean product development/
     Donald G. Reinertsen

          p. cm.
Includes bibliographical references and index.
ISBN-13: 978-1-935401-00-1
ISBN-10: 1-935401-00-9
1. New products.   2. Product management.   I. Title.

Dedicated to my mother and my father

MARY VIKTORIN REINERTSEN

LEIF CHRISTIAN REINERTSEN

Contents

1

The Principles of Flow

It ain't what you don't know that gets you into trouble.
It's what you know for sure that just ain't so.
—Mark Twain

Why write this book? After about 30 years of advising product development organizations, I've been lucky enough to work with many smart and experienced developers. I've had a chance to see what they do, and what outcomes they get. At the same time, I've been exposed to all the standard advice about how product development should be managed. Curiously, what actually works is surprisingly different from the standard advice. Why?

I believe that the dominant paradigm for managing product development is fundamentally wrong. Not just a little wrong, but wrong to its very core. It is as wrong as we were in manufacturing, before the Japanese unlocked the secret of lean manufacturing. I believe that a new paradigm is emerging, one that challenges the current orthodoxy of product development. I want to help accelerate the adoption of this new approach. I believe I can do this by helping people understand it. That is the purpose of this book.

The approach I will describe has always been present in some form in development processes. After all, product developers repeat behaviors that work, even if, in theory, they are not supposed to work. But discovering and repeating successful behaviors is not enough to create large-scale use. Product developers need to extract the underlying mechanisms of action that make these methods work. It is only by generalizing these principles that we can expand their application from a handful of isolated successes into a general approach that transforms the entire development process.

Let's begin with an illustration. Officially, many product developers have phase-gate processes. Work is divided into mutually exclusive phases separated by gates. One phase must be complete before the next one can begin. For example, such processes typically require that all product requirements be defined before beginning design activities. The team appears to do this, and delivers complete product requirements to management at the gate review. Then, they are given approval to exit the requirement definition phase and to begin the product design phase. On its surface, this procedure appears quite sensible, and it seems to work.

What really happens is quite different. When I survey managers in my product development courses, 95 percent will admit that they begin design before they know all requirements. In fact, the average product developer begins design when 50 percent of requirements are known. They simply do not publicize this to management. Instead, they engage in a time-honored ritual of asking for permission to proceed. There is a tacit "don't ask, don't tell" policy. Managers politely avoid asking if the next phase's activities have already begun, and developers discreetly avoid mentioning that they have already moved on. In practice, sensible behavior prevails, despite the presence of a dysfunctional formal procedure.

The underground overlap of design and specification activities is just one simple example of this alternative paradigm in action. Among other things, this paradigm emphasizes small batch transfers, rapid feedback, and limited work-in-process inventory (WIP). These three specific methods are actually broadly applicable throughout the development process. When we recognize why they work, we can adapt them to dozens of situations.

At its heart, this new paradigm emphasizes achieving flow. It bears many similarities to the methods of lean manufacturing and could be labeled lean product development (LPD). However, the methods of lean manufacturing have been optimized for a domain with very different characteristics than product development.

For example, manufacturing deals with predictable and repetitive tasks, homogeneous delay costs, and homogeneous task durations. As a result, manufacturing sequences work in a simple first-in-first-out (FIFO) order. FIFO prioritization is almost never economically optimal in product development, because product development deals with high variability, nonrepetitive, nonhomogeneous flows. Different projects almost always have different delay costs, and they present different loads on our resources.

As you shall see, these new challenges force us to go far beyond the ideas of lean manufacturing. If we are open to advanced ideas from other domains, we can do this. To distinguish this more advanced approach from the ideas of lean manufacturing, we call it Flow-Based Product Development.

What Is the Problem?

Today's orthodoxy has institutionalized a set of internally consistent but dysfunctional beliefs. This has created a tightly interlocking and self-reinforcing system, a system from which it is very difficult to break free. Even when we change one piece, the other pieces hold us back by blocking the benefits of our change. When our change fails to produce benefits, we revert to our old approaches.

Let's look at how our current beliefs reinforce each other. For example, if we combine the belief that efficiency is good, with a blindness to queues, we will load our development process to high levels of capacity utilization. After all, underutilized capacity appears to be waste. High capacity utilization may cause queues, but these queues have no apparent cost. Thus, these two beliefs combine to drive us to disastrous levels of capacity utilization. This, in turn, leads to large queues and long cycle times.

Let's take another example. If we combine the belief that variability is bad with the failure to correctly quantify economics, we will minimize variability by sacrificing other unquantified economic goals. We will create risk-averse development processes that strive to "do it right the first time." We will blindly embrace concepts like Six Sigma product development.

This risk aversion will drive innovation out of our development process. Eventually, we will wonder why our products have no differentiation and low profitability. Thus, our current belief system incorrectly causes us to choose variability reduction over profitability. Yet, it deludes us into thinking that we are increasing profits.

In this chapter, I want to challenge some of the core beliefs of the current orthodoxy and to highlight what is wrong with them. Of course, this is only a brief introduction to these controversial ideas. The orthodox beliefs are quite well-defended, so we will need to assault them with heavier weapons later in this book. For now, I will just fire a few

Problems with the Current Orthodoxy

1. Failure to Correctly Quantify Economics
2. Blindness to Queues
3. Worship of Efficiency
4. Hostility to Variability
5. Worship of Conformance
6. Institutionalization of Large Batch Sizes
7. Underutilization of Cadence
8. Managing Timelines instead of Queues
9. Absence of WIP Constraints
10. Inflexibility
11. Noneconomic Flow Control
12. Centralized Control

Figure 1-1 Twelve critical problems with the current product development orthodoxy.

tracer rounds so you can see where the targets lie. I only request that you be open to the possibility that the current orthodoxy is deeply dysfunctional. Let's pick twelve key problems with the current approach, as shown in Figure 1-1.

Failure to Correctly Quantify Economics

Perhaps the single most important weakness of the current orthodoxy is its failure to correctly quantify economics. The key word is *correctly*. When done correctly, an economic framework will shine a bright light into all the dark corners of product development. Today, we only light up part of the landscape. Then, we focus on these well-lit details. We are like the drunk under the lamppost looking for his keys where the light is best, instead of where he dropped them.

This criticism may surprise product developers since most are convinced they correctly quantify economics today. Yet, it is exactly this conviction that blocks them from making progress. For example, the only way to comprehend the economic importance of queues is to quantify the cost of delay for product development projects. Yet, today, only 15 percent of product developers know the cost of delay associated with their projects.

Today, developers focus on what we call proxy variables. A proxy variable is a quantified measure that substitutes for the real economic objective: life-cycle profits. For example, developers measure development cycle time and seek to make it shorter. However, when you ask them how much life-cycle profit will decrease due to a week of delay, they don't know.[1] Cycle time is only a proxy variable.

Developers measure the percent value-added time and seek to make it higher. But, if you ask them how much life-cycle profit will improve when they do this, they don't know. Percent value-added time is only a proxy variable. By focusing on proxy variables, product developers delude themselves into thinking they understand their economics. They do not.

The danger in focusing on proxy variables is that proxy variables interact with one another. Raising capacity utilization has the beneficial effect of improving efficiency and the negative effect of increasing cycle time. To understand the net impact, we must combine both effects. To do this, we must express changes in all proxy variables in the same unit of measure. This unit of measure should be life-cycle profit impact, which is the ultimate measure of product development success.

It is only when we understand the mapping between proxy variables and life-cycle profits that we can really see the economic consequences of our choices. I will show you how an economic framework helps us do this in Chapter 2.

Blindness to Queues

Few developers realize that queues are the single most important cause of poor product development performance. Queues cause our development process to have too much design-in-process inventory (DIP). Developers are unaware of DIP, they do not measure it, and they do not manage it. They do not even realize that DIP is a problem. For example, product developers will say that they want to be more innovative and never realize that high levels of DIP undermine this objective. When DIP is high, cycle times are long. When cycle times are long, innovation occurs so late that it becomes imitation.

---

[1] More precisely, companies will give answers to this question, but these answers have such high variance that they simply represent quantified ignorance. On average, at companies that do not calculate cost of delay, people working on the same project will give answers that vary by 50 to 1.

There are two important reasons why product developers are blind to DIP. First, inventory is financially invisible in product development. We do not carry partially completed designs as assets on our balance sheet; we expense R&D costs as they are incurred. If we ask the chief financial officer how much inventory we have in product development, the answer will be, "Zero."

Second, we are blind to product development inventory because it is usually physically invisible. DIP is information, not physical objects. We do not see piles of DIP when we walk through the engineering department. In product development, our inventory is bits on a disk drive, and we have very big disk drives in product development.

But if we are blind to DIP, then we are also blind to the danger in operating with high levels of DIP. As you shall see in Chapter 3, queues lie at the root of a large number of product development problems. They increase variability, risk, and cycle time. They decrease efficiency, quality, and motivation.

To understand the economic cost of queues, product developers must be able to answer two questions. First, how big are our queues? Today, only 2 percent of product developers measure queues. Second, what is the cost of these queues? To answer this second question, we must determine how queue size translates into delay cost, which requires knowing the cost of delay. Today, only 15 percent of product developers know their cost of delay. Since such few companies can answer both questions, it should be no surprise that queues are managed poorly today.

I must stress that the ultimate root cause of this queue blindness lies in the failure to correctly quantify our economics. We can learn to see whatever we consider to be important. Once we quantify the cost of delay, we become aware of the cost of queues. Once we recognize the cost of queues, we are motivated to measure and manage them. Without a cost of delay, queues appear to be free and therefore, unworthy of attention.

Worship of Efficiency

But, what do product developers pay attention to? Today's developers incorrectly try to maximize efficiency. This is a natural consequence of queue blindness and the failure to correctly quantify economics.

Any subprocess within product development can be viewed in economic terms. The total cost of the subprocess is composed of its cost of capacity and the delay cost associated with its cycle time.[2] If we are blind to queues, we won't know the delay cost, and we will only be aware of the cost of capacity. Then, if we seek to minimize total cost, we will only focus on the portion we can see, the efficient use of capacity.

This explains why today's product developers assume that efficiency is desirable, and that inefficiency is an undesirable form of waste. This leads them to load their processes to dangerously high levels of utilization. How high? Executives coming to my product development classes report operating at 98.5 percent utilization in the precourse surveys. What will this do? Chapter 3 will explain why large queues form when processes with variability are operated at high levels of capacity utilization. In reality, the misguided pursuit of efficiency creates enormous costs in the unmeasured, invisible portion of the product development process, its queues.

What is the root cause of this problem? Once again, it is the failure to correctly quantify economics. Although efficiency does have economic impact, it is only another proxy variable. We must make decisions based on overall economics. Since high capacity utilization simultaneously raises efficiency and increases delay cost, we need to look at the combined impact of these two factors. We can only do so if we express both factors in the same unit of measure, life-cycle profits. If we do this, we will always conclude that operating a product development process near full utilization is an economic disaster.

Hostility to Variability

The absence of clear economic thinking also leads to a profound misunderstanding of the role of variability in product development. Today, most product developers assume that variability is bad, and they try to eliminate this variability. This emphasis on variability reduction is deeply flawed for three important reasons.

First, without variability, we cannot innovate. Product development produces the recipes for products, not the products themselves.

---

[2] For introductory purposes, we will omit a third cost which is associated with the performance of the subprocess. Later in this book, we will use a more complete economic framework.

If a design does not change, there can be no value-added. But, when we change a design, we introduce uncertainty and variability in outcomes. We cannot eliminate all variability without eliminating all value-added.

Second, variability is only a proxy variable. We are actually interested in influencing the economic cost of this variability. As you shall see in Chapter 4, this economic cost depends on how variability is transformed by an economic payoff-function. It is critical to pay attention to both the amount of variability and the nature of this payoff-function. When we start viewing variability this way, we usually discover it is much easier to alter the payoff-function than it is to reduce the underlying amount of variability.

Third, with a little help from option pricing theory, we will discover that we can actually design development processes such that increases in variability will *improve*, rather than *worsen*, our economic performance.

Unfortunately, today's product development processes are permeated with methods and behaviors that uncritically accept the idea that variability is bad. Developers build buffers into their schedules to reduce variability. They adopt Six Sigma programs to reduce variability. They seek to create repeatable processes to reduce variability.

My surveys of product developers show that 65 percent of product developers consider it desirable to eliminate *as much variability as possible* in product development. Variability is viewed as the enemy. This view is completely disconnected from any deep understanding of product development economics. Minimizing the economic impact of variability is a profoundly different goal than minimizing variability.

Worship of Conformance

In addition to deeply misunderstanding variability, today's product developers have deep-rooted misconceptions on how to react to this variability. They believe that they should always strive to make actual performance conform to the original plan. They assume that the benefit of correcting a deviation from the plan will always exceed the cost of doing so. This places completely unwarranted trust in the original plan, and it blocks companies from exploiting emergent opportunities. Such behavior makes no economic sense.

We live in an uncertain world. We must recognize that our original plan was based on noisy data, viewed from a long time-horizon. For example, we may have started development believing a feature would take 1 week of effort and it would be valued by 50 percent of our customers. As we progressed through development, we may have discovered that this feature will require 10 weeks of effort and it will only be valued by 5 percent of our customers. This is a factor of 100 change in its cost-to-benefit ratio. This emergent information completely changes the economics of our original choice. In such cases, blindly insisting on conformance to the original plan destroys economic value.

To manage product development effectively, we must recognize that valuable new information is constantly arriving throughout the development cycle. Rather than remaining frozen in time, locked to our original plan, we must learn to make good economic choices using this emerging information.

Conformance to the original plan has become another obstacle blocking our ability to make good economic choices. Once again, we have a case of a proxy variable, conformance, obscuring the real issue, which is making good economic decisions.

Institutionalization of Large Batch Sizes

Our blindness toward queues and our focus on efficiency lead us to institutionalize large batch sizes. Large batches seem attractive because they appear to have scale economies that increase efficiency. Furthermore, large batches appear to reduce variability because they pool many activities together. However, this efficiency gain and variability reduction is only an illusion. As you shall see later, in Chapter 5, there can be strong diseconomies associated with large batches. Furthermore, the modest reduction in variability due to the pooling of variances will be completely overwhelmed by the geometric increase in uncertainty caused by the longer planning horizons associated with large batches.

Today's developers are blind to the issue of batch size. They do not measure batch size or try to reduce it. They fail to recognize both the critical relation between batch size and cycle time, and the critical relation between batch size and feedback speed. My surveys of product developers show that only 3 percent of them are trying to reduce batch sizes in their development processes.

Today's orthodoxy encourages maximum possible batch sizes. For example, the majority of product developers use phase-gate processes, which transfer 100 percent of the work product in one large batch to the next phase. We cannot make batch size any higher than 100 percent.

We will devote Chapter 5 to understanding the surprising benefits of smaller batch sizes and the methods we can use to achieve them. In particular, we will examine how we can enable small batch processes by systematically lowering transaction costs.

It should come as no surprise that since the current orthodoxy ignores the effects of large batch size, it also places no emphasis on lowering transaction costs. In fact, only 3 percent of developers have a formal program to reduce transaction costs.

Underutilization of Cadence

Today's development processes typically deliver information asynchronously in large batches. A flow-based process delivers information on a regular cadence in small batches. In fact, cadence helps lower transaction costs and makes small batches more economically feasible.

Let's look at a simple example. In many companies, manufacturing wants to receive a complete design from engineering. They tell engineering that they don't want to see any engineering drawings until engineering has stopped changing the design. Once all drawings are ready, they are reviewed in one large batch. All 200 drawings may be reviewed on a single day. Companies assume this makes reviewers more efficient because they can see the entire design at once.

But these 200 drawings were not completed in a single day. They may have been completed over a 10-week period. The first 20 drawings to be completed may have waited 9 weeks to be reviewed.

What happened during these 9 weeks? If an engineer makes a bad assumption in one of the first 20 drawings, then that bad assumption will go unchallenged until the final review. Without feedback from a review, this bad assumption can be incorporated into 180 more drawings. By breaking drawing review into small batches, we improve quality, efficiency, and cycle time.

But how do we prevent all these small review meetings from driving up overhead? We conduct these review meetings on a regular time-based cadence. Every Wednesday afternoon at 1:00 PM, we review all the drawings completed in the last week. There is no need for a meeting announcement and no need to coordinate schedules. Meetings that are synchronized to a regular and predictable cadence have very low set-up costs. They contribute very little excess overhead.

In Chapter 6, we will see why cadence and synchronization are surprisingly powerful tools for product development. We will discover how cadence helps to control the progressive accumulation of variability in development processes. Today's orthodoxy constrains the scope of work and drives variability into timing. The new paradigm constrains timing and drives variability into the scope of work. These two approaches are fundamentally different.

Managing Timelines instead of Queues

We have already pointed out that companies do not manage product development queues. What do they manage? Timelines. Today's orthodoxy emphasizes managing timelines, rather than managing process queues. We train our project managers how to create these timelines and how to manage them. In fact, this was the same mistake we made in manufacturing before the arrival of the Toyota Production System (TPS). We created detailed timelines using our manufacturing planning systems. The more detailed we made our plans, the longer our cycle times became.

We favor highly granular planning because we don't understand the statistics of variability. Misunderstanding variability is dangerous in the repetitive world of manufacturing, but is it even more dangerous in product development where variability is much higher.

Most product developers do not understand the statistics of granular schedules. A granular timeline subdivides time intervals into very small buckets. When we do this, the coefficient of variation for each of these buckets becomes very high. This makes variance very high and conformance unlikely. Even worse, if we incentivize conformance, people will insert contingency reserves to prevent their tasks from missing the schedule. The more granular the schedule, the larger the schedule reserves. And these reserves aggregate into even longer timelines. The more we increase planning detail and the harder we try to incentivize performance, the worse our problem becomes.

In contrast, when we emphasize flow, we focus on queues rather than timelines. Queues are a far better control variable than cycle time because, as you shall see, queues are leading indicators of future cycle-time problems. By controlling queue size, we automatically achieve control over timelines.

Our blindness to queues and our misunderstanding of variability combine to hide this opportunity. The current orthodoxy focuses on planning and managing timelines, instead of the more powerful approach of managing queues.

Absence of WIP Constraints

One of the most powerful ways to manage queues is to use WIP constraints. This technique is virtually absent in today's development processes. Only 3 percent of developers use WIP constraints. In contrast, this method is widespread in modern manufacturing. One of the most prominent examples is the kanban system used by Toyota.

In Chapter 7, with the help of some queueing theory, we will examine the power of WIP constraints and their effect on cycle time. WIP constraints are even more important in product development than manufacturing, because product development has higher inherent variability.

If we limit ourselves to the relatively simple WIP constraints used in lean manufacturing, we will underexploit the power of WIP constraints. Instead, we will explore some of the more advanced ideas used in the world of telecommunications.

If we showed the Toyota Production System to an Internet protocol engineer, it is likely that he would remark, "That is a tail-dropping FIFO queue. That is what we started with on the Internet 30 years ago. We are now four generations beyond that method." I mention this to encourage you to look beyond the manufacturing domain for approaches to control flow.

As mentioned earlier, manufacturing has an advanced view on how to achieve flow when four conditions are present: predictable and repetitive tasks, homogeneous delay costs, and homogeneous task durations. In product development, these four conditions are virtually never present.

In Chapter 7, I will expose you to the more advanced ideas that come from other domains. What is critically important is that these other domains do not achieve flow by eliminating variability; they have developed methods that achieve flow in the presence of high variability. As a result, these methods are extremely relevant to product developers.

Inflexibility

In pursuit of efficiency, product developers use specialized resources loaded to high levels of utilization. Our current orthodoxy accepts inflexibility in return for efficiency. But what happens when this inflexibility encounters variability? We get delays. So what do we do? The current orthodoxy suggests that we focus on the variability. We can reduce this variability directly, or we can build buffers and reserves to mask the variability.

I have already explained why variability reduction is not the answer. Later in this book, you will see that buffers and reserves are also a dangerous approach. They pay for variability reduction with cycle time, which is a very expensive parameter to trade for variability reduction.

Flow-based Product Development suggests that our development processes can be both efficient and responsive in the presence of variability. To do this, we must make resources, people, and processes flexible. We can learn some lessons on how to do this from our factories, and even more lessons from telecommunications networks. In our factories, we create flexibility by paying more to workers who can work at more stations on a production line. We value flexibility, and we pay for it. In contrast, most product development organizations exclusively reward specialization.

In telecommunications networks, we use adaptive approaches that enable us to adjust to emerging congestion in less than a second. In product development, we have not yet recognized the tremendous value of flexibility as an explicit strategy for exploiting the economic benefits of variability. Instead, we still try to eliminate or hide the variability.

Noneconomic Flow Control

There are many systems used to control flow in today's development processes, but sadly, none of them is based on economics. Some companies follow the approach of manufacturers, where jobs are handled in a FIFO sequence. This makes sense in manufacturing, because jobs are typically homogeneous. They all place the same time demands on resources, and they have the same cost of delay. These two conditions are virtually never present in product development.

Other companies prioritize on the basis of project profitability measures like return on investment (ROI). On the surface, this appears to be an economic approach, but this is just an illusion. By prioritizing, we choose to service one project before another. In general, it is best to delay the project with a low cost of delay. This suggests that we should not prioritize on the basis of project profitability, but rather on how this profitability is affected by delay. Of course, this can only be done when we know the cost of delay, information that 85 percent of developers do not have.

Still, other companies have adopted more complex methods, like Goldratt's Critical Chain concept. This approach provides buffers to each project and gives priority to the project with the smallest remaining buffer. In classic scheduling theory, this method is called minimum slack time first. It can encourage you to apply resources to a low cost-of-delay job with a depleted buffer in preference to a high cost-of-delay job that is ahead of schedule. This is the opposite of what economics would suggest.

Today, there is no current orthodoxy for flow control, unless we consider ignoring economics a method. Again, we can trace this problem back to lack of economic understanding. A good economic framework resolves many scheduling dilemmas.

Centralized Control

Finally, today's product development orthodoxy tends to use centralized control. We create project management offices. We create centralized information systems. We centralize buffers to take advantage of the efficiency gains of this approach. Our focus on centralization arises because we value efficiency more than response time. We shall see that this is a mistake in Chapter 8, when we examine the role of fast feedback.

Product developers often avoid decentralized control because they are afraid decentralization will lead to chaos. I hope to offer a different view of decentralization. One of the most interesting examples of decentralizing control without losing alignment is the way the military deals with the uncertainty of warfare. We will examine their approach in Chapter 9 and consider how it can be applied in product development.

By this point, I hope I have convinced you to look at the current orthodoxy more critically. It has serious problems, and there are logical ways we can resolve them. The first step, as in any change, is to admit that things must be changed.

Major Themes

1. **Economics**
2. **Queues**
3. **Variability**
4. **Batch Size**
5. **WIP Constraints**
6. **Cadence, Synchronization, and Flow Control**
7. **Fast Feedback**
8. **Decentralized Control**

Figure 1-2 The eight major themes of this book.

A Possible Solution

The major chapters of this book will focus on how we can overcome the limitations of the current orthodoxy. We will explore eight major themes, shown in Figure 1-2. These themes are mutually supportive, and they lie at the core of Flow-based Product Development.

Economics

The first key theme is economically-based decision making. It is the ultimate foundation of this book. Our central premise is that we do product development to make money. This economic goal permits us to use economic thinking and allows us to see many issues with a fresh point of view. It illuminates the grave problems with the current orthodoxy.

The current orthodoxy does not focus on understanding deeper economic relationships. Instead, it is, at best, based on observing correlations between pairs of proxy variables. For example, it observes that late design changes have higher costs than early design changes and prescribes front-loading problem solving. This ignores the fact that late changes can also create enormous economic value. The economic effect of a late change can only be evaluated by considering its complete economic impact.

The current orthodoxy uses observation, a powerful tool, but it ignores the bias inherent in all methods based on observation. When we focus on observable phenomena, we can be biased by the fact that some characteristics are more observable than others. This increased visibility biases our findings.

For example, when we benchmark other companies, certain aspects of the development process are very visible. Observers quickly conclude that these visible characteristics are the root cause of superior performance. It is easy to see that the development team wears red hats. It is hard to see the control rule they use for managing DIP. As a result, we tend to focus on the easily visible characteristics that are often the least important drivers of development process performance.

Let me make a simple analogy. Suppose you want to learn how to design a radio. You find a well-designed radio and are allowed to carefully inspect it. You would see certain components, such as resistors, capacitors, transistors, and integrated circuits. If you duplicated exactly what you saw, you could create a functioning radio, but you would still know virtually nothing about radio design.

The essence of radio design is the logical process by which the components were selected. In fact, what you can observe visually tells you little about the way a radio functions. For this, you must understand the signals flowing through the system. Unfortunately, these signals are completely invisible. You may be quite convinced that you have carefully inspected the radio, but the way it works and why it works will remain a mystery. This is also true in product development. Critical process choices with great influence on economics, such as inventory levels and feedback loop design, are virtually invisible.

Queues

The second major theme is the importance of queues. Even a basic understanding of queueing theory will dramatically change your perspective on product development. Fortunately, queues have been studied by very smart people for almost a century. Unfortunately, product developers have a poor quantitative intuition regarding the behavior of queues. They are also unaware of the many problems caused by queues. We must get a deeper sense of how queues affect development processes and what can be done about them.

Our approach in this book is to give you industrial-strength queueing theory, rather than a more simplified version. This differs from the more popular versions such as Goldratt's Theory of Constraints (TOC) in two important ways. First, we are interested in the intersection of economics and queueing theory. TOC suggests that bottlenecks should not run out of work. A careful economic analysis reveals that this is not true. Second, we will treat queueing as the statistical science that it is, which also leads us to some different conclusions. For example, TOC suggests that we cannot reduce cycle time without increasing the capacity of bottlenecks. Industrial-strength queueing theory reaches a different conclusion.

TOC deserves respect because it has been an extraordinarily useful tool for making people aware of queues. However, the time has come to go a bit deeper. The issue is not queues, it is the economics of queues. Rather than saying queues are universally bad, we must treat them as having a quantifiable cost. This allows us to compare both the benefits and the costs of an intervention to reduce queue size.

Variability

The third major theme is variability. I want to present a radically different perspective on the role of variability and how it can be managed. In this case, we are interested in the intersection of economics and the science of statistics. In particular, we will focus on how variability is transformed into economic consequences by an economic payoff-function. Once you realize the critical role of this payoff-function, you will recognize it can be a powerful tool to improve economic performance.

This section of the book will challenge many of your existing beliefs about variability. It will show you methods for reducing variability and for reducing the cost of variability. Some of these methods, like variability pooling, are based on statistical theory. Other methods, such as variability substitution, are based on economic theory. We need to go far beyond the current belief that variability is always bad and that it should always be reduced.

Batch Size

The fourth key theme is the importance of reducing batch size. By recognizing that queues are the problem, we are led to examine methods for reducing queues. We will discover that reducing batch size is usually the single most cost-effective way to reduce queues. Smaller batches do this by reducing unnecessary variability in flow. Once again, we are interested in the intersection between batch size and economics. In this case, batch sizes have their own economic tradeoffs, which lead to U-curve optimization problems.

Batch size reduction is a powerful technique that works for both predictable and unpredictable flows. In manufacturing, where flows are quite predictable, we strive for one-piece flow, which is minimum theoretical batch size. In packet-switching networks, where flows can be completely unpredictable, we manage highly variable flows by breaking them into small packets. However, such networks virtually never use minimum theoretical batch size because there are technical and economic tradeoffs that make this suboptimal. We can learn a lot from both domains.

WIP Constraints

The fifth theme is the power of WIP constraints. WIP constraints are a powerful way to gain control over cycle time in the presence of variability. This is particularly important for systems where variability accumulates, such as in product development. WIP constraints exploit the direct relationship between cycle time and inventory, which is known as Little's Formula.

We will discuss two common methods of constraining WIP: the kanban system and Goldratt's Theory of Constraints (TOC). These methods are relatively static. We will also examine how telecommunications networks use WIP constraints in a much more dynamic way. Once again, telecommunications networks are interesting to us as product developers, because they deal successfully with inherently high variability.

Cadence, Synchronization, and Flow Control

Our sixth theme is the use of cadence, synchronization, and dynamic flow control. Cadence involves processing work at regular time intervals. Synchronization involves making multiple tasks start or finish at the same time. We can synchronize with or without cadence. We can use cadence with or without synchronization. It is best when we combine both.

By flow control, we refer to the sequence in which we process jobs in our product development process. We are interested in finding economically optimum sequences for tasks. Current practices use fairly crude approaches to sequencing.

For example, it is suggested that if subsystem B depends on subsystem A, it would be better to sequence the design of A first. This logic optimizes efficiency as a proxy variable. When we consider overall economics, as we do in this book, we often reach different conclusions. For example, it may be better to develop both A and B simultaneously, despite the risk of inefficient rework, because parallel development can save cycle time.

In this book, our model for flow control will not be manufacturing systems, since these systems primarily deal with predictable and homogeneous flows. Instead, we will look at lessons that can be learned from telecommunications networks and computer operating systems. Both of these domains have decades of experience dealing with nonhomogeneous and highly variable flows.

Fast Feedback

Our seventh theme is the importance of fast feedback loops. The speed of feedback is at least two orders of magnitude more important to product developers than manufacturers. Developers rely on feedback to influence subsequent choices. Or, at least, they should. Unfortunately, our current orthodoxy views feedback as an element of an undesirable rework loop. It asserts that we should prevent the need for rework by having engineers design things right the first time.

We will present a radically different view, suggesting that feedback is what permits us to operate our product development process effectively in a very noisy environment. Feedback allows us to efficiently adapt to unpredictability.

Feedback gives us new information, information that can be used to make better economic choices. Let's take a simple example, shown in Figure 1-3. I will offer you two ways to invest in a two-digit lottery ticket that pays out $100 for a winning number. Using the first method, you can buy a random two-digit number for $1. In such a case, you would have a 99 percent chance of losing $1 and a 1 percent chance of making $99. This bet produces no net gain.

Using the second method, you can buy the first digit for 50 cents, receive feedback as to whether this digit is correct, and then, if it is correct, you can choose to buy the second digit for 50 cents. The economics

The Value of Feedback

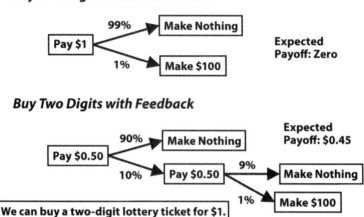

Buy Two Digits at the Same Time

Buy Two Digits with Feedback

Figure 1-3 In this lottery ticket example, the expected payoff is higher if we buy one digit and obtain feedback, than if we buy both digits at the same time. The feedback stops us from buying the second digit 90 percent of the time, since we already know we cannot win.

of the second method is clearly better. You have a 90 percent chance of losing 50 cents on the first digit. You will only go on to invest in the second digit if you picked the first digit correctly. This occurs only 10 percent of the time. Ninety percent of the time you will save the cost of buying the second digit. When you buy the second digit, you have a 9 percent chance of losing $1 and a 1 percent chance of making $99.

By breaking the betting process into two steps, the overall bet produces a net gain of 45 cents. This added value occurs because 90 percent of the time, you will not purchase the second digit, because you already know you will not win.

When we start to view feedback through the perspective of economics and probability, we will discover its power to improve product development economics.

We will also look at feedback from a control engineering perspective. This allows us to consider problems of dynamic response and stability that are not considered in many traditional approaches.

Finally, this theme of fast feedback will include a discussion of metrics. The current orthodoxy uses a set of metrics that is based on a specific belief system about what causes economic success. The new paradigm has different beliefs about what causes economic success, so it tries to control different things.

Decentralized Control

Our final theme is decentralization of control. Decentralization is a logical response to unpredictable situations where response time is important. This occurs in product development, where problems can expand quickly and opportunities can be perishable.

Counterbalancing the response-time benefits of decentralization are the efficiency benefits of centralized control. Centralized control creates scale economies and more efficient alignment of our efforts.

Rather than arguing that we must eliminate all centralized control and create completely decentralized control, we will take a more balanced view. We will use the military as a role model. The military confronts fleeting opportunities and unexpected obstacles in warfare, a domain of high uncertainty. It has experimented for centuries with both centralization and decentralization. In its most advanced form, today's military combines decentralized control with alignment. We will explore how they do this and what lessons can be learned by product developers.

The Relevant Idea Sources

As I explore the major themes of this book, it should be clear that many fields have advanced ideas on the problem of managing flow in the presence of variability. I believe that many of these ideas have the power to transform product development. The science of flow does not reside tidily in a single location. Important insights come from the world of engineering, manufacturing, mathematics, economics, and military science. I have tried to consolidate those ideas that I find most useful. Let's look at where the key contributions come from:

Lean Manufacturing

Lean manufacturing provides us with a mature set of ideas for managing certain types of flow. We owe Toyota a great debt showing us the importance of using small batches in production processes. Many of these ideas can be transferred into design processes. In doing so, we must recognize that manufacturing is a domain with fundamentally different economic characteristics. Its ideas must be significantly extended to make them useful in product development.

Economics

Almost all of the problems of the current orthodoxy can be traced back to the failure to apply economic frameworks to product development. An economic framework enables us to quantify the effects of multiple interacting variables. This is the key to making good economic choices. With an understanding of economics, you will learn that popular ideas, like the customer is the ultimate judge of value-added, actually make little economic sense.

Economics will also help us think in a more sophisticated way about variability. Economists would find the notion that minimizing variability maximizes economic value to be hopelessly simplistic.

Queueing Theory

Queueing theory is a field of applied statistics that studies the formation of waiting lines. It is a century old and has benefited from some very careful thinking by applied mathematicians and engineers. Queueing theory permits us to quantify the relationships between waiting times and capacity utilization, even when arrivals and service times are highly variable. We use queueing theory in the design of telecommunications networks, which are themselves a sophisticated and fertile source of ideas.

Statistics

The field of statistics is a rich source of insight into processes with variability. Yet, the ideas of statistics have only been applied in a very limited way in product development. We will use ideas that go beyond those taught in Six Sigma training.

First, we are extremely interested in the intersection of statistics and economics. This intersection enables us to understand the economics of variability.

Second, Six Sigma teaches us about random variables. Random variables help us to understand the problems of repetitive manufacturing. In product development, we are interested in a more advanced application of statistics called random processes. These are time sequences of random variables. Random processes are much more relevant to product developers, and, as you shall see, often counterintuitive.

The Internet

The Internet is a highly successful application of ideas for managing flow in the presence of variability. Manufacturing networks emphasize variability reduction as the path to improving flow. In contrast, telecommunications networks assume variability is inherent, and adopt design approaches that are robust in the presence of variability. We can learn a great deal about flow control by looking at methods that have evolved in telecommunications networks over the last 100 years. Manufacturing networks only use a small subset of these flow control concepts.

Computer Operating System Design

Computer operating systems have evolved over the last 60 years. They are another rich source of ideas for two reasons. First, they deal with mixed-priority workflows. Different jobs have different priorities. Second, computer operating systems deal with tasks that have unpredictable arrival times and unpredictable durations. As a result, operating systems have developed much more advanced sequencing methods than the simple FIFO sequences used in manufacturing processes. Since product development must also deal with unpredictable and mixed-priority workflows, we can obtain useful approaches from computer operating systems.

Control Engineering

The feedback loops that most readers have been exposed to are the relatively simple feedback loops of the plan-do-check-act (PDCA) cycle. In the field of control engineering, the science of feedback is bit more sophisticated. In particular, this field gives us insights about the importance of dynamic response and the problem of instability. Such issues rarely show up in manufacturing, because manufacturing flow times are measured in hours or days. These issues become much more important in product development where our flow times are measured in months or years. We will draw upon these ideas when we examine the use of feedback loops in product development systems.

Maneuver Warfare

Finally, we will draw upon ideas from the military. Most readers will not be very familiar with military doctrine. What they know will be shaped by ideas received from Hollywood and television. This is unfortunate, because military thinkers actually have very advanced ideas on how to combine decentralized control and alignment of effort.

The organization I have chosen as a model of this approach is the U.S. Marine Corps. Marines believe that they cannot remove uncertainty from warfare, and that this uncertainty does not inherently favor either side. Instead, the side that can thrive in the presence of uncertainty is most likely to win.

Marines view warfare as a domain of unexpected obstacles and fleeting opportunities. They use decentralized control and local initiative to quickly exploit opportunities, but they also recognize that decentralized control can lead to chaos. Their methods are both practical and highly relevant to product developers.

The Design of This Book

Perhaps the most obvious structural feature of this book is that it is organized into 175 principles. It is not a business novel, telling the story of an intrepid manager on his or her journey to success. It is not a collection of company stories reflecting on their successes. It is not a set of rules to be rigidly followed. It is a set of principles. These are patterns and causal relationships that occur often enough to make them useful guidelines. They will help you think more deeply about your choices, but they will not eliminate the need for thinking.

I have chosen to emphasize principles for three reasons. First, I believe that a powerful set of underlying principles can be used to solve an incredibly wide range of problems. I have always admired the field of physics for its ability to distill many phenomena down to a much smaller number of governing principles.

Second, this principle-based approach allows me to increase the density of information in this book. None of us have time to read everything we would like to read. Increasing density helps reduce this problem. I aspire to write books with more content than fluff, and hope this book will achieve that goal.

Third, I hope this principle-based design will make it easier for a wide range of readers to use this book. Experienced developers can skip over ideas they already use, beginners can examine everything. Organizing around principles should also make it easier to retrieve specific information. It offers an alternative to indexes, which are sometimes a bit too detailed, and tables of contents, which are often a bit too general.

I've assumed a moderate degree of technical literacy on the part of the reader. Experience shows that most readers of my previous books have an engineering or scientific background. I have decided to take advantage of this. When working with previous publishers, I heeded their warnings that equations would frighten away readers. Today, I am willing to take the risk of inserting a few equations when they help explain key ideas. People who dislike equations should still find plenty of content in this book. Others, who appreciate the power and compactness of mathematics, may value its presence.

It Will Be a Long Journey, so Start Now

I used to think that sensible and compelling new ideas would be adopted quickly. Today, I believe this view is hopelessly naive. After all, it took 40 years before we recognized the power of the Toyota Production System.

Based on my personal experience, it takes a bit of time for new ideas to obtain traction. I began writing about the importance of calculating cost of delay in 1983. After 26 years, only 15 percent of product developers know the cost of delay on their projects. I began writing about the importance of product development queues in 1991. After 18 years, about 2 percent of product developers measure the size of queues in their development process. The ideas in this book challenge many existing practices. I do not expect they will be adopted overnight.

There are two common but bad reasons to delay adoption. First, some companies will wait until there are role-model companies demonstrating large-scale and mature implementations of these ideas. Once this has occurred, they will be ready to adopt all the ideas in one large batch.

I would suggest that there is a better approach. The methods in this book can be implemented using two general paths. They can be implemented from the top down in one large batch, or from the bottom up in small batches. Everything we will discuss about the advantages of small batch size applies to implementation. Small batches have lower risk, are less expensive, and they produce faster results. They accelerate learning. In fact, companies that are already implementing these ideas in small batches have achieved 5–10 times improvements in portions of their development process.

Furthermore, I believe you will miss a huge economic opportunity if you wait until the full-scale implementations become visible. Did you ever consider why American industry adopted lean manufacturing 30 to 40 years after these methods began to produce benefits in Japan? Was it because the Japanese hid this approach from Western eyes? No. American industry waited until the full-scale implementations of these ideas at Toyota could no longer be ignored. As a result, we missed out on 30 years of economic benefits.

A second bad reason to delay adoption is to wait until this new approach has been carefully studied by academia. You might reflect on how long it took for academia to replace the orthodoxy of traditional manufacturing with the new ideas of lean manufacturing. The new methods of lean manufacturing began emerging in the late 1940s in Japan. They originated from practitioners like Toyota, not academia.

It took approximately 30 to 40 years for these ideas to be acknowledged and accepted by the academic community in the United States.[3] Again, I would stress that you can make a lot of money between the time when useful new ideas appear, and when they are widely accepted in academia.

So, start small, and start quickly. Pay attention to feedback. Above all, think about what you are doing. Good luck!

---

[3] It would be an oversimplification to attribute all this delay to inertia. Responsible academics reach conclusions based on factual evidence and rigorous analysis. It takes time to do solid research.

2

The Economic View

While you may ignore economics, it won't ignore you.

What should we change in our product development process? Eliminate waste? Increase quality? Raise efficiency? Shorten cycle time? The key to answering this question is to step back to a more basic question: *Why* do we want to change the product development process? The answer: to increase profits.

As obvious as this may seem, this economic view of product development is surprisingly uncommon. Instead, product developers create a large number of proxy objectives: increase innovation, improve quality, conform to plan, shorten development cycles, eliminate waste, etc. Unfortunately, they rarely understand how these proxy objectives quantitatively influence profits. Without this quantitative mapping, they cannot evaluate decisions that affect multiple interacting objectives.

Should we delay the project by one month to be more innovative? Innovation is good. Fast time-to-market is also good. If we can justify a 1-month delay to increase innovation, what about 12 months, and what about 12 years? There is simply no way to compare things that lack a common unit of measure. The economic view solves this problem.

If you are convinced that you do not have this problem, because *your* teams understand their economics, let me propose a simple test. Find 10 people working on the same development project. Ask them to independently estimate what it would cost the company, in pretax profit, if their project were 60 days late to market. Rank their answers from the highest to the lowest. In the last 20 years, the typical range of answers that I receive from people working on exactly the same project is 50 to 1.

What would happen if we allowed such people to do what they think is economically correct? We would have an economic catastrophe. Is it any surprise then, that many senior managers are reluctant to delegate important economic decisions? As we shall see later, when high-quality decentralized economic information is absent, it is too often replaced by the mind-numbing bureaucracy of centralized control.

Our primary goal in product development is to make good economic choices. All proxy objectives, such as innovation, waste reduction, design for manufacturing, etc., should be viewed as secondary. They are a means to influence overall economic outcomes, never an end in themselves.

In this chapter, I will try to convince you to view product development economically. We will begin by discussing the critical need for quantification. Then, I will expose you to the single most important tool in the entire book, the project economic framework. After this, we will look at the nature of the decisions we are trying to make and their implications for our control strategy. Finally, we will introduce some very useful economic concepts and debunk two popular fallacies.

The Nature of Our Economics

Let's begin by describing the economic problem that we are trying to solve. It involves multiple variables that interact with one another. Success is only measured in terms of overall economic results. We will need to quantify the economic effect of many secondary factors, like value-added, risk, waste, and schedule delay.

With an economic framework, we can do this. This framework has the power to illuminate the dark corners of the economic terrain of product development. It makes the invisible visible. For example, as we shall see in Chapter 3, with an economic framework, we can quantify the cost of queues in our development process. Without it, it is virtually impossible to recognize the economic damage done by queues.

E1: The Principle of Quantified Overall Economics: Select actions based on quantified overall economic impact.

Let's begin with a simple problem. Should we release a product from the development lab to the factory before we have eliminated all defects? Most companies approach this question as a philosophical debate. One side argues that engineering should finish their work before they give the product to manufacturing. The other side argues that it is foolish to wait for a perfect product before we face the challenges of a hostile factory. Who is right?

We can find out by quantifying the overall economic impact. We begin by gathering the relevant facts. What is the cost difference between correcting a defect on the factory floor and fixing it in the development lab? A factor of 10. How much rework does a typical immature product create on the factory floor? $20,000. How much time would it take the development lab to find the same number of defects that we can find in 1 week on the factory floor? Five weeks.

Now, we can do the math. An early move to manufacturing saves us 4 weeks of cycle time, but it raises the cost of correcting defects from $2,000 to $20,000. The critical question is whether 4 weeks of cycle time savings will pay for this $18,000 of extra cost. If so, we should push the immature product onto the factory floor.

As we progress through this chapter, you will discover the enormous benefit of having an economic framework. You'll see how it enables us to deal with complex multivariable decisions by expressing all operational impacts in the same unit of measure: life-cycle profit impact. You'll see how it dramatically reduces the effort needed to make decisions quickly, correctly, and with logic that everyone can understand. Finally, you'll see how an economic framework allows us to effectively communicate our conclusions to a vital audience, one that places great weight on economic arguments, senior management.

E2: The Principle of Interconnected Variables: We can't just change one thing.

In product development, decisions almost always simultaneously affect multiple variables. Life would be quite simple if only one thing changed at a time. We could ask easy questions like, "Who wants to eliminate waste?" and everyone would answer, "Me!" However, real-world decisions almost never affect only a single proxy variable. In reality, we must assess how much time and effort we are willing to trade for eliminating a specific amount of waste.

This has an important implication. For simple single variable decisions, we only need to know the direction of the change. For multivariable decisions, we also need to know the magnitude of the change, and most importantly, we need a method to express all changes, in all variables, in the same unit of measure. This is the only way we can evaluate

Five Key Economic Objectives

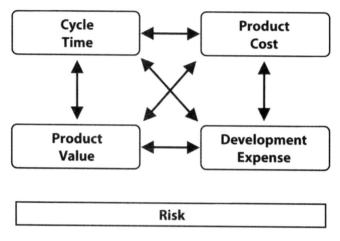

Figure 2-1 Five key economic objectives are commonly used for sensitivity analysis.

the overall economic consequences of changing multiple proxy variables simultaneously.

The Project Economic Framework

Fortunately, there is a straightforward way to solve this problem. We quantify the overall economic impact of decisions using a project economic framework. This framework treats a project as a black box that is designed to produce life-cycle profits. As Figure 2-1 shows, we commonly use five key economic objectives as measures of performance for a project. We vary each measure independently and assess its influence on life-cycle profits. In effect, we are trying to determine the transfer function between each measure of performance and life-cycle profitability. This method is known as sensitivity analysis.

The output of such an economic framework is a set of decision rules that tells us what we should pay for changes in individual measures of project performance. The five most common sensitivities are product cost, product value (measured in life-cycle revenue), development expense, cycle time, and risk. However, we are not limited to these standard sensitivities. It can be very useful to perform economic sensitivities on specific measures of technical performance. What is a kilogram of weight reduction worth? What is a 1 percent increase in efficiency worth? What is 1,000 hours of additional mean time between failure (MTBF) worth?

The key idea is that product and project attributes that have economic value should be quantified using a standardized and useful unit of measure: life-cycle profit impact. We can make good economic choices when we understand the overall economic consequences of our decisions.[1]

E3: The Principle of Quantified Cost of Delay: If you only quantify one thing, quantify the cost of delay.

In theory, by following Principle E1, we will automatically quantify the cost of delay (COD) for our projects. In practice, since 85 percent of companies do not quantify cost of delay, it is worth highlighting this particular sensitivity. We simply have no business trading money for cycle time if we do not know the economic value of cycle time.

Consider the following example. Unhappy with late deliveries, a project manager decides he can reduce variability by inserting a safety margin or buffer in his schedule. He reduces uncertainty in the schedule by committing to an 80 percent confidence schedule. But, what is the cost of this buffer? The project manager is actually trading cycle time for variability. We can only know if this is a good trade-off if we quantify both the value of cycle time and the economic benefit of reduced variability.

In our experience, no single sensitivity is more eye-opening than COD. As this book progresses, you will see that the economics of flow is almost always dominated by the cost of queues. If we cannot quantify

---

[1] For the more mathematically inclined, we can think of our sensitivities as describing a transformation that maps the proxy variable space onto the economic space. We identify a set of basis vectors in the proxy variable space and determine how each basis vector is transformed in the economic space. Since these basis vectors span the proxy variable space, we can describe *any* change in the proxy variable space as a weighted sum of these basis vectors. The economic measure of this change is simply the weighted sum of the transformed basis vectors. Thus, once we know how the basis vectors transform, we do not have to recalculate the transformation each time we confront a new economic decision. By expressing a decision in terms of the proxy-variable basis vectors, we can quickly determine its economic impact as a weighting of transformed basis vectors. This turns out to be incredibly helpful, because it dramatically lowers the effort to evaluate the economic impact of complex decisions. With this lower effort, we can subject many more decisions to economic scrutiny.

the cost of a queue on the critical path, then we cannot quantify the benefit of reducing this queue. If we cannot quantify the benefit, we can't generate support for major changes.

We need COD to evaluate the cost of queues, the value of excess capacity, the benefit of smaller batch sizes, and value of variability reduction. Cost of delay is the golden key that unlocks many doors. It has an astonishing power to totally transform the mind-set of a development organization.

We should also point out that COD, and other sensitivities, can be computed for any milestone, not just for the final milestone of the project. For example, what is the cost of delay when engineering delivers their work product late, but manufacturing still must ship on time? We can find out by determining if compressing the manufacturing activities changes our economics. When manufacturing has insufficient time to ramp production, they may incur expensive expediting, yield problems, scrap, and high warranty costs. If we know the economic consequences of a late release to manufacturing, then we can quantify the delay cost associated with missing this key milestone. Knowing this delay cost enables us to decide what we are willing to pay to meet this milestone.

E4: The Principle of Economic Value-Added: The value added by an activity is the change in the economic value of the work product.

At this point, we must add some rigor to the concept of value-added. Many product developers blindly accept a definition of value-added that is used in the world of lean manufacturing. There, it is popular to say that an informed customer is the sole judge of value-added. This view is both economically incorrect and dangerous. In reality, value-added is a well-established economic concept. The value added by an activity is the difference in the price that an economically rational buyer would pay for a work product before, and after, the activity is performed. The customer is one judge of economic value, but never the sole judge.

Let's illustrate why this economic view is more useful to product developers than the lean manufacturing view. Lean manufacturing experts classify testing as a form of necessary waste, not as a value-added activity. Would an economist view testing this way? Not if testing increases the economic value of the work product.

Let's illustrate this with a simple example. A pharmaceutical company will perform clinical trials when testing a new drug. A Phase I clinical trial, which is a form of testing, may have a 50 percent chance of success. Is this test value-added or necessary waste? Economics provides an unambiguous answer. Would a rational buyer pay more money for this drug candidate after the trial had been successfully completed? Yes. Why? The projected price of the drug has not changed. The number of patients that can be helped by the drug has not changed. The projected manufacturing cost of the drug has not changed. What has changed is the probability of realizing a billion-dollar stream of gross margin.

Reducing risk, which is the primary mission of testing, clearly creates economic value for product developers. In fact, reducing risk is so centrally important to product development that it is indispensable for us to quantify its economic impact.

Of course, since value-added is an economic concept, it follows that non-value-added, or waste, is also an economic concept. This is correct. We can define waste as the failure to optimize our economics. To measure waste in economic terms, we must convert all proxy variables into their economic form. This permits us to trade off different types of waste using a common unit of measure. Why is this important?

Consider an example. Should we operate a computer-aided design (CAD) area at 80 percent utilization with a 2-week queue, or 90 percent utilization with a 4-week queue? We must trade off the economic waste of underutilization against the economic waste of queues. We can only make this trade-off correctly when we convert both forms of waste into the same unit of measure: life-cycle profit.

E5: The Inactivity Principle: Watch the work product, not the worker.

Making all forms of economic waste visible changes our view of product development. Without an economic framework, we tend to focus only on the most visible form of waste, inefficient activity. But, making activities more efficient is much less important than eliminating *inactivity*. In product development, our greatest waste is not unproductive engineers, but work products sitting idle in process queues.

Yet, most observers focus on the activities. Some praise Toyota because its engineers report that they spend 80 percent of their time adding value compared to lower numbers at other companies. They encourage American companies to imitate Toyota. Does this make economic sense?

In product development, value-added time is a proxy variable that interacts negatively with other proxy variables. As you shall see in Chapter 3, when we increase value-added time in a process with variability, we will create queues. The cost of these queues is usually far greater than any efficiency savings that come from increasing the percent of value-added time.

We've already learned this lesson in manufacturing. Long ago we believed that an idle manufacturing resource was the most important form of waste. Managers would walk the factory floor, worrying about underutilized machines. They knew that idle machinery raised overhead and hurt profits. They assumed it was better to use an idle machine to make anything than it was to let the machine be idle. This practice led to excess inventory, low quality, high overhead, and long cycle time.

Today, we realize that inventory is the biggest source of waste in manufacturing. Work product lying idle on the factory floor destroys quality, efficiency, and cycle time. Today, no competent manufacturer believes that high utilization rates will optimize manufacturing.

So, let economics enable you to see the inactivity, as well as the activity. Pay attention to the work product as it lies idle in the queues between activities, not just to the busy workers.

As we shall see in Chapter 3, our management systems conspire to make these product development queues invisible. We don't know how big they are or what they cost us. It is not surprising that we do nothing about them.

Fortunately, COD makes these invisible queues visible. With it, you can discover the enormous economic leverage that lies in queues. In product development, our problem is virtually never motionless engineers. It is almost always motionless work products.

The Nature of Our Decisions

Now that we understand the nature of our economics, let's look at the nature of the decisions we are trying to make. This is important because the nature of these decisions dictates the type of decision support system we must create. It affects the type of information we need, the required accuracy of the information, and when we will need it.

Economic Batch Size

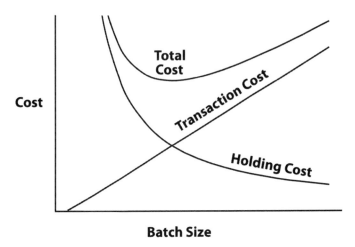

Batch Size

Figure 2-2 Economic batch size is a U-curve optimization. We do not need to find the perfect optimum to capture most of the value.

E6: The U-Curve Principle: Important trade-offs are likely to have U-curve optimizations.

What sort of decisions are we trying to make? After almost 30 years of analyzing product development trade-offs, I am struck by the frequency with which U-curve optimizations occur. Such U-curves are common in multivariable problems.

Figure 2-2 shows a classic example of batch size optimization which trades off a hyperbolic function against a linear function. Knowing that important optimizations take this form is surprisingly useful, because U-curves have two important properties. First, optimization never occurs at extreme values. If optimization occurred at extreme values, then quantification would be unnecessary. We would only need to know the direction that maximizes performance. In contrast, U-curve optimizations virtually always require quantification, because we must balance two or more competing factors.

Second, and very importantly, U-curve optimizations do not require precise answers. U-curves have flat bottoms, so missing the exact optimum costs very little. For example, in Figure 2-2, a 10 percent error in optimum batch size results in a 2 to 3 percent increase in total cost. This insensitivity has a very important practical implication. We do not need highly accurate information to improve our economic decisions. This is indeed fortunate, because many inputs to our economic framework, such as unit sales, are difficult to estimate with high accuracy. If our answers were highly sensitive to noisy assumptions, our economic framework would be much less useful.

E7: The Imperfection Principle: Even imperfect answers improve decision making.

The other thing to realize about our economic decisions is that we are trying to improve them, not to make them perfect. We want to make better economic choices than we make today, and today, this bar is set very low. We simply do not need perfect analysis.

Some companies worry that imperfect economic frameworks will lead workers to make bad decisions. They act as if the absence of these frameworks will magically protect them from bad decisions. Sadly, the lack of an economic framework does not prevent people from making economic decisions. It simply causes these decisions to be driven underground and to be based on intuition instead of analysis. As we pointed out at the beginning of this chapter, this intuition typically produces a 50 to 1 difference in the price people pay for cycle time. With an economic framework, we can normally bring this range down to 2 to 1, a 25-fold improvement.

The economic framework also improves decision making in a more subtle way. As we try to analyze economics, we uncover those assumptions that have the greatest impact on our answers. This permits us to invest more effort on getting these assumptions correct. Thus, the economic view regeneratively improves our understanding of economics. We can create enormous improvements in decision making with surprisingly imperfect answers. Do not let fear of inaccuracy prevent you from creating economic frameworks.

E8: The Principle of Small Decisions: Influence the many small decisions.

We must also recognize the size of the decisions that we are trying to influence. Many companies assume that the path to economic success lies in making a handful of big economic choices correctly. This leads them to concentrate decision-making authority at high levels and to design information systems that support this high-level decision making.

While big decisions are important, this bias means that most companies have weak systems to ensure that the many small economic decisions are made correctly. Collectively, these small decisions have enormous economic impact.

Sadly, this is a blind spot for many modern managers who are heavily influenced by the concept of the Pareto Principle, which observes that 80 percent of the leverage lies in 20 percent of problems. The dark side of the Pareto Principle is that we tend to focus excessively on the high payoff 20 percent. We overmanage this 20 percent, and undermanage the other 80 percent. This leads to what we might call the Pareto Paradox: There is usually more actual opportunity in the undermanaged 80 percent than the overmanaged 20 percent.

For example, consider the problem of cycle time in a traditional factory. Such a factory might take 100 days to do what a lean factory could do in 2 days. Where was the extra 98 days? Was it in two or three big 30-day queues? No! It was actually caused by 98 little 8-hour delays. Each individual delay was too small to manage, but collectively, they accounted for virtually all of the delay. Factory cycle time only improved when we learned to attack the many small opportunities.

As we shall see later, the fact that we are trying to influence many small decisions has important implications. In Chapter 5, we will discover that it is best to process these decisions in small batches, and that this requires a low fixed transaction cost per decision. More on this later.

E9: The Principle of Continuous Economic Trade-offs: Economic choices must be made continuously.

It is also important to consider the timing of the economic trade-offs that we make in product development. We do not make a few, big, predictable trade-offs at the start of our development process. Instead, we make many small trade-offs, at random times, throughout our development process.

This is, in fact, quite different from the decision pattern in manufacturing. In the factory, we create a work order to establish the sequence of operations needed to manufacture a part before we release a part to the factory floor. Work is typically planned by planners and manufacturing engineers and executed by workers on the factory floor. We can make excellent plans because the work is inherently repetitive. Our plan represents the optimum course of action, and any deviation from this plan will create economic damage. As a result, it makes enormous sense to measure conformance against this preestablished optimum plan. In manufacturing, higher conformance yields better economic performance. In manufacturing, it is both feasible and beneficial to make all our economic choices in one large batch before we start the work.

Some product developers aspire to use the same approach in product development. They prepare a minutely detailed plan at the beginning of the project and measure performance against this plan. When they deviate from this plan, they take corrective action. They aspire to front-load their decisions. While this is a superb strategy in repetitive environments like manufacturing, it is a terrible one in product development.

Why? In product development, we continuously receive new information from the market and from the design process. Customer preferences change. Engineering tasks that looked easy at first may now require breaking the laws of physics.

Originally, we believed a feature was important to 50 percent of the customers and it would take 2 weeks of work. As time passed, we discovered it was important to 1 percent of the customers and would require 2 months of work. This means the economics of the decision have changed by a factor of 200.

When economics change, we must reevaluate the economic wisdom of our choices. Remember Principle E1, our primary objective is to make good economic choices. To blindly conform to the original plan when it no longer represents the best economic choice is the act of a fool.

E10: The First Perishability Principle: Many economic choices are more valuable when made quickly.

Not only do these emergent opportunities arrive continuously and randomly, but they are also quite perishable. Opportunities get smaller with time, and obstacles get larger. The longer we wait to exploit an opportunity or to deal with an obstacle, the less economic value is available.

This, too, has important implications for our decision-making process. It means we must explicitly measure, and shorten, the time it takes to make a decision.

It follows that if most opportunities and obstacles are first visible to people at the lowest level of the organization, then this level should be able to make these decisions. This suggests a strategy of decentralized control, which we will examine in Chapter 9. Is this what we do today? Not even close. Instead of moving towards decentralization, many companies are centralizing control and decision making. They use massive phase reviews where unempowered teams must ask for permission to enter the next phase. Later in this chapter, we will explain how an economic framework enables decentralized control without risking bad economic choices.

E11: The Subdivision Principle: Inside every bad choice lies a good choice.

Finally, we should recognize the nonmonolithic nature of our decisions. Most of our decisions can be decomposed into component parts that individually have distinct economics. This means that we can often isolate a good choice inside a bad one.

Let's illustrate this with an example. Consider the choice to create a backup solution for a high-risk primary solution. One semiconductor company was using an outside contractor to provide important design intellectual property (IP) for their project. They did not have enough resources to develop this content internally, but their risk assessment identified outside IP as a major program risk. They concluded that the only realistic contingency plan would be to develop this IP internally. However, they did not have enough resources to do a parallel internal development. After all, lack of resource was the reason they were using external IP. Doing a full-scale parallel program was a bad choice.

What else could they do? The company recognized that there were alternatives to a full-scale internal program. They could allocate a single engineer to carefully monitor the status of the external program. If they had to pull the program inside, they would understand exactly where the issues were and what had already been tried to solve them. By investing a small fraction of the resource needed for a full-scale parallel program, they could ensure that the backup plan could be executed very quickly. They had found the economically attractive good choice hidden inside the bad choice.

It is always useful to look for a way to reshape a bad choice into a better one. Decompose the choice into its pieces and keep the good parts. How do we know what the good parts are? Our economic framework permits us to evaluate the components of a decision on the basis of cost and benefit. We can decide which parts to keep and which ones to discard. Decomposition and recombination are enabled by having a way to measure the economics of the individual pieces. This allows us to recombine these pieces in a more economically desirable configuration.

Our Control Strategy

Now, let's develop a control strategy to improve these decisions. Remember the nature of the problem. We have many small decisions. These decisions create the most value if they are made quickly. We need to provide simple, easy-to-use methods that enable many people to make good economic choices.

In this section, we will examine how we can harvest the best economic opportunities and how we can decentralize control with decision rules. We will look at ways to motivate decision makers and the optimum timing of decisions. So, let's begin.

E12: The Principle of Early Harvesting: Create systems to harvest the early cheap opportunities.

When people first obtain a COD, they use it as a blunt instrument to justify expensive damage-control actions at the end of the development process. COD is certainly useful for this purpose, but experienced users use a different approach. They recognize that the cheapest opportunities to buy cycle time appear early in the development cycle. They devise a system to capture these cheap opportunities.

One organization does this by setting limits on the authority of engineers to buy cycle time. Every engineer is permitted to buy up to 4 weeks of schedule improvement, at a cost of no higher than $500 per week. Their manager has higher authority limits, and the director has even more authority. This is shown in Figure 2-3.

What happens when the engineers reach their limit? Their decisions are reviewed, and they are granted authority to buy up to 4 more weeks. This system allows the company to harvest the many small, cheap, early opportunities to improve cycle time, instead of the expensive ones that occur later in the development process. It does this without taking any significant risk, because authority is carefully controlled.

Authority Limits for Buying Cycle Time

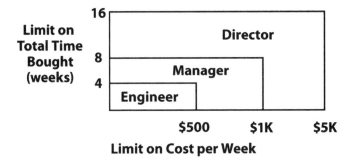

When you've spent your limit, see the boss to get your card refilled.

Figure 2-3 Each level of the organization is given a specific level of authority to buy cycle time. This enables the organization to exploit the cheap opportunities that occur early in the project.

E13: The First Decision Rule Principle: Use decision rules to decentralize economic control.

If the majority of the opportunity lies in the small decisions made at the lowest level of the organization, then we should decentralize authority to this level. To do this, we must provide high-quality decision support information to this level of the organization. How can we do this?

The most important tool for influencing the many small decisions is economic decision rules. Such decision rules accomplish four things. First, they align all the economic choices on the entire project. Second, they ensure that these choices are optimum at the system level. Third, they enable us to push control down to low levels with limited risk. Finally, they streamline the process of making decisions. By dramatically reducing the marginal effort required to make good economic choices, they make it possible to control many more decisions. The combined impact of these four effects is astonishing. We can make more decisions, faster, more easily, more correctly, and with less risk.

Let's illustrate how economic decision rules enable people at low levels to make good economic choices without the involvement of their superiors. Consider the case of the Boeing 777. Traditionally, weight and cost are allocated to each subsystem on an aircraft at the beginning of the program. This allocation is difficult and imperfect. As each subsystem tries to meet its allocated objectives, it trades one performance parameter against another. The feasible trade-offs within a subsystem are highly dependent on the subsystem's original allocations.

For example, if a subsystem has been underallocated weight and overallocated cost, it might seek to buy weight for $5,000 per pound. Another subsystem that has been overallocated weight and underallocated cost may choose to ignore opportunities to buy weight for $50 per pound. How could Boeing avoid this economic inconsistency?

One approach would be to funnel all decisions through a single expert, but this would create major decision-making delays. Instead, Boeing calculated a decision rule for trading off weight and unit cost, a rule that was correct at the system level. Any designer was authorized to increase unit cost by up to $300, by making design changes or material substitutions, to save a pound of weight. As a result, Boeing had 5,000 engineers making system-level optimum trade-offs without the need to ask for permission from their superiors.

The intrinsic elegance of this approach is that the superiors didn't actually give up control over the decision. Instead, they recognized that they could still control the decision without participating in it. They simply had to control the economic logic of the decision. Control without participation is control without decision-making delays.

Decision rules are a powerful tool for controlling the quality and consistency of decisions, but they actually do more than this. They also reduce the effort required to make good economic choices. We shall see in Chapter 5 that reduced effort means less transaction cost, and this permits fast processing in small batches. Decision rules make it practical to drive good economic decision making very deep into the organization.

E14: The First Market Principle: Ensure decision makers feel both cost and benefit.

After decentralizing control to low levels, we should consider how we can motivate decision makers to make good economic decisions. Ideally, decision makers should feel both the cost and benefit of their decisions.

Today's reality is less than ideal. Today, most product developers enjoy benefits while being insulated from costs. For example, we let the program manager who requests head-of-the-line privileges pay the same price as those who wait for the same service. We let a forceful program manager grab an unfair share of resources without paying any premium price.

Does this make economic sense? If we make resources available for free, they will tend to be infinitely utilized. But wait, you say, we don't have infinite utilization in product development. This is only because we force management to allocate these underpriced resources. Unfortunately, this solution is often as bad as the problem. It funnels too many decisions through limited management bandwidth, leading to decision delays.

Is there an alternative? Use pricing to control demand. This is how economic markets work. When prices rise, demand falls. Markets work because decision makers experience both the benefit and the cost of their decisions. Pricing enables such decentralized control.

Today's development organizations are managed like centrally-controlled economies of the twentieth century. Resource is allocated by an infinitely wise centralized decision maker. There is no explicit cost for requesting priority or excess resource. In theory, the decision maker has the scarce global knowledge needed to allocate resources. In reality, this creates a massive incentive for projects to exaggerate their needs. Skillful lobbying can often get more resources than legitimate needs.

How could we substitute market mechanisms for this central control? Use pricing to manage demand. For example, a manager at one defense contractor wanted to regulate demand for limited CAD resources. He decided to provide two classes of service to his customers. If a project accepted his standard turnaround time, it paid standard cost. If the project wanted the premium service, 48-hour turnaround time, they would have to pay 125 percent of standard cost. This 25 percent premium funded the capacity margin needed to create fast turnaround time.

Why does this work? The project, not management, is making the choice to use the premium service. The project can make the correct economic choice because it experiences both the cost and benefit of premium service. Under such conditions, project managers will only request rush service when they truly experience benefits over standard service.

But, what if everyone is willing to pay for premium service? This would tell us that the CAD department had incorrectly balanced efficiency and quality of service. When nobody wants to buy our standard service, we need to increase capacity for premium service.

E15: The Principle of Optimum Decision Timing: Every decision has its optimum economic timing.

Principle E9 suggested that we cannot front-load all our decisions. What about the opposite approach, delaying our decisions to the "last responsible moment"? Should we delay all decisions as long as possible? Again, economics helps clarify this issue. If the cost, payoff, and risk of our decisions are time-dependent, then each decision will have an optimum economic timing.

Consider, for example, an airline ticket purchase. Airlines use load management software to carefully manage the number of tickets available, and their price, as a function of time. If a flight is not filling as expected, more seats become available at lower prices. As the day of the flight approaches, there are fewer seats left. These scarce seats will be sold at premium prices to last-minute travelers. We are likely to overpay if we buy our ticket either too early or too late.

The same phenomenon occurs with product development decisions. There is little value in locking down the color of a consumer product at very long time horizons. Color preferences change over time, so a color choice is best deferred. Yet, if this choice is deferred too long, it becomes expensive to implement. In contrast, some decisions, such as the form of the product, should be decided early. The shape of the product can be much more expensive to change late in the schedule. As a result, we normally freeze color late and form early.

The general principle is that we should make each decision at the point where further delay no longer increases the expected economic outcome. By avoiding "front-loading," we can take advantage of the fact that market and technical uncertainty decrease with time.

Instead of waiting for the "last responsible moment," we can recognize that the cost of certain decisions can rise steeply past a certain point, or that the value created by waiting may have stopped increasing. The timing of economic choices should be based on their economics, not broad philosophical concepts like "front-loading" or "responsible deferral."

Profit vs. Marginal Profit

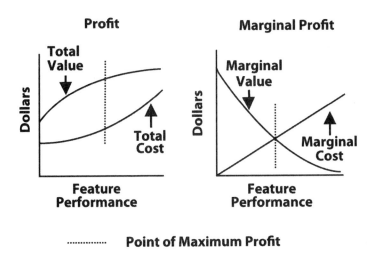

Point of Maximum Profit

Figure 2-4 Maximum profit occurs when marginal value drops to equal marginal cost. This is different from maximizing total value.

Some Basic Economic Concepts

Let me now introduce you to three general economic principles that can lead to better economic choices. We will examine the importance of marginal economics, the concept of sunk costs, and the concept of buying information.

E16: The Principle of Marginal Economics: Always compare marginal cost and marginal value.

When we evaluate the economic impact of an incremental decision, we should compare marginal value and marginal cost. The term "marginal" refers to the amount by which parameters change when we make very small changes in other parameters. For example, the marginal cost of a feature is the increase in product cost caused by adding that feature. As Figure 2-4 shows, comparing marginal economics is quite different from comparing total cost with the total value.[2] Whenever marginal value exceeds marginal cost, the action improves economic value. Importantly, marginal profit and total profit reach zero at different points.

---

[2] Marginal cost and marginal value are simple concepts mathematically. They are just partial derivatives of the value and cost functions.

Product developers frequently fail to pay attention to marginal economics. For example, many products experience "feature creep," in which more and more low-priority features are crammed into a product. Since each of these features contributes value, some companies assume it is desirable to add them. When one considers marginal economics, however, the picture changes. We might discover that the small increase in value cannot be justified when compared to the extra expense and cycle time necessary to add that feature.

Let's look at a more subtle example of marginal economics. A project which is currently 80 percent complete has two important features. One feature has met its objective, and the other has fallen short by 10 percent. Which one should the team work on?

Most companies would work on the feature that has fallen short. They assume that achieving planned objectives maximizes economic outcomes. The correct economic choice is to work on the feature which has the greatest difference between marginal cost and marginal benefit. Interestingly, this is often the feature that has already met its objectives, since it is most likely to have additional unexploited opportunities for improvement. In contrast, the feature that has fallen short may have already exhausted all cheap opportunities for improvement.

Let's look at a final example. Projects may achieve 95 percent of their performance objectives quite quickly, but they may struggle to attain the last 5 percent. Should they fully consume their allotted schedule or opt to deliver 95 percent of the value without further delay? The economic question is whether that last 5 percent is truly worth the expense and cycle time that will be consumed. Again, the decision should be made based on marginal economics. Marginal economics is a simple but very useful concept.

E17: The Sunk Cost Principle: Do not consider money already spent.

If you follow Principle E16, the issue of sunk costs is simple. Money we have already spent is a "sunk cost" and should not enter into an economic choice. We should make the choice on marginal economics.

Let's consider an example. We are working on a project with an average financial return. This project is 90 percent complete. Now, a high-return project becomes available. Should we preempt the average-return project to give priority to the high-return project?

The correct way to analyze this problem is to look at the return on the *remaining* investment for the current average-return project, excluding the money that has already been spent. A project that is 90 percent complete produces its entire incremental return after 10 percent remaining investment. For the new project to be more desirable, it would have to have a return equal to 10 times the average return.

E18: The Principle of Buying Information: The value of information is its expected economic value.

Information reduces uncertainty. When we reduce the uncertainty of an economic outcome, we create economic value. But, what should we pay for this increased certainty? We should not pay more than the economic value that it creates. Let's take a simple example. What is a fair price for a lottery ticket that offers a one-in-a-million chance of paying off $1 million? One dollar.

Now, suppose I offered to sell you perfect information about the first digit of this number. This would increase the odds of winning by a factor of ten, so it raises the value of this ticket to $10. What should you rationally pay for this information? No more than $9.

It is important to recognize that investments in product development can create economic value even when they do not lead to successful products. This is because they can create information that has economic value.

For example, the first version of Microsoft Windows,® Windows 1.0, was a market failure. However, it generated valuable information that influenced later versions of the product.

Consider also the clinical trials that are done on new drugs. Each phase of clinical trials is more expensive than the last. Why do we break the screening process into a series of stages? At the end of each phase, we have better information. This information alters the conditional probability of success for the next phase. This information has clear economic value because it allows us to force early attrition of

Sequencing Risk Reduction

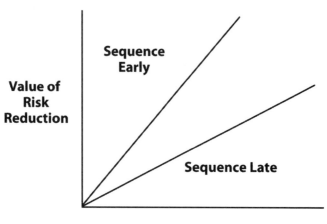

Expense of Risk Reduction

Figure 2-5 We should sequence first those activities that remove the most risk for the least expense. These activities vary from project to project.

doomed products. This prevents them from proceeding to expensive trials and thereby accruing costs that will later be written off. Information reduces uncertainty, and this reduction in uncertainty has a quantifiable economic value.

Finally, let me point out one more subtle implication of this approach towards buying information. It implies that there is an economically optimum sequence for risk-reduction activities. Low-cost activities that remove a lot of risk should occur before high-cost activities that remove very little risk.

We can plot the value of risk reduction compared to its cost, as shown in Figure 2-5, and use this to determine the correct sequence for de-risking the project. Developers sometimes do this intuitively by searching for the "killer test," one capable of removing very high amounts of risk. With the economic view, we can do this more systematically. Our economic framework enables us to assess the value of risk reduction. This can be compared with the cost of risk reduction. The activities that create the maximum value at the minimum cost should be sequenced first.

Debunking Some Popular Fallacies

Now let's evaluate two popular concepts using the economic view. First, we will consider the concept of parallel development of backup solutions, known as set-based concurrent engineering (SBCE). Then, we will examine the perennial question, "Why are so many new product development projects unsuccessful?"

E19: The Insurance Principle: Don't pay more for insurance than the expected loss.

At the moment, it is popular to advocate parallel development of multiple backup solutions as a "best practice" in product development. This approach is called set-based concurrent engineering. Unfortunately, advocates tend to ignore the economic trade-offs inherent in this approach.

We can easily analyze this issue using Principle E16, the principle of marginal economics. When we develop backup solutions, we trade development expense for risk reduction. Risk decreases because parallel solutions have a lower probability of failure than a single solution. This probability of failure drops exponentially.

For example, if a single solution had a 10 percent failure rate, two parallel solutions would have 1 percent failure rate, and three parallel solutions would have 0.1 percent failure rate. But note that the incremental value added by each additional backup solution decreases geometrically. At the same time, the incremental cost added by each additional solution is constant or possibly increasing.

The optimum number of parallel paths occurs when incremental value equals incremental cost. As Figure 2-6 shows, this is clearly a U-curve optimization. There is always a correct number of parallel paths. Since this economic optimum can equal one, parallel paths don't always make economic sense.

This economic view of SBCE contrasts with the popular view, which argues that SBCE is a best practice regardless of the economic context. In this book, we view SBCE as helpful under specific economic conditions. Parallel development of a backup solution is an insurance policy; we pay money to reduce risk. Whenever the economic benefit of this risk reduction is less than the cost of insurance, it is not a good investment.

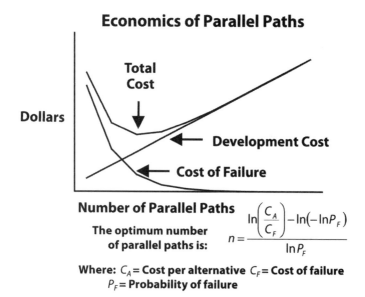

Economics of Parallel Paths

Dollars

Total Cost

Development Cost

Cost of Failure

Number of Parallel Paths

The optimum number of parallel paths is:

$$n = \frac{\ln\left(\frac{C_A}{C_F}\right) - \ln(-\ln P_F)}{\ln P_F}$$

Where: C_A = Cost per alternative C_F = Cost of failure
P_F = Probability of failure

Figure 2-6 The incremental benefit of adding parallel paths progressively decreases. Multiple paths increase development costs. The minimum point is frequently a single path.

E20: The Newsboy Principle: High probability of failure does not equal bad economics.

In any course on decision theory, one is exposed to a classic problem in applied economics known as the "newsboy problem." If a newsboy makes 50 cents on each newspaper he sells and loses 25 cents on each newspaper that is not sold, how many papers should he have in stock to deal with uncertain demand? If he holds exactly enough newspapers for the average demand, he will be as likely to lose a sale as he is to have an extra newspaper. But because he loses less money with an overstock than he makes when he sells a newspaper, he would rather experience an overstock. This is another problem of marginal profit.

The anticipated demand level that optimizes expected profits is known as the "critical fractile." In this case, he should run out of newspapers one-third of the time. This equalizes the cost of overstock and the cost of shortage, which, in turn, maximizes profit. Whenever there are strong economic asymmetries in loss and gain, the optimum success rate can be surprisingly low. For example, if the newsboy made $1 on each sale and lost 1 cent on each overstock, he should target to have excess newspapers about 99 percent of the time.

What can a product developer learn from this problem? At a recent conference, a speaker warned that 96 percent of new products fail to meet their economic objectives. He proposed that better management could raise product development ROI by almost 20 times, and advocated more aggressive filtering of opportunities. For the last 30 years, I have heard similar arguments in many articles and speeches.

Let's look at the economics of this problem. Product development has remarkable asymmetries between the payoff of success and the cost of failure. For example, a new drug might produce $1 billion in profits, but it may be possible to knowledgeably truncate investment in a candidate molecule after investing a mere $10,000 in evaluation costs.

What would happen if drug companies filtered out all molecules with less than a 50 percent chance of success? Such aggressive filtering, before acquiring sufficient information to make a good economic choice, would eliminate all uncertain and poorly understood opportunities. However, it is precisely these uncertain opportunities that have large payoff asymmetries, making them the best sources of new drugs. Opening the filter to pass these asymmetric opportunities actually increases economic value.

In fact, economics would suggest that the 96 percent failure rate tells us more about the asymmetry of payoffs from product development than it does about our management competence. When we make much more money from success than we lose from failure, then we should be willing to invest in opportunities that have considerably less than a 50 percent chance of success. This problem appears to be better understood by economists than by observers of product development.

E21: The Show Me the Money Principle: To influence financial decisions, speak the language of money.

We end this chapter with some practical advice. Most corporations give control over financial resources to people who worry about the economics of their choices. To influence these people, we must speak the language of economics, not the language of proxy variables. If you use the tools in this chapter, you will be able to frame your proposed actions in an economic context. When we speak to those who control the money, using the language of money, we can get fast decisions and enthusiastic support.

Whenever I am told that management makes decisions too slowly, I ask to see the specific proposal that went to management. Invariably, I discover that the cost and benefit of the decision are either unquantified or poorly quantified. In my experience, most managers make amazingly fast decisions when they are presented with compelling economic arguments. Our economic framework does not simply help us make better decisions, it helps us get support to implement them.

Conclusion

The economic view of product development enables us to approach product development decisions as economic choices. This is quite different from chasing after whichever proxy variable is popular at the moment. By transforming all proxy variables to the same unit of measure, life-cycle profits, we can make the multivariable trade-offs that lie at the heart of product development. We use an economic framework to make this transformation, and we express our results as decision rules.

Even imperfect decision rules improve decision making. These decision rules are critically important because they permit us to quickly process the small, perishable, economic decisions that arrive continuously and randomly. They enable us to gain the benefits of decentralized control without losing economic alignment. They enable us to communicate with management in the language of economics.

Of all our decision rules, the one that most transforms our thinking is the one that is missing today in most companies, a quantified cost of delay. This decision rule will be used continuously throughout this book. With it, we can bring the hidden cost of queues into the bright daylight of economic understanding. We can use this decision rule to quantify the economic impact of work product sitting idle in queues, a key concept that we will develop in the next chapter.

3

Managing Queues

Festina lente[1] — Latin Proverb

In the last chapter, I showed you how to use an economic framework to guide your product development decisions. When we use such a framework, we often discover that cycle time has high economic leverage. If we can find cheap ways to reduce cycle time, our profits go up. But what causes long product development cycle time? I hinted at the answer in the last chapter. Our real problem is periods of inactivity, not slow activities. But why do we have inactivity when we have enough resources to do all the work?

To answer this question, we need to understand a little queueing theory, the focus of this chapter. I will begin by providing a brief introduction to queueing theory. Then, we will examine the behavior of queues, and their economic impact. Finally, we will discuss six principles that can lead to better queue management, and nine examples of specific product development queues.

Queueing Theory

Queueing theory originated in 1909 with a paper by a mathematician named Ågner Krarup Erlang at the Copenhagen Telephone Company. Telephones were a growing technology, and network managers were trying to determine how many phone lines were needed for a specific number of people. This was a nontrivial problem because phone calls arrived at random times and they had random durations.

Erlang was the first person to tackle this problem using probability and statistics. He was able to accurately estimate the probability

---

[1] Translation: Make haste slowly. In Aesop's fable, "The Tortoise and the Hare," the hare excelled at adding value quickly, but still lost the race due to inactivity. Eliminating periods of inactivity, such as time spent in queues, can be far more important than speeding up activities.

that a call would be blocked at different levels of capacity utilization. Queueing theory can provide important insights to product developers because we wrestle with similar problems of unpredictable work arrival times and unpredictable task durations.

Before we discuss queues, we must introduce a little vocabulary. When we describe queueing systems, we refer to the queue, which is the waiting work, and the server, which is the resource performing the work. The pattern with which work arrives, which is usually unpredictable, is known as the arrival process. The time it takes the server to accomplish the work may also be unpredictable. This is known as the service process. We handle waiting work in a certain sequence, such as first-in-first-out (FIFO). This sequence is known as the queueing discipline.

There are many different types of queueing processes, but we can gain enormous insight by looking at one of the simplest of queues, what is called an M/M/1/∞ (infinite) queue. This way of labeling a queue is known as Kendall notation. It is named after the British statistician David Kendall, who first used it in 1953.

The first letter "M" refers to the arrival process, in this case a Markov process. In a Markov process, the elapsed time between arrivals is exponentially distributed. This simply means that short interarrival times are more probable than long ones. This is also known as a memoryless arrival pattern, because each arrival is statistically independent from the next.

The second "M" refers to the service process. It tells us that the service process is also a Markov process. This means the time it takes to perform the service is also exponentially distributed and memoryless.

The number "1" refers to the number of parallel servers in the system, and the final term "∞" (infinite) describes the upper limit on queue size. In this case, there is no upper limit on the size of the queue. Later in this book, I will discuss other types of queues, and I will describe them when I introduce them.

Queueing processes have various measures of performance. Two of the most important are occupancy and cycle time. For example, we can measure the number of items in the queue, the number in service, and the number in the entire system. Likewise, we can measure the time spent in the queue, time spent in service, and the total time in the system.

Why Queues Matter

Queues matter because they are economically important, they are poorly managed, and they have the potential to be much better managed. Queues profoundly affect the economics of product development. They cause valuable work products to sit idle, waiting to access busy resources. This idle time increases inventory, which is the root cause of many other economic problems. As we shall see in this chapter, among other things, queues hurt cycle time, quality, and efficiency.

Despite their economic importance, queues are not managed in today's development processes. Few product developers are aware of the causal links between high capacity-utilization, queues, and poor economic performance. Instead, developers assume that their cycle times will be faster when resources are fully utilized. In reality, as we shall see later, high levels of capacity utilization are actually a primary cause of long cycle time.

Fortunately, queues can be managed better. The economic framework of the last chapter allows us to logically and systematically attack this problem. With this framework, we can quantify the economic cost of queues, justify interventions that reduce queues, and access an enormous untapped opportunity to improve economic performance. To begin, we must understand why queues frequently escape scrutiny and how they cause waste.

Q1: The Principle of Invisible Inventory: Product development inventory is physically and financially invisible.

Why are we so blind to the existence of product development queues? In manufacturing, we are keenly aware of our inventory. We see it every time we walk the factory floor. Our chief financial officer (CFO) can report the exact amount of work-in-process inventory (WIP) by simply reading it off the balance sheet. If we cut WIP by $10 million, the CFO is overjoyed because we just freed up $10 million in cash.

Unfortunately, our situation is quite different in product development. If we ask our CFO, "How much design-in-process (DIP) inventory do we have?" we will get a puzzled look and the reply, "There is nothing on our balance sheet called design-in-process inventory. We have no inventory in product development."

If we don't believe the CFO, we can walk through the engineering department and look for inventory. But since the inventory in a product development process is not physical objects but information, it is virtually invisible. Inventory could double overnight in an engineering department, and we would see no change in the physical appearance of that department.

One engineering manager from Hewlett-Packard (HP) remarked, "Our inventory is bits on a disk drive, and we have very big disk drives here at HP!" Inventory in product development is both physically and financially invisible.

But just because this inventory is invisible doesn't mean it doesn't exist. Product development inventory is observable through its effects: increased cycle time, delayed feedback, constantly shifting priorities, and status reporting. Unfortunately, all of these effects hurt economic performance.

Q2: The Principle of Queueing Waste: Queues are the root cause of the majority of economic waste in product development.
Product development queues do much more damage than manufacturing queues for two reasons. First, product development queues tend to be much bigger than manufacturing queues. It takes orders of magnitude more time for work products to flow through the product development pipeline compared to the manufacturing pipeline.

Even worse, because these queues are invisible, there are no natural predators keeping them under control. Companies do not measure queues, they do not manage queues, and most don't even realize that queues are a problem. Ironically, some companies are even proud of their queues, boasting of the size of their product development pipeline.

Second, queues in product development create many forms of economic waste. This waste comes from six different sources, as shown in Figure 3-1.

First, queues increase cycle time. It takes longer to reach the front of a large line than a small one. By quantifying cost of delay, we can attach a specific financial cost to this queue time. Usually, delay cost rises linearly with queue size.

Second, queues increase the riskiness of a product development process. Queues increase the transit time through the product development pipeline. When the transit time goes up, we are more vulnerable

The Effect of Queues

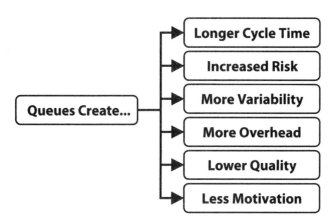

Figure 3-1 Queues are the underlying cause of many economic problems in product development. Yet, they remain unmeasured at 98 percent of product developers.

to changes in customer preference, preemption by competitor product introductions, and shifts in underlying technology. In the next chapter, we will explain why risk rises exponentially with cycle time.

Third, queues increase the variability of our development process. When we load our development process to high levels of utilization, we are at an operating point that tends to amplify variability. As we shall see later in this chapter, this means that small deviations in loading will turn into very large deviations in cycle time.

Fourth, queues raise the costs of our process. The more projects we have in process, the more projects we have to track and report status on. Even worse, we will ask for more progress reports per project because queues lead to long transit times.

It is worth noting that lean factories do far less status reporting than traditional factories, primarily because they have much faster cycle times. A traditional factory with a 16-week lead time may use 60 move transactions to maintain visibility on a work order moving through the factory. A lean factory making the same product might do two transactions, one to start the work order and the other to close it out. Bigger queues inevitably create higher overhead costs.

Fifth, queues reduce quality by delaying feedback from downstream processes. If a programmer makes a bad assumption about a protocol and gets feedback one day later, she stops making this bad assumption. If she must wait for 30 days to get this feedback, she will embed the bad assumption into 30 days' worth of code.

Queues delay feedback, and delayed feedback leads to higher costs. This feedback effect is orders of magnitude more important in product development than manufacturing because manufacturing work is inherently repetitive.

In contrast, in product development, we are constantly trying new ideas and we rely on rapid feedback to truncate unproductive efforts. We cannot truncate a bad path quickly when feedback is slow.

This is actually a more serious problem than most developers realize because the waste created by following a bad path typically increases exponentially, not linearly, as we progress down the path.

Sixth, queues have a negative psychological effect. They undermine motivation and initiative. When the next process will be ready to use our work product within an hour, we feel a sense of urgency. When the next process has a 4-week queue, we feel there is little value in hurrying to finish our work. After all, our work product will simply wait in queue. Widespread queues demotivate workers and undermine initiative.

Some companies incorrectly assume that a queue off the critical path has no cost. When you examine these six wastes, you will realize this is not true. Only one of these wastes arises from the cost of delay. The other five wastes are still present even when the queue is off the critical path. For example, queues delay feedback and raise overhead, even when they are not on the critical path.

Do product developers realize that queues are a severe problem? I'll let you decide. From time to time, I speak at conferences on product development metrics. Whenever I do so, I ask the audience two questions. Do you measure cycle time, and do you measure queues? The answer: 100 percent of product developers measure cycle time, and about 2 percent measure queues. When 98 percent of product developers do not even measure queues, we have an important problem.

The Behavior of Queues

Let's now look deeper at what queueing theory tells us about the behavior of queues. To do so, we need to understand how capacity

Queue Size vs. Capacity Utilization

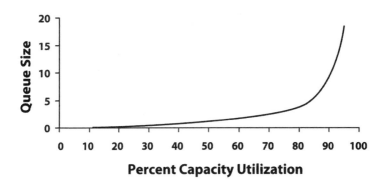

Percent Capacity Utilization

Note: Assumes M/M/1/∞ Queue

Figure 3-2 Queue size increases rapidly with capacity utilization.

utilization and variability affect the size of queues. We need to understand the relative frequency of high-queue states and why they are
important. We also need to understand how the structure of a queueing system affects its performance, and what will happen if we link
queues together.

Q3: The Principle of Queueing Capacity Utilization: Capacity utilization increases queues exponentially.

The single most important factor that affects queue size is capacity utilization. Sadly, few product developers recognize this. For
13 years, I collected data from attendees of my executive courses
at Caltech. The average product developer loads their development
process to 98.5 percent utilization. What would queueing theory say
about this?

Figure 3-2 shows the actual relationship between capacity
utilization and cycle time for a M/M/1/∞ queue. As we approach 100
percent utilization, queues become exponentially large. In fact, each
time we halve the amount of excess capacity, we roughly double the
average queue size. As we move from 60 to 80 percent, we double
the queue. As we move from 80 to 90 percent, we double it again.
As we move from 90 to 95 percent, we double it again. Most product

Effect of Capacity Utilization

If Percent Capacity Utilization $= \rho$

Then, Percent Unblocked Time $= 1 - \rho$

Number of Items in Queue $= \dfrac{\rho^2}{1-\rho}$

Number of Items in System $= \dfrac{\rho}{1-\rho}$

Percent Queue Time $= \rho$

$$\dfrac{\text{Cycle Time}}{\text{Value-Added Time}} = \dfrac{1}{1-\rho}$$

Note: For M/M/1/∞ Queue

Figure 3-3 Capacity utilization allows us to predict many important characteristics of an M/M/1/∞ queue. At the same time, we can use these characteristics to estimate capacity utilization.

developers load to utilization levels that would only work in a deterministic process.

It is worth developing a quantitative understanding of the critical effect of capacity utilization on the behavior of a queue. In queueing theory, the symbol for capacity utilization is "ρ," the Greek letter rho. This single number tells us a surprising amount about queue behavior. Figure 3-3 shows how capacity utilization affects key measures of performance for a M/M/1/∞ queue. Knowing capacity utilization allows us to predict:

1. The percent of time arriving work will find the resource busy.

2. The average number of items in queue.

3. The average number of items in the system.

4. The percent of overall cycle time that is queue time.

5. The ratio of cycle time to value-added time.

Some of these formulas surprise many product developers. Few product developers realize that percent capacity utilization and percent queue time are identical for a random queue. When we choose to operate an M/M/1/∞ queue at 95 percent utilization, we are choosing to operate with 95 percent queue time. Also, most product developers underestimate how steeply queues grow when we approach 100 percent utilization.

It is worth noting that these formulas work in both directions. We can use capacity utilization to predict queue size and cycle time, and we can also use queue size or cycle time to calculate capacity utilization. This property is quite useful from a practical perspective, because it is often very difficult to directly measure capacity utilization in product development processes. This difficulty arises because capacity utilization is the ratio of two factors, demand and capacity, that are individually hard to estimate.

Even the best product developers can easily have a 10 percent error in estimating demand, which is the work content of tasks they have never done before. Even the best product developers can easily have a 10 percent error in estimating capacity, which is the productivity of an engineer on a task they have never done before. When these errors combine, they may not be sure if they are operating at 55 percent or 95 percent utilization. But this can cause a 25 to 1 difference in queue size.

In practice, although capacity utilization lies at the heart of queue behavior, we rarely measure it directly. As you shall see throughout this book, we find it more practical to measure factors like queue size and WIP.

Q4: The Principle of High-Queue States: Most of the damage done by a queue is caused by high-queue states.

The probability we will find a queue in a specific quantitative state is a function of capacity utilization. Low-queue states are more probable than high-queue states, however, high-queue states are usually more important.

Figure 3-4 shows the probability of different queue states for an M/M/1/∞ queue operating at 75 percent utilization. Although each increasingly high-queue state is less likely, we must remember that high-queue states delay more jobs. As a result, they have a surprisingly strong influence on cycle time.

Let's look at an example. The economic damage done by a queue state is a product of its probability and its consequences. The

System States at 75% Utilization

Number in System	Probability	Cumulative Probability
0	25.0 %	25.0 %
1	18.8 %	43.8 %
2	14.1 %	57.8 %
3	10.5 %	68.4 %
4	7.9 %	76.3 %
5	5.9 %	82.2 %
6	4.4 %	86.7 %
7	3.3 %	90.0 %
8	2.5 %	92.5 %
9	1.9 %	94.4 %
10	1.4 %	95.8 %

State Probability = $(1-\rho)\rho^n$

Figure 3-4 When a M/M/1/∞ queue is loaded to 75 percent utilization, it has two or fewer jobs in the system 57.8 percent of the time. Nevertheless, the average number of jobs in the system is three, because of the disproportionate impact of high-queue states.

probability that we will find two units in the queue is 75 percent of the probability that we will find one unit in the queue. However, delaying two units creates twice the delay cost. This means that over time, the less probable state of a two-unit queue does 150 percent of the economic damage done by a one-unit queue. Thus, the improbable tail of high-queue states has a very important effect on average cycle time. In Chapter 6, we shall exploit this fact to achieve better control of cycle time.

Q5: The Principle of Queueing Variability: Variability increases queues linearly.

Variability also has an important effect on queues, but one that is much less significant than capacity utilization. Figure 3-5 shows how queue size varies with variability. The equation shown in this figure is known as the Allen-Cuneen heavy traffic approximation.

A heavy traffic approximation applies when systems are operating at high-capacity utilization, which is virtually always the case for product development processes. Thus, the equation is useful for

Queue Size with Different Coefficients of Variation

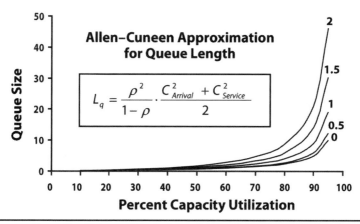

Note: Coefficient of Variation = Standard Deviation/Mean
An exponential distribution has a coefficient of variation equal to one.

Figure 3-5 Queue size is linearly proportional to variability. As a result, reducing variability has much less effect on queue size than lowering capacity utilization.

product developers. It shows that queues are proportional to the average of the squares of the coefficient of variation for arrivals and the coefficient of variation for the service process.

The coefficient of variation is a measure of variability that is computed as the ratio between the standard deviation and the mean of a probability distribution. You can think of it as a general measure of the relative breadth of a probability distribution. Since the square of the standard deviation is the variance of a distribution, this means that queues vary linearly with variance, a point worth remembering.

Different distributions have different coefficients of variation. A Poisson distribution, which characterizes the arrivals and service times in an $M/M/1/\infty$ queue, has a coefficient of variation of one because its mean and its variance are equal. A deterministic process with no variation would have a coefficient of variation equal to zero.

It is worth noting that under heavy traffic, queue size depends on both the arrival process and the service process. This should make sense. Even if arrivals were perfectly predictable, queues would still form if the service process had variability. Likewise, even if the service process were perfectly predictable, queues would still form if random arrivals created periods of high arrival rate. Later in this chapter, in Principle Q8, we will examine how this affects the behavior of linked queues.

We should consider carefully what this equation implies about the consequences of reducing variability. If we were able to make the processing time in a heavily loaded M/M/1/∞ queue exactly the same for every job, which is a very ambitious goal indeed, the service time coefficient of variation would drop to zero.[2] However, this would only cut the average queue size in half. It would not make queues disappear, because it would have no effect on the randomness of arrival times.

So, be very cautious if you think you can solve the problem of queues by reducing variability. The folly of this approach will become even clearer when you discover the economic importance of variability in Chapter 4.

Q6: The Principle of Variability Amplification: Operating at high levels of capacity utilization increases variability.

Let's now look more deeply at this queueing curve. The effect of changes in loading depends on where we are operating on this curve. This is because the slope of the queueing curve affects how changes in loading are transformed into changes in queue size. This slope is inversely proportional to the square of capacity utilization, as shown in Figure 3-6. Thus, as we move up the queueing curve and the slope gets steeper, random changes in loading will have a larger effect on cycle times.

For example, a change in loading at 95 percent utilization produces a cycle time impact that is 25 times higher than the same change in loading at 75 percent utilization. Thus, when product developers choose to operate their processes at high levels of utilization, they create unnecessary and wasteful variability in their processes. It is important to realize that this variability is a self-inflicted wound.

Q7: The Principle of Queueing Structure: Serve pooled demand with reliable high-capacity servers.

In queueing theory, we distinguish between different process structures. For example, we can service a demand stream with a single server in an M/M/1 queue, or with "n" servers in an M/M/n queue. As shown in Figure 3-7, we can have single or multiple servers with a

---

[2] Since this new queue would have deterministic rather than Markovian service times, it would be classified as a M/D/1/∞ queue, rather than a M/M/1/∞ queue.

Queues Amplify Variability

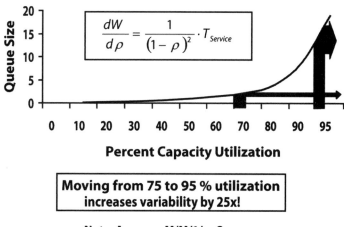

$$\frac{dW}{d\rho} = \frac{1}{\left(1-\rho\right)^2} \cdot T_{Service}$$

Percent Capacity Utilization

Moving from 75 to 95 % utilization increases variability by 25x!

Note: Assumes M/M/1/∞ Queue

Figure 3-6 As we increase capacity utilization, small changes in loading produce increasingly large changes in queue size and cycle time. Our processes become increasingly unstable at high levels of capacity utilization.

single shared queue, or we can have individual queues for each server. The performance of these structures differs.

Most people have experienced some of these structures at airport check-in lines. Some airlines feed a group of ticket agents from a single queue, while others have a queue for each agent. The performance of these two structures is different, even when they both have the same demand and capacity. If there is one queue per server, a single bad job can block everything behind it in the queue. This means that all customers in that server's queue will be severely delayed, while the other queues will not experience this delay.

In contrast, with a shared queue, all customers experience a smaller delay. The mathematical consequences of this are that the variance in processing times is lower when we use shared queues. Unfortunately, one queue per server structures are very common in product development processes. Such structures lead to unnecessarily large queues.

An alternative to a single-queue, multiple-server structure is a single queue with a single high-capacity server. This choice is a bit

Queueing System Structure

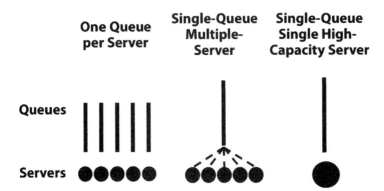

|One Queue
per Server|Single-Queue
Multiple-
Server|Single-Queue
Single High-
Capacity Server|

Figure 3-7 Single-queue multiple-server systems will have less variation in processing time than systems that have a dedicated server for each queue. The lowest variation occurs with a single high-capacity server, but only when it is very reliable.

more complex. The advantage of a single server is that processing times will be faster. Imagine 100 slow ticket agents processing at the same rate as five fast ticket agents. The slow agents would take 20 times longer to accomplish their task. A slow service process from multiple low-capacity servers is particularly burdensome when the system is lightly loaded. Under such conditions, service time is the majority of cycle time.

However, there are two practical disadvantages to using a single high-capacity server. First, it is less robust with respect to server failure, since a failure of the single server will stop all flow. Second, a single server can be blocked by a single bad job. For example, if one engineering job requires breaking the laws of physics, it will stop many jobs for a very long time. This does not happen in a multiple server system where flow will simply continue at a reduced rate. In Chapter 6, we will discuss strategies for dealing with tasks that explode to very long duration, a very real possibility in product development.

Q8: The Principle of Linked Queues: Adjacent queues see arrival or service variability depending on loading.

The behavior of linked queues is interesting because the departure process for one queue becomes the arrival process for the next one.

Depending on the size of the queue at a process, its output pattern will either look more like its arrival pattern or its service pattern. In effect, the queue can function as a buffer isolating the variability of the arrival pattern from the departure pattern.

Some nice examples of linked queues occur in traffic systems. At rush hour on the Los Angeles freeway system, stoplights operate at the freeway on-ramps. We hold arriving cars in this queue and release them at a regular cadence onto the highway. This conditions the flow arriving on the freeway and prevents us from injecting cars onto the freeway at highly variable rates. This, in turn, is important because highly variable arrivals generate what are called "shock waves" when freeways are congested. If a group of cars merges onto the freeway, this causes nearby cars to slow. The following cars react later and have to decelerate even more quickly. This, in turn, leads to an accordion-like pattern of turbulence in traffic flow.

This turbulence can be reduced if the injection rate is conditioned by a metered queue at the on-ramp. The exit rate of this queue becomes the low-variability cadence of the stoplight, instead of the high-variability pattern of driver arrivals at the on-ramp. Of course, when there is no queue at the on-ramp, the injection rate onto the freeway will be identical to the arrival pattern at the on-ramp.

Another example of interacting queues is the way we reduce the number of lanes on a freeway in a construction zone. We do not narrow down over a short distance, but instead, reduce the width from four lanes to three over a distance of at least a mile. Any narrowing process creates turbulence in the flow, since cars must change lanes. We do not want this turbulence to be present at the bottleneck, because it would reduce the flow rate of the bottleneck. Instead, we move the turbulence of the narrowing process away from the bottleneck. This permits smoother flow at the bottleneck and thus, higher throughput at the bottleneck, which is the rate-limiting process.

Thus, it is important to go beyond the popular but simplistic idea that the capacity of the bottleneck controls system flow. In fact, flow through a bottleneck is affected strongly by the process that precedes the bottleneck. The upstream process determines the variation in the arrival rate at the bottleneck, and this affects the queue. Managing the process upstream of the bottleneck is a valuable tool for improving flow at the bottleneck.

The Economics of Queues

Now that we understand how queues work, let's look at the economics of queues. First, we will look at the problem of optimizing queue size. The higher we make capacity utilization, the more we pay for queues, but the less we pay for excess capacity. If we use our economic framework to express these two factors in the same economic unit of measure, we can make quantitative trade-offs between them. Second, we will look at how we can use queueing discipline to reduce the economic cost of a queue without reducing the size of queue.

Q9: The Principle of Queue Size Optimization: Optimum queue size is an economic trade-off.

We can quantitatively trade off queue size against capacity utilization. To do so, we must calculate the total cost of our process, combining the cost of capacity and the cost of the queue, and determine where this is minimal.

The solution for a M/M/1/∞ queue is shown in Figure 3-8. The first term in this equation is the capacity we would need if there were no variation in arrival times or service times. The second term can be viewed as the excess capacity margin required to compensate for variation. We can see that the required margin is proportional to the cost of delay and inversely proportional to the cost of capacity. This should make sense. When delay cost is high, we prevent delays by having excess capacity. When capacity is expensive, we can afford less margin.

Note the striking difference between a quantitative approach to optimizing queues and a qualitative approach. When we use a quantitative approach, we focus on the idea of trade-offs. Because the correct queue size is based on analysis, our answer automatically changes along with changes in our environment. If either cost of delay or cost of capacity change, the optimum point for our U-curve changes.

Contrast this with the simpler qualitative approach. If we decide that "Queues are evil," we will seek the smallest possible queue size. Our goal will be unaffected by changes in the economic environment. Approaching queues as a philosophical problem rather than a quantitative one decouples our solutions from economics. When economics change, our solutions will remain static.

Theoretical Optimum Capacity

Total Cost = Cost of Capacity + Cost of Delay

$$C_T = C_C + C_D$$

$$C_T = C_C \mu + C_D (\frac{\lambda}{\mu - \lambda})$$

Total Cost is optimum at:

$$\mu_o = \lambda + \sqrt{\frac{C_D \lambda}{C_C}}$$

μ = Average Capacity C_T = Total Cost
λ = Average Arrival Rate C_D = Project Cost of Delay
μ_o = Optimal Capacity C_C = Project Cost of Capacity

**Note: Solution for M/M/1/∞ Queue,
Taha, H., Operations Research, Macmillan, New York, 1987**

Figure 3-8 Optimal capacity for a process must be higher when cost of delay increases because queues become more expensive. When the cost of capacity rises, then optimal capacity decreases.

Some readers may observe that we could also reduce queue size by reducing variability. This is true, but we should remember that variability has less impact than capacity utilization, as explained in Principle Q5. For example, we would have to eliminate all variability in our service process to cut queues in half. In contrast, we can create the same results by adding 10 percent more capacity to a system loaded at 90 percent utilization. In practice, capacity margin is a better weapon for fighting queues than variability reduction.

Q10: The Principle of Queueing Discipline: Queue cost is affected by the sequence in which we handle the jobs in the queue.

In product development, our goal is to reduce the economic cost of queues, not simply to reduce the size of queues. What makes these two factors different? The cost of a queue is not just determined by its size; it depends on which items are delayed, and how long they are delayed. By changing the sequence in which we service the jobs in the queue, we can significantly reduce the cost of the queue.

As mentioned earlier, the sequence in which we handle the jobs in a queue is called the queueing discipline. When all the items in the queue are homogeneous, queueing discipline doesn't matter. Under such conditions, the only way to reduce queue cost is to reduce queue size. This is the common situation in manufacturing, where all jobs take the same amount of time to complete, and they all have the same cost of delay. In such cases, for example, in the Toyota Production System, we use a first-in-first-out (FIFO) queueing discipline.

In product development, the situation is quite different. Our jobs have different delay costs, and they block resources for differing amounts of time. As a result, we can create value with a thoughtful queueing discipline. For example, if two jobs take the same amount of time, it is better to service the one with the highest delay cost first. If two jobs have the same cost of delay, it is better to process the shortest job first.

In Chapter 7, we will examine more advanced scheduling methods, including those that can be used when the actual duration of a job is unknown. For now, I'll just give you two simple heuristics: high cost of delay before low cost of delay, and short jobs before long jobs.

To roughly assess whether a different queuing discipline could improve your economics, ask three questions. First, is there a difference in the cost of delay of different jobs in the queue? Second, is there a difference in the time a job will block a resource? Third, is the average length of the queue large? In most product development processes, all three of these conditions apply, so we can make money with better queueing discipline.

The third factor, average queue length, is quite important. The payoff from queueing discipline is highest when queue sizes are large. In such circumstances, moving a high cost-of-delay job to the head of the line leads to a significant cycle time reduction and large economic benefits. When queue sizes are small, the payoff of queueing discipline is much lower.

Think of a hospital emergency room. When there is a 6-hour wait, critical patients must be moved to the head of the line. When waiting times are very short, patients can be processed in FIFO order. Ideally, our goal is to make queue size so small that we don't need queueing discipline. Since we are so far from this point today, queueing discipline is, in practice, a very useful tool.

Finally, let's stress that any economically grounded queueing discipline relies on knowing the cost of delay for projects in the queue. This method of setting priorities has an interesting side benefit. When we base priorities on economics, they tend to remain more stable than priorities based on opinions. Opinions can be changed by the last phone call received from a customer. In contrast, economic facts change less abruptly. The key to stable priorities is to link them to economic facts.

Managing Queues

In this section, we would like to provide six principles that will help you manage queues. First, we want to provide an indispensable practical tool for managing flow: the cumulative flow diagram (CFD).

Second, we will show you a simple but powerful tool called Little's Formula. Then, we will provide two important principles for controlling queue size. Finally, we will expose you to the counterintuitive nature of random processes. This will help you to recognize the great value in reacting to emergent queues, a topic we will discuss in more detail in Chapter 6.

Q11: The Cumulative Flow Principle: Use CFDs to monitor queues.

One of the most useful tools for managing queues is the cumulative flow diagram (CFD), depicted in Figure 3-9. This diagram uses time as its horizontal axis and cumulative quantity as its vertical axis. We plot cumulative arrivals at a process as one variable and cumulative departures as a second variable. The vertical distance between the arrival line and the departure line is work that has arrived but not yet departed, thus, the instantaneous size of the queue. The horizontal distance between the arrival and departure line tells us the cycle time through the process for an item of work. The total area between these two lines tells us the size of the queue.

We can also use this diagram to determine demand and capacity. The slope of the arrival line tells us the demand feeding into the queue. The slope of the departure line tells us the capacity of the process emptying the queue. Thus, the CFD visually presents a great deal of information about our queue.

Cumulative Flow Diagram

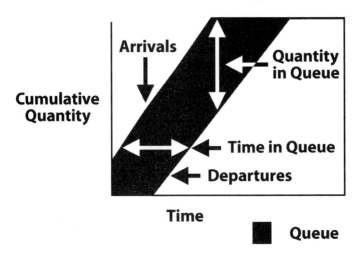

Figure 3-9 The cumulative flow diagram visually depicts what is happening to a queue over time. It is a powerful tool for understanding queueing problems and for diagnosing the causes of queues.

Most organizations do not yet use CFDs. If they track queues at all, they simply track queue size as a function of time. Of course, this is a great starting point. It is easy to do, and it starts to focus attention on managing queues.

I prefer using the CFD because it provides more information. Why? Queue size only shows us the balance between arrivals and departures. But a change in queue size doesn't tell us if the queue is caused by excess arrivals or by insufficient departures. With a CFD, we can see exactly which of these factors is the problem. Furthermore, on a CFD, we can observe the time dependency of demand and capacity.

Changes in the slope of the arrival and departure lines inform us of trends in demand and capacity. Moreover, as we shall see in Chapter 5, batch size problems are also visible on a CFD. When arrivals or departures occur in large batches, they appear as jagged lines on the CFD.

In fact, with a CFD we can detect an emerging queue, determine the size of our problem, identify what we have to do about it, and determine when it will be corrected. We will discuss this more in Chapter 7. As a practical tool for controlling queues, few methods rival the CFD.

Little's Formula

For Time in Queue: $\quad W_Q = \dfrac{L_Q}{\lambda}$

Queue time for average job $= W_Q$

Number of customers in queue $= L_Q$

Average processing rate $= \lambda$

For Time in System: $\quad W_S = \dfrac{L_S}{\lambda}$

Time in system for average job $= W_S$

Average number of jobs in system $= L_S$

Average processing rate $= \lambda$

Figure 3-10 Little's Formula relates queue size, cycle time, and processing rate. It is most often used on the queue or the entire system.

Q12: Little's Formula: Wait Time = Queue Size/Processing Rate

Another valuable tool is one of the most famous principles of queueing theory, Little's Formula. It describes the relationship between wait time, queue size, and processing rate. It is named after the MIT professor John D. C. Little, who proved it in 1961.[3] The formula states that average queue time will be equal to the average queue size divided by the average processing rate. This formula is amazingly robust; it applies to virtually all queueing disciplines, all arrival processes, and all departure processes.

Little's Formula is shown in Figure 3-10. I think of this like the problem of emptying a tank of water. If the tank holds 10 liters, the queue size, and we can remove 1 liter per minute, the processing rate, then it will take 10 minutes to empty the tank, the time in queue.

Little's Formula can be applied to either the queue or to the system as a whole. Applying it to the system as a whole is particularly useful, especially if we have trouble distinguishing which items are in queue

---

[3] Little's Formula appears in books on queueing that predate Little's 1961 publication, such as the book, *Queues, Inventories and Maintenance,* by Philip M. Morse, John Wiley & Sons, Inc. 1958, p.75. Professor Morse was also a professor at MIT. Professor Little formalized its proof.

and which ones are in service. This problem is common when we first start measuring queues.

When people learn that queues are bad, the easy way to eliminate this problem is to report that all jobs are in process and none are in queue by stating, "We are working on everything." We avoid this problem by using Little's Formula at the system level. We simply pay attention to total DIP and don't try to determine what portion of it is in queue. This allows us to predict cycle time directly from the quantity in the system and the processing rate. We can do such a prediction either at the level of the overall system or at the level of any individual process.

For example, if our development process has 50 projects in process and completes an average of 10 projects per year, it will take an average of 5 years to complete a project. If our testing area has 50 tests in process and completes an average of 10 tests per week, it will average 5 weeks to complete a test.

Little's Formula also gives us a quick way to assess our overall cycle times. If we simply determine the amount of DIP in each process stage, we can divide this by the average completion rate and determine the cycle time through each stage of our process. Knowing the cycle time for each process stage, we can determine our overall process cycle time. And once we know the cycle time for each process stage, we can also compute the delay cost for each stage.

Of course, when we calculate total cycle time, we must be careful to focus on critical-path activities. Queue time off the critical path does not increase total cycle time and does not generate delay cost.

However, as mentioned earlier, a queue off the critical path is not a free queue. It can actually be quite expensive for two reasons. First, tasks are actually not either on or off the critical path; instead, they have probabilities of getting on the critical path. The cost of delay for a task that is not on the critical path is the cost of delay for the project times the probability that the task will get on the critical path.

Second, as mentioned earlier, delay cost is not the only economic cost of queues. Even queues with no delay cost do economic damage. They delay feedback, add overhead, reduce quality, and raise variability.

Sometimes we can use Little's Formula to determine the equivalent number of jobs in queue, even though people claim that they are "working on everything." In such cases, we multiply queue time by processing rate to get queue size.

But where do we get queue time? There are two relatively easy ways to obtain it. First, we can compare queueless cycle time for a process with average cycle time. Mark a job as a "hot lot" and give it preemption privileges in all queues and processes. It will experience no queue time, so its cycle time is 100 percent service time. Compare this with average cycle time and the difference is queue time.

A second approach is to calculate average service time by dividing a department's applied hours by its throughput. Then queue time is simply the total processing time minus service time. For example, if the process applies 40 hours a week and completes 10 jobs, then each job receives 4 hours of processing. If average cycle time through this process is 40 hours, this process has 10 percent value-added time and 90 percent queue time.

Q13: The First Queue Size Control Principle: Don't control capacity utilization, control queue size.

When product developers first discover the importance of capacity utilization, they are tempted to try to control cycle time by controlling capacity utilization. Unfortunately, this is not practical in product development, since we cannot estimate either demand or capacity to sufficient accuracy, as discussed in Principle Q3. Capacity utilization is almost useless as a metric for real-time control.

Fortunately, there is an alternative. Why not take advantage of the steep slope of the queueing curve? Why not choose queue size as the control variable, instead of capacity utilization? Small changes in capacity utilization will translate to large changes in queue size and cycle time. This means that a relatively wide control band of queue size will force the system into a very tight range of capacity utilization. Controlling queue size directly controls cycle time.

Is this a novel concept? Not to readers who use supermarkets. Many supermarkets cross-train check stand operators to perform other tasks. These stores monitor the size of queues at check stands. As soon as they have more than three customers in line, they open up a new check stand. When the queues are cleared, they close the extra check stand. This is a highly effective way to provide quality of service in the face of uncertain demand. We will discuss the mathematics and economic logic behind these methods in Chapter 6.

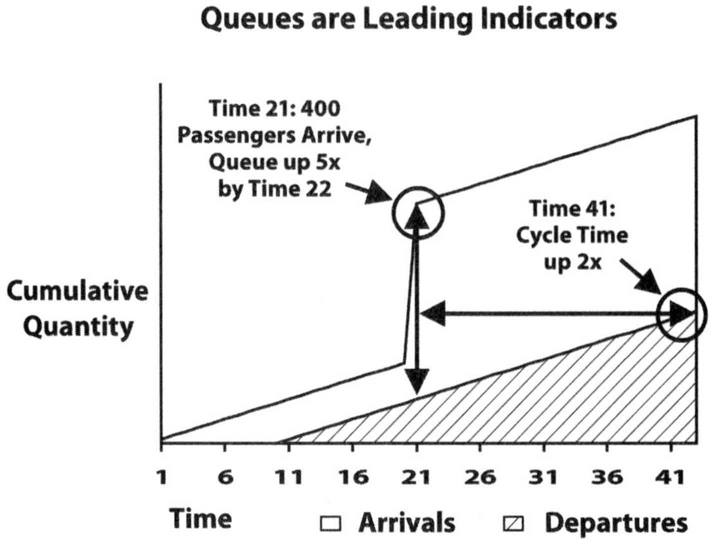

Queues are Leading Indicators

Figure 3-11 If 400 passengers arrive in an immigration area at time 21, then queue size has more than doubled by the next time period. In contrast, the first passenger to report a doubling of cycle time will leave the system at time 41. Queue size detects the problem 20 times faster than cycle time.

Q14: The Second Queue Size Control Principle: Don't control cycle time, control queue size.

Queue size is also a much better control variable than cycle time. Cycle time is always a lagging indicator, because cycle time is not measurable until a job exits the system. Figure 3-11 uses a CFD to illustrate what happens when there is an unanticipated heavy arrival rate at an airport immigration area. If 400 passengers are added to an existing queue of 100 passengers, the queue size more than doubles instantly. In contrast, if the extra passengers arrive at time 21, the cycle time will not double until time 41. In this case, monitoring queues alerts us to a problem 20 times faster than monitoring cycle time.

Q15: The Diffusion Principle: Over time, queues will randomly spin seriously out of control and will remain in this state for long periods.

Six Sigma programs have introduced many workers to statistical thinking. However, such programs primarily focus on the statistics of random variables. There is another domain of applied statistics

One Thousand Coin Tosses

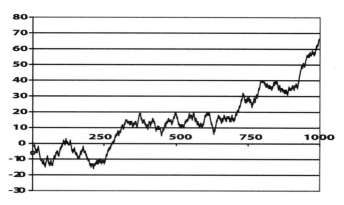

Note: Add one for each head; subtract one for each tail.
Based on example from, *Introduction to Probability Theory and Its Applications*, by William Feller, John Wiley: 1968.

Figure 3-12 The cumulative total for the flips of a balanced coin will progressively drift away from the zero line. There is only a 50 percent chance it will ever return to zero during the last 500 flips. Random variation will create problems that random processes will not correct.

called random processes, which are sequences of random variables. A single roll of the dice generates a random variable. If we track the specific values delivered by a series of dice rolls, we are observing a random process. In general, even numerate people (such as engineers and scientists) have limited intuition for the behavior of random processes.

Let me illustrate this with an example from a classic book on probability, William Feller's, *An Introduction to Probability Theory and Its Applications*. Take a fair coin, one that will come up heads exactly 50 percent of the time. Flip it 1,000 times in a row. Each time we get a head, we add one to our total, and each time we get a tail, we subtract one. We plot our cumulative total on a graph. How many times will this cumulative total cross the zero line in the course of 1,000 flips? Most people, even trained mathematicians and statisticians, have poor intuition on this problem. They assume that the cumulative total will hover around the zero line.

Figure 3-12 is a typical example of how this cumulative sum actually behaves. It tends to diffuse further and further above or below

Diffusion of the Cumulative Total

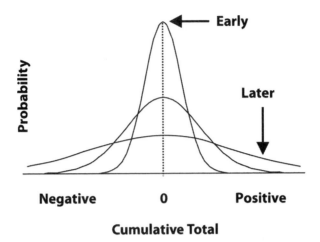

Figure 3-13 The most probable value for the cumulative total is zero, but this value becomes less and less probable over time. The mean distance from the zero line constantly increases. The variance in random processes accumulates over time, which makes intervention very important.

the zero axis. In fact, as Feller points out, there is only a 50 percent probability that the cumulative total will ever cross the zero axis during the last 500 flips. Although the zero value is the most probable value, the variance of the cumulative total grows larger and larger with time.

Mathematically, this cumulative total has a binomial distribution. As the number of flips gets large, a well-known theorem of statistics, the Central Limit Theorem, states that we can approximate this binomial distribution with a Gaussian distribution. As Figure 3-13 shows, this Gaussian distribution becomes flatter over time. Although the most likely value of the cumulative sum is zero, this value becomes less likely with time. The cumulative sum drifts further and further away from its mean.

Why is this important? In our coin flipping problem, we have much less variation than a product development process. Flips occur at predictable times. Each flip represents a uniformly distributed random variable with much less variance than the exponentially-distributed interarrival times of a Poisson process. Yet, even in this low-variance case, we spin out of control. This has important implications for managers who want to avoid expensive, high-queue states in their processes. We simply cannot rely on randomness to correct the problems that randomness creates.

Q16: The Intervention Principle: We cannot rely on randomness to correct a random queue.

Because queues randomly spin out of control, they can drift into a sustained high-queue state that causes grave economic damage. Because they have no memory of how they got there, they will not be gracious enough to quickly drift back to a low-queue state.

Consider the math. If we have drifted 10 heads above the zero line in our coin flip experiment, what is the probability of getting 10 tails in a row to return us to zero? About 1 in 1,000. Future arrivals are totally independent of the queue state we are starting from. It is as likely that the next arrival will make the cumulative total go up, as that it will make the total go down.

In Principle Q4, we explained that high-queue states do disproportionate damage. When there are 20 jobs in line, a 5-minute delay generates 100 minutes of delay time. When there are only two jobs in line, a 5-minute delay generates 10 minutes of delay time. Thus, queue size acts as a multiplier, increasing our delay cost.

The damage done by a high-queue state also depends on how long this state lasts. But in Principle Q15, we showed you that these high-queue states can last for a very long time. Therefore, it is critical that we react quickly to emerging queues. If a queue is allowed to persist, it does much more economic damage. If we intend to intervene, we should intervene quickly and decisively. The longer we delay adding capacity or shedding demand, the more expensive the problem becomes.

As Figure 3-14 shows, if we respond quickly, we can limit the size of our queue. This has strong implications for our control strategy, as we shall see in Chapter 7. We can rely on randomness to create a queue, but we cannot rely on randomness to correct this queue.

You can undoubtedly see the road ahead. We need to make quick, forceful interventions when queues get large. This suggests that we might set limits on maximum queue size and intervene as

Slow Interventions Increase Queues

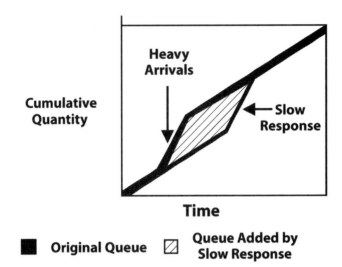

Time

■ **Original Queue**   ▨ **Queue Added by Slow Response**

Figure 3-14 The size of the black shaded area is the size of the original queue. When we respond slowly to an emerging queue, we add the lightly shaded area. Slow responses to emerging queues cause them to do more damage because they delay more jobs for a longer time.

we approach these limits. It also suggests that the more frequently we monitor queues and the more quickly we intervene, the less queues will cost us. We will explore both these ideas in much more depth in later chapters.

Round Up the Usual Suspects

The bad news is that we have lots of queues in product development. The good news is that they are very easy to find. Let's look at nine typical offenders.

Marketing

Marketing is a common source of queueing at the front end of the development process. Marketing usually has a mismatch between capacity and demand. Capacity is restricted because marketing resources tend to be spread across many opportunities with a low duty-cycle on each activity. Demand is high because most organizations like to have a surplus of opportunities. This leads to queues that are typically unmeasured and unmanaged. Even when companies recognize delays, they usually underestimate the cost of queues in very early process stages. They assume that low spending rates will limit costs. They fail to realize that delay costs can be very high even when spending rates are low.

Analysis

Analysis frequently has queues because of high capacity-utilization and high variability. Capacity is scarce because resources are highly specialized and expensive. Although demand is only limited, it is extremely variable. This creates queues, but this queue size and its associated flow time are rarely monitored. Instead, analysis resources are typically measured and incentivized on efficiency, which reinforces the queues. It makes more economic sense to measure analysis groups on response time than efficiency.

CAD

Computer-aided design (CAD) is another common location of queues. Capacity is often restricted. In the presence of variable demand, this leads to queues. As in the case of analysis groups, these resources are commonly measured on efficiency when they should be measured on response time.

Purchasing

Purchasing has queues for slightly different reasons. Purchasing support for R&D is a small portion of their overall workload. Their processes tend to be optimized for the high-volume purchasing needs of manufacturing. Their incentives are also aligned to manufacturing needs, so they typically focus on quality, expenses, and cost.

For example, it is common for purchasing to delay purchases to search for lower cost sources of supply. While this makes sense for large manufacturing purchases, it is often the wrong measure of performance for R&D support. In fact, purchasing queues are so common that most organizations don't even think they have queues.

Prototyping

Prototype shops are also a common location for queues. Such shops are specialized resources that service variable demand. They are commonly measured on efficiency and usually operate with limited excess capacity. This is a prescription for queues. This is a particularly dangerous place to have queues, because it occurs late in the development process. Even worse, slow prototyping leads to delayed feedback, an issue that we will cover in Chapter 8.

Testing

Testing is probably the single most common critical-path queue in most R&D organizations. It is also one of the most dangerous, because it is on the critical path near the end of the development process. Its queues are caused by limited capacity and variable demand. Testing also has queues, because tests are often done with larger batch sizes than are desirable. We will examine this issue more in Chapter 5.

Management Reviews

Management reviews can also create queues. The biggest single reason for this is the widespread phase-gate processes that are popular in development organizations. Sequential phase-gate processes have inherently large batch transfers. As we shall see in Chapter 5, this leads to large queues.

Tooling

Tooling is a common location of queues. The reasons are similar to those we have already mentioned. Tooling shops are specialized resources that are measured on efficiency. They often wait until all information is available before they begin work. They justify this because it appears more efficient.

Even outside tooling shops tend to have delays. Often, purchasing waits until complete information is available before they let outside shops begin work. Waiting for complete information improves efficiency, but it leads to queueing.

Specialists

Finally, we should point out that almost any specialist can become a queue. This occurs because specialists are scarce resources and they are typically managed for efficiency. Furthermore, the pressure for efficiency leads to late involvement, which can raise costs even more.

Conclusion

Queues are the hidden source of most development waste. They are concealed from view in our financial systems. Because they are composed of information, not physical objects, they are hard to spot in the workplace. Queues increase cycle time, expenses, variability, and risk. They slow feedback, reduce quality, and decrease motivation. Reducing queues is the key to improving product development performance.

Queues are caused by variability and high capacity utilization. Increasing capacity utilization increases queues exponentially. Increasing variability increases queues linearly. Most of the damage done by queues occurs when they are in high-queue states. These high-queue states can be very persistent. They must be corrected with decisive and quick responses.

We can affect queues by the structure of our queueing systems. In particular, when we share a common queue for multiple servers, we can take advantage of variability pooling, a topic we cover in more detail in the next chapter.

The optimum queue size occurs when we balance the cost of capacity against delay cost. Since this is a U-curve optimization, we can capture most of the benefits without finding a perfect answer. However, we must avoid high cost points on this U-curve, such as operating near 100 percent capacity utilization.

Queueing discipline provides a way to reduce the cost of a queue without reducing the size of the queue. It does this by servicing jobs with a high cost of delay before we service jobs with a low cost of delay. We examine this problem in more detail in Chapter 7.

We discussed two extremely useful tools in this chapter, the CFD and Little's Formula. The CFD is one of the most useful ways to visualize and analyze queues. It is a practical tool for day-to-day control. Little's Formula provides us with a powerful way to relate queue sizes and cycle time. We will use it again in Chapter 8, when we discuss control systems.

In this chapter, I suggested that we cannot solve the problem of queueing by eliminating variability. In the next chapter, we will take a deeper look at variability and examine its role in product development.

4

Exploiting Variability

We cannot add value without adding variability,
but we can add variability without adding value.

There is probably no aspect of product development that is more misunderstood than variability. Because variability *sometimes* leads to bad outcomes, it is inevitable that some observers will incorrectly generalize that variability *always* leads to bad outcomes. They compound this faulty logic by reasoning that if the presence of variability leads to bad outcomes, then the absence of variability must lead to good outcomes. Energized by this insight, they advocate variability reduction.

The quest for low variability has marched under different banners over the years: do it right the first time, zero defects, repeatability, process maturity models, and Six Sigma. What these approaches have in common is the sweeping assertion that it is always desirable to reduce variability in product development.

Today, advocates can bolster their argument by pointing to the unquestionable success of variability reduction in lean manufacturing. They assert that if variability creates waste in manufacturing, surely it must also create waste in product development. Why not eliminate this waste? These advocates meet little resistance because few managers want to appear in favor of waste, lack of repeatability, immaturity, or defects.

We will carefully examine the problem of variability in this chapter. Our examination will be based on economics, statistics, and a few insights from information theory. We are particularly interested in the intersection of statistics and economics.

Most readers are familiar with a purely statistical view of variability. This view describes random variables using parameters such as the mean and variance of their probability distributions. The variance of a probability distribution quantifies the *amount of variability*. In this chapter, I hope to convince you that the *amount of variability* is actually less important than the *economic cost of variability*. The economic cost of variability is a function of how variability is transformed into economic consequences. This transformation is performed by an economic payoff-function. This payoff-function is critically important because it can be changed more easily than we can reduce the amount of variability.

This chapter should provide you with a fresh perspective on product development variability. We will begin by examining the economic role of variability in product development. Then we will examine specific techniques to reduce the amount of variability and the economic cost of variability.

The Economics of Product Development Variability

Let's start by examining the economic role of product development variability. Product development creates economic value by producing the recipes for products, information, not by creating physical products. If we create the same recipe twice, we've created no new information, and consequently, no economic value. If we wish to create value, it is necessary, but not sufficient, to change the design. But changing the design introduces uncertainty in outcomes. In fact, we must introduce uncertainty to add value in product development. Risk-taking is central to value creation in product development.

Risk-taking plays no equivalent role in manufacturing processes. We can manufacture the same product one million times, and we will create value every time. For a manufacturer, reducing variability always improves manufacturing economics. This is not true in product development. In product development, we must carefully distinguish between variability that increases economic value and variability that decreases it. Rather than eliminating all variability, we must actively put it to work to create economic value.

The four principles in this section will help you understand why variability is not necessarily bad, how payoff asymmetries affect the economics of variability, why there is an optimum amount of variability, and how variability affects the efficiency with which we can generate information.

Taking Rational Risks

Choice	Stakes	Payoff	Probability	EMV
A	$15,000	$100,000	50%	$35,000
B	$15,000	$20,000	90%	$3,000
C	$15,000	$16,000	100%	$1,000

EMV=Expected Monetary Value

> **We cannot maximize economic value by eliminating all choices with uncertain outcomes.**

Figure 4-1 Expected monetary value is a function of both probability and payoff-functions. While choice C has the lowest variability, it is not the best economic choice.

V1: The Principle of Beneficial Variability: Variability can create economic value.

To refute the blanket assertion that minimum variability always results in optimum economic performance, let's consider a simple example. Figure 4-1 offers you three technical paths. Each of them costs $15,000 to investigate. Path A has a 50 percent probability of success, and, if successful, will result in $100,000 in savings. Path B has a 90 percent chance of success, and, if successful, will result in $20,000 of savings. Path C has 100 percent chance of success, and, if successful, will result in $16,000 of savings. Which is the best economic choice? Path A, with an expected value of $35,000. But which path has the minimum uncertainty in its outcome?

Path C has zero uncertainty, yet it is not the best economic choice. It only has an expected value of $1,000. The economics of each discrete choice depend on two factors: the probability function and the payoff-function. When we focus on the probability function alone, we are excluding the critical economic dimension of this decision. We cannot make good economic choices if we only pay attention to

Asymmetric Payoffs

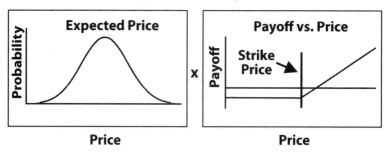

Figure 4-2 To calculate the value of an option, the lognormal probability function of expected price is multiplied by an asymmetric economic payoff-function.

probabilities.[1] Yet, this is exactly what we are doing in our quest to eliminate variability. We are ignoring the critically important economic payoff-function. Paying attention to the payoff-function radically transforms our view of variability.

V2: The Principle of Asymmetric Payoffs: Payoff asymmetries enable variability to create economic value.

Only certain payoff-functions will cause variability to create economic value. Such payoff-functions are asymmetric. Let's take a closer look at the last example. The one-time choice in the last example is known in statistics as a Bernoulli trial. Though simple, it points the way toward more general principles. An investment makes economic sense when its expected value exceeds its expected cost. This expected value is computed as the payoff-function weighted by the probability of each payoff.

In the example of V1, the high-risk alternative made economic sense, even though success and failure were equally likely, because of the payoff-function: we gained $85,000 half the time and lost $15,000 half the time. We call this an asymmetric payoff-function.

The effect of variability on asymmetric payoff-functions has been examined by some brilliant minds. In 1997, the Nobel Prize for eco-

---

[1] Most readers are familiar with probability functions and their key parameters, such as their mean and variance. To make economic decisions, we are interested in the expectation of an economic function. The expectation of the economic function $g(x)$, $E[g(X)]$, is the sum of individual values of $g(x)$ weighted by the probability function $p(x)$. Since economic choices depend on economic expectations, it is a mistake to evaluate these choices by only focusing on the statistical parameters of the probability function, such as its mean and variance.

Expected Payoff vs. Price

Figure 4-3 The expected payoff of an option occurs because the left side of the expected payoff distribution has less area than the right side. This difference occurs because of the asymmetry of the payoff-function.

nomics was awarded to Robert Merton and Myron Scholes for their work on the Black-Scholes option pricing model. (Fisher Black was deceased, so he could not be awarded the prize.) This model enabled financial professionals to compute the fair price for a financial option.

The underlying logic of this model is shown in Figure 4-2. An option gives its holder the right, but not the obligation, to buy a stock at an agreed price, known as the "strike price." This right can be exercised on or before the option expiration date. If the actual stock price on the expiration date is higher than the strike price, then the option holder will exercise the option. For every dollar the actual price exceeds the strike price, the option holder will make one more dollar per share. If the actual stock price on the expiration date is lower than the strike price, the option holder will not exercise their option. They will lose all the money they paid for the option, but never more than this amount. Thus, the payoff-function of an option is asymmetric with respect to stock price, as shown in the right-hand graph in Figure 4-2.

What is the probability of receiving any particular payoff? Research shows that stock prices have a log-normal probability distribution. This distribution is a slight modification of the well-known Gaussian, or bell-curve distribution, as shown in the left-hand graph of Figure 4-2. When we multiply the probability distribution for stock price by the asymmetric payoff-function, we get the probability distribution of expected payoff, shown in Figure 4-3. It is the difference in the areas on the left and right sides of this payoff curve that causes options to have financial value.

Higher Variability Raises Payoff

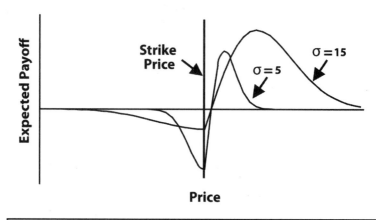

Option Price = 2,   Strike Price = 50,   Mean Price = 50

Figure 4-4 When the underlying volatility of a stock option increases, it has more value. The higher volatility increases the right-side payoff by extending the tail deeper into the high payoff region.

But, how does variability (known as volatility in option pricing theory) affect the price of an option? When variability increases, options are more valuable. This is shown in Figure 4-4.

Why is this example relevant to product developers? We frequently encounter strongly asymmetric payoffs in product development. The value of a success can be much higher than the cost of a failure. I first discussed this asymmetry in the newsboy problem of Principle E20. In the presence of payoff asymmetries, higher variability can create higher economic value.

Consider a pharmaceutical company selecting a new drug candidate to investigate. Which would be a better choice, a new, poorly understood molecule, recently scraped out of the Amazon mud, or a well-understood molecule that had been around for 20 years? The payoff-function for new drugs is very asymmetric. Success can produce a $1 billion blockbuster drug, whereas failure may simply waste the $10,000 cost of an experiment. In the presence of such asymmetries, it makes much more sense to investigate the high variability candidate, because the tail of its performance distribution extends deeper into the high payoff region.

V3: The Principle of Optimum Variability: Variability should neither be minimized nor maximized.

Higher variability can create higher economic values, but we should remember that this value is not created by the variability, but by the way the variability is transformed by the asymmetry of the economic payoff-function. Simplistic notions like "eliminate variability," or "celebrate variability," miss the central economic argument. Variability is not intrinsically desirable or undesirable. Variability is only desirable when it increases economic value. This occurs when the positive tail of the probability distribution extends far enough into a high payoff region to overcome the cost of the negative tail.

There is an important difference between the payoff-functions of stock options and those of product development. Stock options have limited downside and unlimited upside. Under such conditions, we would like to maximize variability. Development projects have unlimited downside and limited upside. Downside has no limit because we can invest unlimited time and expense when we fall short on performance. Upside is limited because once we have sufficient performance to create customer preference, adding more performance produces little incremental profit. Therefore, the payoff-function in product development looks more like that in Figure 4-5.

With such payoff-functions, we cannot maximize our payoff by maximizing variability. As variability increases, the left-hand tail extends deeper into the zone of increased losses. Meanwhile, our right-hand tail extends into the flat zone that produces no incremental benefit. We reach a point where further increases in variability actually diminish our economic returns. As a result, there is normally an optimum amount of variability for a development project.

Let's illustrate this with a simple example. What happens if we increase performance by adding a highly risky but marginally valuable feature? We increase the spread of the probability distribution, but our upside payoff changes very little. On the other hand, our downside can

Product Development Payoff-Function

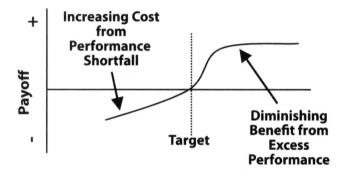

Performance

Figure 4-5 Payoff-functions in product development are different from those of financial options in two important ways: upside can be limited, and downside can be unlimited.

increase considerably. Under such circumstances, we will not increase economic value by adding the feature.

It is important to recognize that it is possible to shape these product development payoff-functions by our management choices. This is an important tool that we will discuss in Principle V12.

Never confuse seeking economic payoffs with seeking variability. Optimal variability is the amount that maximizes the expectation of payoff. This is the difference between the area on the right side of the curve and the area on the left side. Whenever the area on the left side of the curve increases faster than the area on the right side, stop increasing variability. This is simply another application of the principle of marginal economics, Principle E16.

V4: The Principle of Optimum Failure Rate: Fifty percent failure rate is usually optimum for generating information.

Now, let's look at variability from a different perspective, that of information theory. In 1928, R. L. Hartley first suggested that the information contained in an event could be quantified as a logarithmic function of the probability that this event occurs. An event with high probability has low information content. An event has low probability has high

Information and Testing

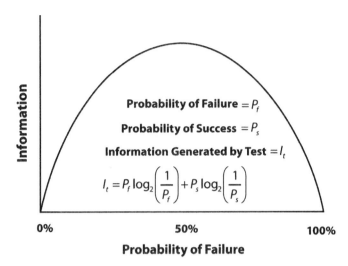

Figure 4-6 The information generated by a pass/fail test maximizes when the failure rate is 50 percent. Very low failure rates and very high failure rates make a test inefficient at generating information.

information content. We can use this quantified view of information to evaluate information-generating events such as tests. We can view the outcomes of such tests as messages bearing information from the physical world. The two messages of success or failure occur with certain frequencies, and they provide quantifiable information. The average information generated by such a test is a function of its failure rate, as shown in Figure 4-6. On this curve, maximum information generation occurs when the probability of failure equals 50 percent.[2] Software programmers will recognize this as the logic behind the binary search algorithm.

Unfortunately, most product developers aim for much lower failure rates. As a result, they expend unnecessary time and money to obtain information. For example, if we test at a low level of integration and get a low failure rate, we should test at a higher level of integration. If our failure rate is too high, we should test at a lower level of integration.

---

[2] Fifty percent is only optimal for a test with two outcomes. When tests have multiple outcomes, we will maximize information generation by making the outcomes equally likely.

Either excessive or insufficient probability of failure reduces the efficiency with which we generate information.

This curve shows why testing to failure is so valuable. The point where there is a 50 percent chance of failure lies at the peak of this information curve. No point in the testing space contains more information. When pharmaceutical companies evaluate the toxicity of new drugs, they determine LD50, the dose that is lethal to 50 percent of the animal subjects. Again, this lies at the peak of the information curve.

The equation in Figure 4-6 shows that the information content of a test comes from the degree of surprise associated with each possible result. Any unexpected success has high information content, as does any unexpected failure.

Unfortunately, most companies do a far better job of communicating their successes than their failures. They carefully document successes, but fail to document failures. This can cause them to repeat the same failures. Repeating the same failures is waste, because it generates no new information. Only *new* failures generate information.

Of course, not all tests should be designed to maximize information generation. Some tests exist to validate the design, not to generate information. On such validation tests, we should strive for 100 percent success rate. Product developers should clearly distinguish exploratory testing, which should be optimized for information generation, and validation testing, which should be optimized for high success rates.

Finally, we should recognize that we are not simply interested in resolving all uncertainty, we are interested in resolving the uncertainty that is worth money to resolve. It is more valuable to know which of two envelopes contains a $100 bill, than which of two envelopes contains a penny. We pay for tests with time and money. We should try to determine if the economic value created by these tests exceeds the cost of the test.

So, avoid oversimplifications, like "eliminate failures" or "celebrate failures." There is an optimum failure rate. Higher or lower rates create economic waste. In fact, the variability at the optimum failure rate point is higher than it is at any other point. We cannot exploit this point if we minimize variability.

Reducing Variability

There are two main approaches to improving the economics of variability. First, we can change the amount of variability. Second, we can change the economic consequences of the variability. In this section, we will focus on methods to reduce variability. In the next, we will focus on changing its economic impact.

Let's look at seven principles that enable us to reduce variability. We will begin with variability pooling and short-term forecasting. Then, we will discuss small experiments, reuse, and repetition. Finally, we will discuss the use of negative covariance and buffers.

V5: The Principle of Variability Pooling: Overall variation decreases when uncorrelated random tasks are combined.

Variability pooling exploits a somewhat subtle mathematical characteristic of variability. When we sum two or more uncorrelated random variables, the variance of the sum is equal to the sum of the individual variances. Similarly, the mean of a sum is the sum of the individual means.

What does this tell us about the variability of pooled variables? One of the most useful measures of variability is the coefficient of variation,[3] the ratio of the standard deviation of a distribution to its mean. Since standard deviation is the square root of variance, total standard deviation is the square root of the sum of the squares of individual standard deviations. This means that if we combine two random variables with the same coefficient of variation, the coefficient of variation for the new combined variable is only 71 percent of the original coefficient of variation. Thus, we can reduce overall variability by pooling variation from multiple uncorrelated sources.

We exploited this principle previously when we used a single consolidated queue with multiple servers, as we did in Principle Q7. The combined demand stream from multiple sources has less relative variation than any its components. For example, let's say we have nine project teams and nine manufacturing engineers. We could assign a single manufacturing engineer to each team. This would be a good approach if the demand for manufacturing engineering had very low

---

[3] The coefficient of variation is useful because it is a dimensionless measure of the variability of a distribution.

variability. However, if the variability were high, it would be better to operate the nine manufacturing engineers as a single resource pool, combining the variable demand of all nine projects. This would reduce the variability by roughly a factor of three, leading to smaller queues and better response times.

We also see the effect of variability pooling whenever we try to estimate the work content of a project. If we estimate the work content of 1,000 individual tasks, each individual estimate will have a high coefficient of variation. However, when we aggregate these estimates, there is less noise in our overall estimate than any of the individual estimates. This is one of the wonderful times in mathematics where, "Garbage in equals quality out." Figure 4-7 shows the effect of pooling uncorrelated variability.

This pooling effect works in the reverse direction when we try to schedule a project that has been decomposed into many small activities. When our task list becomes very granular, the noise in each estimate is very high compared to the signal. Granular estimates produce good estimates of aggregate scope, but we should never schedule tasks at this level of detail. Instead, it makes more sense to aggregate many small tasks and to schedule them as a group. Aggregation pools variability and improves the signal-to-noise ratio of our estimates.

Of course, this is the same principle that is exploited in the stock market when we diversify a financial portfolio. By combining multiple stocks with uncorrelated volatility, we can generate the same average return with less variation.

V6: The Principle of Short-Term Forecasting: Forecasting becomes exponentially easier at short time-horizons.

Forecasting errors are a major source of variability in product development. We can reduce this variability by forecasting at shorter time-horizons.

How much benefit do we get by shortening the forecast horizon? When I was an officer on nuclear submarines, we often had to search for other submarines in the middle of the ocean. If the other submarine's position was known at a particular point in time, the area that we had to search was an expanding circle. Uncertainty was proportional to the square of time, since location is time-dependent with two degrees of freedom. Compare this with the uncertainty in a

Variability Pooling

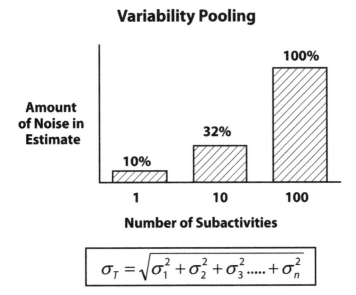

$$\sigma_T = \sqrt{\sigma_1^2 + \sigma_2^2 + \sigma_3^2 ..... + \sigma_n^2}$$

Figure 4-7 When we combine activities with uncorrelated variability, the total standard deviation grows as a square root function. The more we subdivide activities, the higher the coefficient of variation in each subactivity. We can reduce variability by pooling activities together.

product requirement when we forecast at a long time-horizon. Market requirements have many degrees of freedom. This makes requirements exponentially more difficult to forecast at long time-horizons. Forecasting 2 years ahead is not twice as hard as forecasting 1 year ahead; it can be 10 times harder.

The irony of this is that many companies try to reduce the risk of poor forecasts by taking more time to do a careful forecast. They insert more high-level reviews and more approval levels for their plans. Although this may slightly improve assumptions, it pushes out the planning horizon, leading to massive increases in uncertainty. Pretty soon, the only person with sufficient insight to pierce the fog at this long horizon is the CEO. But when we get the CEO involved, the decisions can take even longer.

The most powerful way to reduce variability in forecasts is to shorten our planning horizons. As we shall see in Chapter 5, this is a key payoff from using batch size reduction to decrease the scope of our projects. Smaller scope leads to faster development, which shortens

A Virtuous Cycle

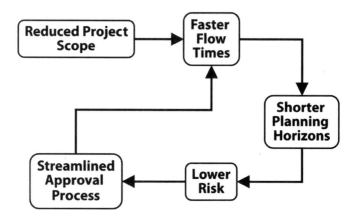

Figure 4-8 By reducing project scope, we trigger a regenerative cycle of faster cycle times and lower risk. This reduced risk leads to less need for oversight.

time-horizons. Reduced scope and shorter time-horizons combine to reduce risk. Lower risk means we don't need high levels of management involved. This further reduces decision-making delays. Obviously, this approach creates regenerative feedback, as shown in Figure 4-8.

Short time-horizons do not just help us to forecast requirements better; they also help us forecast technology. When we are dependent on multiple evolving technologies, long planning horizons lead to large compound errors. We can reduce the size of these errors by shortening our planning horizons.

Again, we must remind you that queues create long planning horizons. When queue sizes are large, it takes a long time for work to flow through a system. This forces us to forecast at long time-horizons. Reducing queues directly reduces forecasting risks and variability.

V7: The Principle of Small Experiments: Many small experiments produce less variation than one big one.

Another lesson we can learn from statistics is the value of decomposing a large risk into a series of small risks. We are tempted to think that there would be little value in doing this since the total risk remains the same.

But, let's return to the example in Principle V1. What if we were interested in technology A, but we did not want to expose ourselves to the 50 percent chance of losing $15,000. How could we structure this choice to reduce this risk? As we mentioned, in statistics we call this one-time choice a Bernoulli trial. When we repeat a series of Bernoulli trials, the probability distribution of our outcome is called a binomial distribution.

What happens to the mean and variance of a binomial distribution as we divide an experiment into a larger number of small trials? The mean increases faster than the standard deviation.[4] If we break our experiment into a series of smaller experiments, we reduce its coefficient of variation. In fact, the coefficient of variation decreases proportional to the square root of the number of trials.

We can see this intuitively if we think of the chance of ruin on a single coin flip: 50 percent. If we broke this bet into four smaller bets, it would take four sequential failures to result in ruin. The probability of four sequential failures is 1 in 16, only 6.25 percent. Thus, when we break large risks into many small independent risks, we reduce the variation in our outcomes.

We can exploit this statistical principle in many areas of product development. For example, consider product line strategy. Should we introduce a single blockbuster product with 10 innovations in it, or should we break this up into a series of smaller steps? A series of smaller steps makes much more economic sense because the likelihood of complete failure is much lower.

V8: The Repetition Principle: Repetition reduces variation.

The effect of breaking large tasks into many smaller tasks is more than statistical. When we have many similar small tasks, we have an economic incentive to systematize the accomplishment of these tasks. This systemization further reduces variation. We uncover a superior approach and standardize around it. This reduces variability even further.

---

[4] Mathematically, we are evaluating the values of X/n, where X is the cumulative number of successes and n is the number of Bernoulli trials. If the probability of success on each trial is p, the mean of X/n is equal to p and independent of n. The variance of X/n is equal to (p)(1-p)/n. Thus, variance decreases inversely with n. With more trials, the tails of the distribution become smaller.

For example, as a software development organization moves towards daily build/test cycles, they increasingly routinize their process. If code check-in occurs once per year, there is little incentive to invest the one-time effort to structure and optimize this process. If code check-in occurs daily, we have both the economic incentive and the opportunity to optimize the process. We shall see in Chapter 5 that the drive to reduce batch size provides the perfect opportunity to reduce variability by increasing repetition.

V9: The Reuse Principle: Reuse reduces variability.

One of the greatly underutilized methods of reducing variability is design reuse. Reuse is powerful for two reasons. First, reuse eliminates variability in completion time. Second, reuse reduces capacity utilization. As we mentioned in Principle Q5, reducing capacity utilization further reduces variability.

We should be clear that reuse must still be justified economically. We may be tempted to reuse our vacuum tube radio design instead of adopting the uncertain new technology of transistors, but this would be an economic mistake. In this case, the economic benefits of the new technology outweigh the benefits of reduced variability. As always, we should make decisions on the basis of overall economics, rather than maximizing reuse, which is another proxy variable.

V10: The Principle of Negative Covariance: We can reduce variance by applying a counterbalancing effect.

A more subtle way of reducing variability is to counterbalance it. For example, when a sailboat is in strong and shifting winds, it runs a risk of being capsized by a strong gust. This risk can be eliminated by taking down the sails, but such an approach sacrifices speed. Instead, the crew of the sailboat will shift to the windward side of the boat to generate a force that counterbalances the wind. They will hike out even further when the wind becomes stronger. Although the wind gusts are random, the active response of the crew reduces the effect of the randomly varying wind. This permits them to safely expose more sail area than they could in the absence of an active response.

In statistical terms, we often have performance that depends on the combined effect of two random variables. Sometimes we can make one of these random variables counterbalance the other, creating what is called a negative covariance. A negative covariance will reduce the total variance obtained when we combine two random variables.

For example, in manufacturing, we might choose to cross-train workers from our assembly area to assist testers during periods of peak demand. Whenever the queue of work gets to a certain size, we shift more resources to the queue. This allows us to offset random increases in demand with compensating changes in capacity. Thus, the separate effects on the queue of changes in demand and capacity, will have a negative covariance. This reduces the average queue size in the presence of variable demand. We can use this same approach by cross-training product development personnel to perform the tasks of adjacent processes.

V11: The Buffer Principle: Buffers trade money for variability reduction.

We can also insulate the project from variability by using a buffer. Buffers are currently popular with some product developers. To prevent the embarrassment of missing a schedule, they pad the schedule with a safety margin. This reduces the chance that the promised completion date will be missed.

As Figure 4-9 shows, we can think of a schedule as having a probability distribution. In this case, it is useful to focus on the cumulative distribution function. Such a function describes the probability that a variable will be less than or equal to a certain value.

Let's say our original schedule had 50 percent chance of being complete at 12 months. To increase certainty, we commit to the 90 percent confidence point, 15 months. We have inserted a 3-month buffer, decreasing the chance that the project will be late.

But what is the economic cost of this buffer? If we had committed to the 50 percent confidence date, then our expected delay would be the shaded area above the cumulative distribution in Figure 4-9. If this area was broken into horizontal slices, then the length of each horizontal slice is an amount of delay and its height is the probability that this particular delay will occur.

What would happen if we commit to a 100 percent confidence schedule? We would completely eliminate the chance of incurring a delay by adding a buffer large enough to absorb the worst case delay.

The Effect of Time Buffers

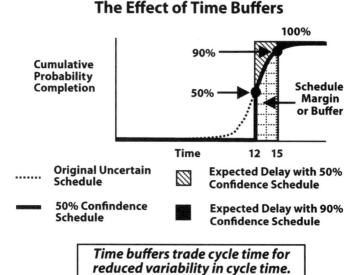

Time buffers trade cycle time for reduced variability in cycle time.

Figure 4-9 We can insert time buffers to reduce the probability of missing a schedule. This trades cycle time for reduced variability. If cost-of-delay is high, time buffers can be an expensive way to reduce variability.

It should be apparent that the expected delay reduction associated with a buffer is always less than the total delay generated by the buffer itself. A buffer converts uncertain earliness to certain lateness. Thus, it is generally a bad idea to trade cycle time for reduced variability in cycle time. Instead, we should trade a different performance parameter, an idea that we will explore in Principle V14.

Reducing Economic Consequences

So far, we have focused on reducing the amount of variability. This is a smart strategy when variability decreases economic value. But what happens when the variability creates economic value? In such cases, we should change the consequences of the variability. This approach offers great opportunity, but it is underexploited in most development processes.

In this section, we will discuss five principles that can be used to reduce variability. We will begin by discussing consequence reduction in general and the importance of preventing nonlinear excursions.

Then, we will discuss the approaches of variability substitution, iteration speed, and variability displacement.

V12: The Principle of Variability Consequence: Reducing consequences is usually the best way to reduce the cost of variability.

When we alter the consequences of variability, we are changing the economic payoff-function, rather than the probability function. We can think of this payoff-function as having a "left side" and a "right side." We can improve both sides. For example, we can decrease cost on the left side by quickly truncating a bad path. If a feature is much harder to implement than we expected, we can drop it from the product. We can also increase the payoff on the right side. For example, if a feature is easier to implement than we expected, we may choose to overachieve on this feature.

This concept of altering payoff-functions is a common blind spot for people experienced in lean manufacturing. In manufacturing, our payoff-function is symmetrically bad whenever we deviate from the mean. Under such circumstances, our only sensible choice is to reduce variability, because both the "left side" and the "right side" do economic damage. In product development, "left side" outcomes represent bad variability, but "right side" outcomes represent good variability.

This difference in payoff-functions is shown in Figure 4-10. As we observed in Principle V2, asymmetry in the economic payoff-function can invert the relationship between economic payoff and the amount of variability. Under such conditions, we can increase economic payoffs when we raise variability. Such an outcome is almost totally unheard of in manufacturing.

I carefully say "almost," because the concept of altering payoff-functions is actually present in lean manufacturing, but it is hidden well. The Japanese term *jidoka* refers to stopping a process from making waste. Before Toyota was a car company, it made textile looms. A key innovation was the feature of stopping the loom whenever a thread broke. This stops the creation of defective WIP. Toyota uses the same principle when it gives any worker the ability to stop the flow of the production line. Toyota actually does not simply try to decrease the frequency of defects, it also tries to decrease the consequences of these defects.

Payoff-Functions

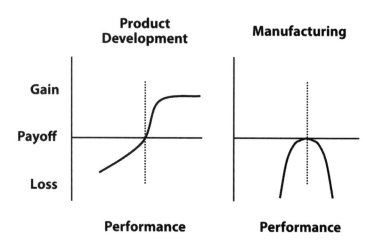

Figure 4-10 Product development payoff-functions are very different from those found in manufacturing. This difference leads to different approaches to managing variability.

Let's illustrate this idea of consequence reduction with a simple example from software development, an example we will discuss in more detail in Chapter 7. Let's say a programmer makes a bad assumption about a communication protocol in the code he is writing. The cost of this type of bad assumption depends on the frequency with which it occurs and the amount of economic damage it does. We can reduce both the frequency of this problem and its consequences by providing rapid feedback. If we provide programmers with test results in 24 hours instead of after 30 days, they will stop making the bad assumption, lowering the frequency of the problem.

Rapid feedback also reduces the consequences of the defect. If feedback is slow, we will write a lot of dependent code before the problem is identified. All this code may have to be modified if we discover underlying assumptions were incorrect. Interestingly, these two beneficial effects can combine to produce order of magnitude reductions in the cost of variability.

V13: The Nonlinearity Principle: Operate in the linear range of system performance.

It is important to understand how the magnitude of variation affects cost. Most systems behave linearly within a certain range. When the operating point of the system moves outside of this range, performance can degrade dramatically. It is desirable to avoid these zones of nonlinearity.

For example, a sailboat has natural stability when it tilts or lists. The relative locations of its center of gravity and its center of buoyancy cause a force (called a righting moment) that returns it to an upright position. However, if a sailboat lists too far, the center of gravity will shift to the point where this natural righting moment reverses direction. At this point, the sailboat will capsize.

As mentioned earlier, in heavy winds, sailors avoid listing to this critical angle by trimming the sails, reducing sail area, and applying force to counterbalance the wind. Most systems have this dangerous zone where assumptions of linearity break down. We want to stay away from it.

A simple example of this nonlinear response occurs in the way project profits are affected by delays. Very short delays can often be compensated for by extra sales and marketing efforts. As delays get longer, the damage done by delay becomes geometrically larger.

How can we protect against the economic cost associated with extreme left-side events? To do this, we need circuit breakers to stop consuming resources and time when we enter this zone. We will explore this concept in Chapter 7, when we discuss congestion control.

V14: The Principle of Variability Substitution: Substitute cheap variability for expensive variability.

Another method to reduce the cost of variability is substituting variability in an inexpensive measure of performance for variability in an expensive measure of performance. For example, missing schedule may be expensive, whereas a low manufacturing yield during the first 30 days of production may be cheap. In such cases, we may be willing to accept a variation in yield to avoid variation in cycle time.

We use this principle continuously in product development. For example, we are willing to pay expedite charges to ensure that the arrival of a part does not delay a project. We do this because we recognize that overspending our expense budget does less economic damage than missing our schedule. As Figure 4-11 illustrates, we can use variation in expenses to stabilize cost, schedule, and performance. Obviously, we need to understand the economic cost of variability to make these trade-offs wisely.

Variability Substitution

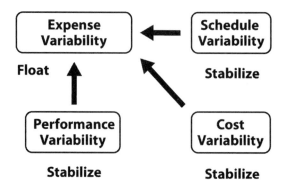

Figure 4-11 We can limit variability in an expensive measure of performance by channeling variability into a cheaper measure of performance. In this case, we are accepting variability in expenses to stabilize schedule, performance, and cost.

V15: The Principle of Iteration Speed: It is usually better to improve iteration speed than defect rate.

When we perform a series of iterations, our ultimate defect rate is proportional to the defect rate per iteration raised to the power of the number of iterations. This suggests two basic approaches for reducing defects. The first is to decrease the defect rate per iteration; the second is to increase the number of iterations we can complete in a given time. The number of iterations is the exponent, and the defect rate per iteration is the base. If the cost of improving iteration speed is comparable to the cost of lowering the defect rate, improving iteration speed will have more influence mathematically.

For example, consider the difference between halving defect rate and halving cycle time. Compare improving from a 2 percent defect rate to a 1 percent defect rate, with improving from a 2-week cycle time to a 1-week cycle time. Two iterations at a 2 percent defect rate produce a quality level that is 25 times higher than one iteration at 1 percent defect rate.[5]

---

[5] Iteration speed has higher leverage when defect rates are below 50 percent. When defect rates are above 50 percent, reducing defects has higher leverage.

Improving iteration speed is particularly attractive because it is usually cheaper to improve than iteration success rate. In most product development processes, iteration time is dominated by queue time, so our emphasis on reducing queues creates enormous payoff.

V16: The Principle of Variability Displacement: Move variability to the process stage where its cost is lowest.

Just as variability can be driven into different performance parameters, it can be driven into different stages of a process. It is better to place variability in a process stage where the economic cost of variability is low, rather than where the economic cost is high.

For example, in air traffic control systems, the landing rate at a busy airport is typically a variable bottleneck. To ensure we load this bottleneck effectively, we have a small inventory of planes in a holding pattern waiting to land. However, it is very wasteful to fly planes around in circles. We can hold additional inventory en route to the destination by slowing them in flight. This ensures they spend very little time circling.

However, holding inventory in transit is still not the cheapest place to hold inventory. We hold the bulk of the inventory on the ground. It is safer and cheaper to have planes wait before takeoff than in any other place in the system. By doing so, we have coupled the downstream variation of the landing process into cheaper upstream stages. Instead of letting planes circle in a holding pattern for varying amounts of time, we let them wait varying amounts of time to take off. This drives variance into the cheapest stage of the process.

The same principle applies in other areas of product development. For example, consider the process of starting new projects. When we permit a project to enter the pipeline, it begins accruing cost. Our investment in the project is perishable, and it is affected by the time it takes to pass through the pipeline. If we invest in market research only to have the product crawl forward slowly for 2 years, our market research will be 2 years out of date. We are better off holding this new product in a ready queue, than letting it enter our pipeline.

There are, of course, some special circumstances when it is better to start a project immediately. This might occur when precedence dates for patents can be established with an early start or when initial activities significantly alter the conditional probability of success for the later activities. For example, we might want to do an early patent search and allocate more project resources if it looks like we have a winning idea. This small early investment to buy information is common in venture capital-based activities.

Another good example of letting variation create queues in the cheapest process stage occurs in the process of correcting software bugs. Rather than permitting a development organization to start fixing all bugs, we are better off restricting the number of bugs that we work on at any time. As we shall see in Chapter 6, permitting too many active tasks leads to slow transit times. Slow transit times increase the chance we are working on old bugs. It is usually not productive to work on old bugs, since they may die of old age or irrelevance before we get around to fixing them. Instead, it is better to hold this inventory in a ready queue, delaying investment until we can allocate serious resources and quickly fix the bug.

Conclusion

If you began this chapter believing variability is always bad, I hope I have changed that belief. If you already suspected that variability is necessary in product development, I hope I have given you additional support for your views.

In this chapter, we explored the intersection of statistics and economics. Economic decisions should be made using economic expectations. These expectations are the result of an economic payoff-function transformed by a probability function. In product development, our payoff-functions are frequently asymmetric. This creates conditions where reducing variability can reduce economic payoffs. Variability is not the enemy; it is a tool to create economic value.

We also explored some practical methods for reducing variability, such as variability pooling, creating covariance, and exploiting reuse. We examined the use of buffers and pointed out how they tend to substitute certain delays for uncertain delays. This illustrates why it is so important to understand the cost of variability when you choose to spend money to reduce it. This is the only way you can determine if variability reduction is actually worth its cost.

When thinking about variability, it is important to focus on the cost of variability instead just worrying about the amount of variability. There are many ways to reduce this cost without changing the amount of variability. In the next chapter, we will consider a very high payoff method for variability reduction—reducing batch size.

5

Reducing Batch Size

Don't test the water with both feet.
—Charles de Gaulle

Ask a typical product developer what their batch size is, and why, and you will get a puzzled look. They are likely to respond, "What do you mean by batch size, and why should I be interested in it?" Product developers simply don't think in terms of batch size. As a result, they underutilize one of the most important tools to improve flow.

I am careful to say underutilize, because product developers have unconsciously made enormous improvements in batch size over the past few decades. In fact, many of the most important improvements in product development, such as concurrent engineering, rapid proto-typing, and agile software methods, are recognizable as batch size reductions. However, because developers fail to recognize the under-lying mechanism of action behind these improvements, they lose the chance to apply this principle much more broadly throughout their development processes.

In this chapter, we will start by building a compelling case for batch size reduction. We will explain the 10 ways that smaller batch sizes improve the economics and performance of product development. Then, we will examine the economic trade-offs associated with using smaller batch sizes. Finally, we will provide seven key principles that will help you get the most out of batch size reduction along with a dozen typical places to look for opportunities.

The Case for Batch Size Reduction

To begin, we must understand why batch size reduction represents such a compelling opportunity. In this section, we will discuss the

10 principles that enable batch size reduction to improve product development performance.

B1: The Batch Size Queueing Principle: Reducing batch size reduces cycle time.

Figure 5-1 uses a CFD to depict a steady arrival rate being processed with different batch sizes. Remember that, on a CFD, the size of the shaded area is the size of the queue. As you can see, queue size is directly proportional to batch size. And, since Little's Formula says average queue size determines average cycle time, this means that we can directly reduce cycle time by reducing batch size.

It is worth pointing out that we have reduced cycle time in Figure 5-1 without making any change in the average arrival rate or the average departure rate. This means we have reduced cycle time *without changing either demand or capacity.* This is quite important since throttling demand and increasing capacity can have significant economic cost. Batch size reduction can enable us to shorten cycle time, often by an order of magnitude or more, without changing capacity utilization.

B2: The Batch Size Variability Principle: Reducing batch sizes reduces variability in flow.

Batch size reduction does not just improve cycle time. Its second effect is to reduce variability in flow. Large batches inherently increase the variation in flow, which causes periodic overloads. For example, a restaurant may be able to handle a continuous stream of customers arriving in groups of three or four people, but a bus full of 80 tourists will overload its processes. This large batch behaves like an elephant traveling through a boa constrictor, progressively overloading the seating process, the ordering process, the kitchen, and the table clearing process.[1]

Sometimes the lower variability due to batch size reduction can completely eliminate a queue. For example, if we sent a 100-person engineering department to lunch at exactly the same time, they might complain about the queue in the cafeteria. If we assume this queue is

---

[1] The overloads propagate through the system unless we decompose the large batch into smaller batches. Smaller intermediate batches will significantly help overall cycle time and reduce intermediate queues. For example, we could seat and serve this large group as many small groups. Of course, the final process step may require that the large group be recombined, since the bus departure is a single large batch. Nevertheless, it is often very practical to sandwich smaller intermediate batch sizes between larger batches.

Batch Size and Queues

Large Batches   **Small Batches**

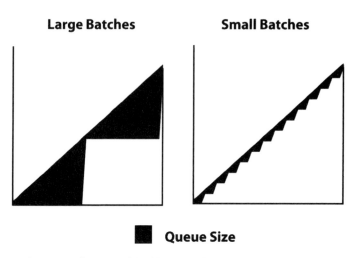

■ **Queue Size**

Figure 5-1 The size of the black shaded area indicates the size of the queue. Small batch sizes reduce queues.

caused by insufficient capacity, then we may be tempted to increase the size of the cafeteria.

It makes much more sense to stagger lunch hours, sending half the engineers to lunch at 11:30 AM and half at 12:00 noon. By staggering lunch hours, we are reducing the batch size, and thus, the variability in arrivals. The variability reduction alone may eliminate the queue. In fact, batch size reduction is one of the cheapest, simplest, and most powerful ways to reduce variability and queues.

B3: The Batch Size Feedback Principle: Reducing batch sizes accelerates feedback.

The third effect of batch size reduction is particularly important in product development: small batches accelerate feedback. In the stable, repetitive world of manufacturing, this feedback benefit occurs infrequently and is of minor economic importance. In product development, this feedback is continuous and extremely important economically. We constantly try new things and expose ourselves to the risk of failure.

As mentioned in Principle V4, the optimum failure rate in product development is much higher than that of manufacturing. We depend on feedback to control the consequences of these failures, which, as we explained in Chapter 4, is the most important way to lower the economic cost of variability.

In product development, fast feedback also provides disproportionate economic benefits because the consequences of failures usually increase exponentially when we delay feedback. Each engineering decision acts as a predecessor for many subsequent decisions. The number of dependent decisions generally grows geometrically with time. Consequently, a single incorrect assumption can force us to change hundreds of later decisions. When we delay feedback, rework becomes exponentially more expensive. With accelerated feedback, we can truncate bad paths before they do significant economic damage.

The benefits of fast feedback can be present for any product development task. They do not require that a task be on the critical path or that a project has a high-delay cost.

B4: The Batch Size Risk Principle: Reducing batch size reduces risk.

The fourth effect of batch size reduction is decreased risk. This lower risk comes from three factors. First, small batch sizes lead to smaller queues, which decrease cycle time and expose us to exponentially less change in technology and requirements, as explained in Principle V6. Second, decomposing a large batch into several smaller batches reduces the risk of failure, as explained in Principle V7. Third, as mentioned in the previous section, B3, smaller batch sizes accelerate feedback, which makes the consequences of an error much smaller.

It is not an accident that a packet switching network like the Internet breaks its messages into many small packets. Consider what would happen if we sent a 10 megabyte file as a single large packet and we had one error per million bytes. We would average 10 errors in our transmission. We would have one chance in 22,026 that the file would reach the destination without an error. In contrast, if we break this large file into 10,000 packets of 1,000 bytes apiece, there is only 1 chance in 1,000 that an individual packet will become corrupted. We will have to resend an average of 10 of the 10,000 packets, an overhead of 0.1 percent.

Put another way, if we didn't break messages into smaller packets, our overhead would be 22 million times higher. We achieve such high reliability by using small packets that the Internet can actually forward packets between nodes without error checking at the network level.

Virtually all of the responsibility for quality is given to the two ends of the communications link, the sender and the receiver. This lowers cost and improves throughput, because we can quickly forward messages with low computational overhead at each node.

B5: The Batch Size Overhead Principle: Reducing batch size reduces overhead.

But, wait, there's more. A fifth benefit of small batches is its unexpected reduction of overhead. I say unexpected, because most developers incorrectly assume that small batches will raise the overhead in their processes. They assume that the extra transaction cost, caused by a larger number of small batches, will become a dominant economic factor. In fact, as we will see in Principle B12, these costs do not become dominant because we can dramatically reduce the cost of these repetitive transactions.

It surprises many product developers to discover that it is large batches that increase overhead, not small batches. For example, consider what happens when we test software in large batches. This increases the average number of open bugs in the code. Why is this bad? If we have 300 open bugs, when we find bug number 301, we need to check to see if this bug duplicates any of the 300 previously reported bugs. If we only have 30 open bugs, then we must only check bug number 31 against 30 previously reported bugs.

Even worse, increasing WIP increases the need for status reports. When we have 300 open bugs, marketing will be asking us for the status of 300 bugs instead of 30. At the same time, the larger queue makes flow-through time 10 weeks instead of 1 week. If marketing asks for weekly status reports, we will provide 10 times as many status reports during the life of each bug.

Just as we were surprised to discover that small batch-size manufacturing plants have lower overhead than large-batch plants, we are discovering the same phenomenon in product development.

B6: The Batch Size Efficiency Principle: Large batches reduce efficiency.

The sixth beneficial effect of smaller batches is that they normally improve overall efficiency. Again, this is an unexpected finding for most product developers. They assume that the long periods of uninterrupted work, created by large batches, improve the efficiency of an individual engineer. In fact, this efficiency gain is local to the engineer, and it often comes at the expense of destroying important feedback loops and lowering overall efficiency. Consider these two examples.

Manufacturing may insist that engineers finish all their work before they hold a manufacturing readiness review. They may feel it is more efficient for them to review 200 drawings in a single meeting.

But what is the system level effect of this choice? The engineers embed incorrect assumptions in all 200 drawings without the benefit of early feedback. The problems in all 200 drawings are identified at the same time. Engineers spend extra time correcting these problems, and manufacturing spends extra time verifying that the additional problems have been corrected. The efficiency of the large batch review was a complete illusion.

If feedback had been provided after the first 20 drawings, then the next 180 drawings would have benefited from the feedback. Engineers would spend less time correcting drawings, and manufacturing would spend less time reviewing these corrections. In engineering, it is very common that the local efficiency improvements due to large batches are completely wiped out by the added rework caused by delayed feedback.

Another interesting example occurs in software. When programmers work in large batches, they change many lines of code in a single release. What does this do to debug complexity?

The complexity of the debug task grows as 2^n when we change n things simultaneously (due to the number of system level interactions created by multiple changes). It is much more expensive to debug large changes than small ones. Again, the local efficiency gains of uninterrupted coding and large batch testing have been completely wiped out by the system-level losses due to increased complexity.

Fast feedback also improves efficiency because engineers are more efficient when something is fresh in their mind. Engineering work is so complex that it remains fresh in an engineer's mind for a limited time. Give a programmer feedback on their code 24 hours after they wrote it and they will probably remember exactly what they were doing. Give them identical feedback 90 days after they wrote the code and they may barely recognize their own work.

B7: The Psychology Principle of Batch Size: Large batches inherently lower motivation and urgency.

The seventh beneficial effect of small batches is their power to motivate people. Large batches demotivate people in two ways. First, large batches dilute responsibility. If I am responsible for delivering one module of code in the next 5 days, I have no place to hide. If I am responsible for one of the 100 modules that are required for the next integration point 100 days from now, I feel much less urgency. After all, even if I am behind schedule, there appears to be plenty of time left before the integration point, and there are many other people who are more likely to get in trouble than I am.

With 100 modules traveling together in a large pack, it is highly probable that somebody else will delay the integration point. As a result, the person responsible for a single module, quite correctly, feels less responsible for the overall outcome.

Second, large batch sizes demotivate by delaying feedback. When engineers are experimenting with a new idea, rapid feedback is enormously energizing. Rapid feedback quickly supplies the positive reinforcement of success, and fast positive reinforcement always increases motivation. Rapid feedback causes us to subconsciously associate our delivery of a work product and the beginning of the next process step. This attribution of causality gives us a sense of control, instead of making us feel we are the victim of a massive bureaucratic system.

Even when ideas fail, engineers prefer to get rapid feedback, because it allows them to truncate a bad path quickly. It is inherently demotivating to invest a lot of effort proceeding in the wrong direction, and this ultimately leads to risk avoidance and reduced innovation. Small batch sizes are a powerful tool to increase urgency, motivation, and accountability.

B8: The Batch Size Slippage Principle: Large batches cause exponential cost and schedule growth.

If you are still not convinced that large batch sizes cause significant problems, let me suggest a simple empirical analysis. Look at the projects you have undertaken in the last 10 years and do a simple regression between the original planned duration and the percentage slippage from the original plan, as shown in Figure 5-2. What is striking about this analysis is the unusually high slippage of long-duration

Slippage Effects

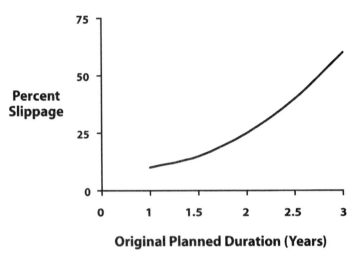

Original Planned Duration (Years)

Figure 5-2 Slippage in projects rises exponentially with duration.

projects. One organization told me that they got a best fit on their data with time to the fourth power. This means that a project of twice the duration experienced 16 times as much slippage. Large batches make cost and schedule grow exponentially.

B9: The Batch Size Death Spiral Principle: Large batches lead to even larger batches.

It gets even worse. The damage done by large batches can become regenerative when a large batch project starts to acquire a life of its own. It becomes a death march where all participants know they are doomed, but no one has the power to stop. After all, when upper management has been told a project will succeed for 4 years, it is very hard for anyone in middle management to stand up and reverse this forecast.

Furthermore, whenever we choose to invest time and effort proceeding in a particular direction, a psychological phenomenon called cognitive dissonance causes us to distort the way we process information related to this project. We evaluate noisy and ambiguous data with a consistent bias towards positive interpretations. The degree of distortion is proportional to the amount of effort we have invested.

It doesn't end there. Our problems grow even bigger when a large project attains the status of the project that cannot afford to fail. Under such conditions, management will almost automatically support anything that appears to help the "golden" project. After all, they want to do everything in their power to eliminate all excuses for failure.

Have you had trouble buying a new piece of test equipment? Just show how it will benefit the "golden" project and you will get approval. Do you have a feature that nobody would let you implement? Find a way to get it into the requirements of the "golden" project. These large projects act as magnets attracting additional cost, scope, and risk. They inevitably become the black holes of product development, uncontrollably devouring resources.

At the same time, large batches encourage even larger batches. For example, large test packages bundle many tests together and grow in importance with increasing size. As importance grows, such test packages get even higher priority. If engineers want their personal tests to get high priority, their best strategy is to add them to this large, high-priority test package. Of course, this then makes the package even larger and of higher priority.

B10: The Least Common Denominator Principle of Batch Size: The entire batch is limited by its worst element.

If the previous nine problems were not enough, large batches create a tenth problem. When we batch together a number of items, the entire batch acquires the properties of its most limiting element. For example, if we create a large test package with 30 tests, one or two of these tests may be safety-related. This typically forces us to treat the entire test package as safety-related, which means we must complete the entire package before we can authorize the next activity. A small batch approach would recognize that only one or two tests actually have to be performed on the critical path. The others can be done in parallel with other activities.

This least common denominator effect is particularly damaging to cycle time. We frequently use precedence-based techniques like PERT to schedule project activities. Such methods virtually always embody the concept of strict precedence, assuming that the prior activity must be completed before starting the current activity. They recognize that we cannot *complete* the current activity unless all activities upon which it depends are complete, and incorrectly assume that we cannot *start* the activity until prior activities are complete. We can avoid this problem by decomposing larger activities into smaller batches so that downstream activities can begin before upstream activities are complete.

Software Testing Example

Let us illustrate how the beneficial effects of small batches can be combined by using the example of software testing. When a software development process moves to daily test cycles, we gain the benefits of smaller changes, fewer open bugs, faster feedback, and faster cycle time. Smaller changes reduce debug complexity and make debugging more efficient. Fewer open bugs means less status reporting. It also makes testing more efficient because the system has more uptime and the validity of testing is higher. Faster feedback accelerates learning and improves quality because bugs are not repeated. It also enables changes to be made at an earlier and cheaper process step. Shorter flow-through times expose us to less requirements change and lower risk. Figure 5-3 shows the complex web of benefits that arise from the simple change of reducing batch size.

If reducing batch size is desirable, does it follow that we should endlessly make batch size smaller? Should the code be tested after each line is written? Should we show it to the customer for feedback each time a line of code is written? As you may already suspect, there is another U-curve optimization lurking up ahead.

The Science of Batch Size

Now, let us take a look at the science of batch size. The optimum batch size for a process is found by making an economic trade-off. While the fundamentals of this trade-off have been known since the early twentieth century, companies like Toyota deserve credit for providing critical insights on how to change the economics of this trade-off.

In this section, we will look at the math behind batch size reduction and discuss why it can sometimes overestimate optimum batch size. Then, we will discuss two technical aspects of batch size, its effect on capacity utilization, and its relationship to product architecture.

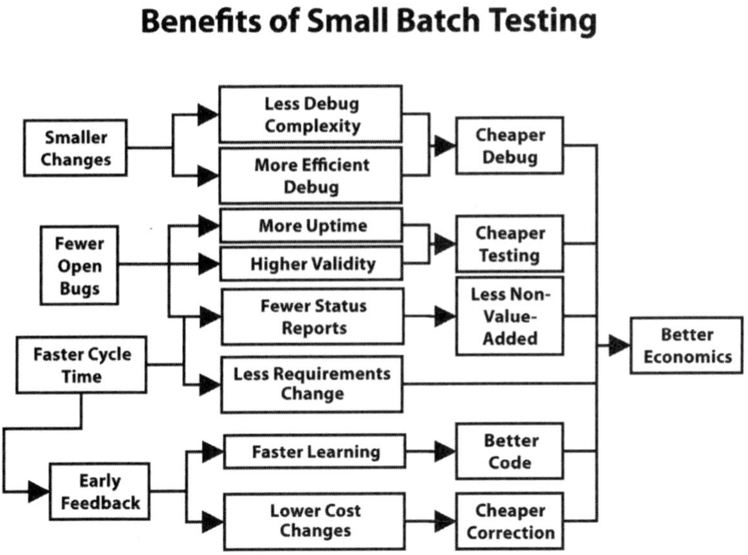

Benefits of Small Batch Testing

Figure 5-3 Smaller batch sizes produce a wide range of benefits. The impact on overall economics is surprisingly large.

B11: The Principle of Batch Size Economics: Economic batch size is a U-curve optimization.

Batch size is yet another U-curve optimization problem. We are trying to minimize total cost, and this cost comes from balancing a transaction cost against a holding cost. The equation that governs this trade-off is known as the Economic Order Quantity (EOQ) or Economic Lot Size (ELS) equation. It was introduced by Ford W. Harris in 1913. It is commonly used for inventory management and production run-length calculations.

We can view the transaction cost as the cost of sending a batch to the next process and the holding cost as the cost of not sending it. We can find the minimum total cost by combining these two costs and finding the minimum. The basic equations for optimum batch size are shown in Figure 5-4.

The U-curve for optimum batch size, which is shown in Figure 5-5, has three interesting and useful properties. First, it is for all practical purposes a continuous function. There are no large steps. This means we can creep up on optimum batch size. If we are using a batch size of 300 tests in our test process, we could take the bold step of reducing this to 299 tests.

Theoretical Optimum Batch Size

$$C_T = C_t + C_h$$

C_T = Total cost per year
C_t = Transaction cost per year
C_h = Holding cost per year
F = Fixed cost per batch
N = Items per year
Q = Items per batch
H = Holding cost per item per year

$$C_T = \frac{FN}{Q} + \frac{HQ}{2}$$

$$\frac{dC_T}{dQ} = 0 = -\frac{FN}{Q^2} + \frac{H}{2}$$

$$\frac{FN}{Q^2} = \frac{H}{2}$$

$$Q^2 = \frac{2FN}{H}$$

$$Q_o = \sqrt{\frac{2FN}{H}}$$

Figure 5-4 Optimum batch size is a function of holding cost and transaction cost.

In contrast, when we use capacity additions to solve queueing problems, we often must make step changes. Once we are running 24 hours per day on a test stand, we cannot increase internal capacity without adding another test stand, causing a step function increase in capacity.

Second, batch size reduction is reversible. If we discover we have moved in the wrong direction, or too far, we can move back. In contrast, when we incorrectly add capacity, it can be difficult to reverse this decision. More importantly, this reversibility allows us to continually modulate batch size in response to changing conditions.

For example, during a stage of development with high uncertainty, we might hold frequent meetings with our vendors to process issues in small batches. Later, when things become more routine, we might choose to process information less frequently in larger batches. We are simply recognizing that the trade-off between holding cost and transaction cost has changed.

Third, as we explained in Principle E6, a U-curve is very forgiving of errors. If we are already at the optimum point, a moderate step below this point will not drive us into a region with disastrous economics. This has very practical implications; we do not need a perfect answer when we select a batch size.

Optimum Batch Size

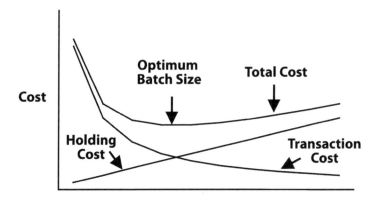

Items per Batch

Figure 5-5 Optimum batch size is another U-curve optimization. Higher transaction costs shift optimum batch size higher. Higher holding costs shift it lower.

B12: The Principle of Low Transaction Cost: Reducing transaction cost per batch lowers overall costs.

The primary controllable factor that enables small batches is low transaction cost per batch. If we reduce batch size without reducing transaction cost, we will be forced to pay the transaction cost more often, raising our total costs.

The brilliant insight of Japanese manufacturers was that what Americans called a "fixed" transaction cost was not "fixed" at all. The Japanese took the 24-hour changeover times for die stamping machines, which were accepted in American factories, and they relentlessly reduced them. Eventually, they were able to change over dies in less than 10 minutes.

These methods of set-up reduction, pioneered by the famous Japanese manufacturing engineer, Shigeo Shingo, are known today as single minute exchange of dies (SMED). This reduction of more than two orders of magnitude completely changed the economics of batch size. It unleashed dramatic reductions of batch size with *no* increase in transaction costs.

The same logic applies in product development. For example, huge improvements in software testing batch size are virtually always triggered by automation of testing. If it takes 24 hours to set up a test, we cannot test every 24 hours. We must invest in reducing transaction cost to enable the use of smaller batches.

If we look carefully at the total cost equation, we notice something else interesting. As we lower transaction costs and shift to the new optimum batch sizes, we also lower total costs. In fact, if we cut transaction cost in half, we create a new minimum cost operating point where total costs have been cut in half. Figure 5-6 shows how total costs decrease when fixed costs come down.

B13: The Principle of Batch Size Diseconomies: Batch size reduction saves much more than you think.

The optimum batch size in the EOQ equation is calculated based on three important assumptions. First, we assume that transaction cost is fixed. We discussed the fallacy of this assumption in the previous section. Transaction cost reduction almost always has a regenerative effect. As we reduce transaction costs, the transaction volume goes up. As transaction volume goes up, we can justify investing more in transaction cost reduction.

Second, the EOQ equation assumes that transaction costs are independent of batch size. What would happen if there were actually *higher* costs associated with large batches? In fact, such batch size diseconomies are common in product development. As mentioned earlier, debug complexity increases exponentially with batch size. Status reporting increases exponentially with batch size. Under such circumstances, batch size reduction lowers costs by reducing both holding *and* transaction costs.

Third, in the EOQ equation, we assume that holding costs increase linearly with batch size. All evidence suggests that holding costs increase at faster than a linear rate in product development. For example, as explained in Principle V6, the perishability of product development work products increases with holding time. This perishability is the most likely reason for the exponential growth effect discussed in Principle B8.

What does this mean? Our calculated optimum batch sizes are likely to be too large. In the presence of the hard-to-quantify large batch diseconomies, it is important to aggressively test our assumptions

Enabling Lower Total Costs

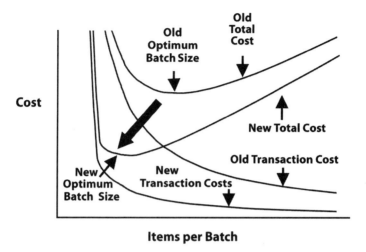

Figure 5-6 By lowering transaction costs, we create a lower optimum batch size. This also creates a new minimum process cost.

about optimum batch size. When one printer company reduced batch size in their software process, they got savings that were twice what they expected. This suggests that they had been unable to make accurate assumptions about diseconomies of scale associated with large batches.

It is generally safe to assume that we really don't know where the optimum point is on the batch size response surface. As a result, we must test the response of the product development process to batch size reduction by reducing batch size and measuring the results.

A useful heuristic is to assume that the hidden costs of large batch size are about twice as high as you think. This would imply that optimum batch size is actually about 70 percent of whatever number you may calculate as optimum. Therefore, as a minimum, you should aim for a batch size that is 30 percent smaller than whatever you think is optimal. And what if you are wrong? The total cost equation would suggest that if you accidentally drop 33 percent below optimum batch size, you will only increase total cost by 8 percent. This is a risk worth taking.

B14: The Batch Size Packing Principle: Small batches allow finer tuning of capacity utilization.

A more subtle advantage of small batches is that they allow us to fine-tune capacity utilization. Small batches make it easier to maintain good utilization, even under conditions when some batches must be large.

Think of it like filling a jar with rocks. Filling it with rocks alone generates wasted space. Filling it with rocks and sand will utilize space just as efficiently as filling with pure sand.

If we have some large batches, we should schedule them first and fill in the gaps with small batches. This is analogous to putting the big rocks in the jar before we add the sand.

This fine-tuning principle is used extensively on the Internet. Traditional telephone service uses what is called a "circuit-switching" approach. When we make a phone call, we acquire the channel capacity for the full duration of our call. This capacity belongs to us until we hang up.

In contrast, the Internet is a packet switching network. A message is broken into small packets, each packet is assigned a number, and the packets are routed on whatever routes are available to the destination. Since packets are small, we can exploit each tiny window of capacity, available on any link, to pass pieces of the message towards its destination. We do not have to find an open channel big enough to transmit the entire message to the receiver. These small savings in capacity have enormous leverage because queueing curves can be very steep. Shunting a small amount of demand from a heavily utilized link can lead to a large reduction in queues and cycle time.

Smaller batches inherently help us get better resource utilization with smaller queues. In Chapter 7, we will further discuss the opportunities for routing flexibility that are created by smaller batches.

B15: The Fluidity Principle: Loose coupling between product subsystems enables small batches.

Working effectively with small batches requires that we reduce dependencies between the batches. If we want to start testing subsystems before the entire system is designed, we need to create independently testable subsystems. As we reduce dependencies, we gain flexibility in routing and sequencing.

The Internet improves throughput using a similar strategy by making it possible to send packets independently. It assigns a specific sequence number to each packet, which enables us to reassemble the entire message independent of the sequence in which the packets arrive at their final destination. Once we are freed from the constraint of sequence, we can use multiple routes and we need no longer wait for one packet to be acknowledged before the next one is sent. By eliminating the need for strict sequence, we can take our system to much higher levels of performance.

This illustrates the extremely important relationship between product architecture and development process design. Once a product developer realizes that small batches are desirable, they start adopting product architectures that permit work to flow in small, decoupled batches. These loosely coupled architectures, with stable interfaces, enable us to work in parallel on many subsystems. We can work in parallel with low risk, if we are confident that the work we do will ultimately integrate well at a system level.

Subsystem reuse has an important influence on interface stability. We discussed the value of reuse in Principle V9, but now we can add a bit more detail. In theory, we could reuse either large or small modules. In practice, we are more likely to achieve effective reuse with small modules. Small modules have less complex interfaces and more potential applications. It is easier to reuse a capacitor, than it is to reuse a complex integrated circuit.

Reuse brings surprising benefits because reused subsystems are already defined, designed, and tested. When we reuse a subsystem, we also reuse testing, documentation, system-level interactions, and reliability-related learning.

We should not limit ourselves reusing the work products of design. Sometimes it is even more productive to reuse the logic of the design, rather than a specific instantiation of this logic. For example, a company I once worked for designed gearboxes for power transmission which had to meet certain design standards. The VP of engineering embedded the entire logic of gearbox design in a computer program. The parameters of a new gearbox could be fed into this program, and it would automatically generate the design. Although each design might be unique, the logical process by which the design was generated was not. New parameters would automatically generate new designs with the same rigor as the old ones.

In another case, I saw a division of a telecommunications company cut their design cycle time by a factor of 30 by increasing the amount of design reuse. They created a database of previous designs and interpolated new solutions between existing qualified designs.

By reducing the dependencies between subsystems, we can free ourselves from the need for strict sequence. This allows us to process work into even smaller batches.

Managing Batch Size

Now let us consider seven principles that help us manage batch size reduction. We will discuss the important role of transport batches, the value of physical proximity, and the importance of infrastructure. Then, we will discuss the critical issue of batch content, the importance of reducing batch size before we attack bottlenecks, and the concept of dynamic batch size.

B16: The Principle of Transport Batches: The most important batch is the transport batch.

In manufacturing, we make a distinction between the batch size of a process that changes the state of the product and the batch size of a process that changes the location of the product. I will refer to these two batch sizes as the production batch size and the transport batch size.

It is important to recognize that production batch size and transport batch size are two separate batch size decisions. Each of these batches has its own optimum economic batch size. The batch size for production is dictated by set-up time. The batch size for transport is dictated by fixed transaction cost associated with transportation.

These same concepts apply in product development. For example, we may do an extensive qualification test on our products. The production batch size of this test would be the portion of the test that we complete uninterrupted on a single setup. The transport batch size for this test is the portion of the test results that we transfer in one batch to the next process stage. Even when we use a large production batch size, we can still use a small transport batch size. We can run an uninterrupted test suite of 1,000 tests while still transferring test results as each test is completed.

Transport batches are generally more important than production batch sizes for two reasons. First, small transport batches allow us to overlap activities which leads to faster cycle time. Second, small transport batches accelerate feedback, which is of critical importance in product development.

As we have explained several times in this chapter, it is small transport batches that make packet switching networks like the Internet work so effectively. We break messages into small packets and begin forwarding a received packet before we receive the next packet. If we waited for the entire file to reach each node before we forwarded it, transport times would be much higher. By using small packets, most of the message will reach the receiver even before the final packet leaves the sender. This dramatically shortens cycle time.

B17: The Proximity Principle: Proximity enables small batch sizes.

For physical objects and many types of information, the transaction cost for transport batches is a function of distance. In manufacturing, collapsing distances is one of the most powerful ways of enabling small transport batches. This is also true in product development. When we colocate development teams, we make it possible to communicate in small batches. Furthermore, communications on colocated teams are face-to-face, which makes them synchronous and real-time. The sender gets instant feedback, verbally and nonverbally, from the receiver.

This is a striking contrast to physically-dispersed teams. Dispersed teams tend to use large batch asynchronous communications. Even when they use small batch e-mail communication, this communication is asynchronous with long delays between a question and a response. This is small batch size deprived of many of its benefits.

Proximity is the main tool used in manufacturing to enable one-piece flow. In a traditional factory, we grouped all the lathes together and had a group of lathe operators supervised by a lead operator, who was an expert on turning operations. This optimized efficiency but forced us to use large transport batches. Now, we organize production lines around products and aim at achieving one-piece flow.

Proximity also promotes flexibility. We use U-shaped production lines so that a worker can easily assist another station on the line. This allows us to quickly respond to emerging queues. We organize work into cells so that workers can move with the work from machine to machine. This reduces time in queue.

B18: The Run Length Principle: Short run lengths reduce queues.

While transport batches are our biggest opportunity, we can also gain benefits by reducing production lot sizes in product development processes. For example, we can avoid overloading a project with features, which results in infrequent product introductions and long development cycles. Instead, if we limit the number of new features and introduce products more frequently, we will get faster feedback from the market.

A subtle advantage of shorter run lengths is that we can sequence tasks in such a way that variances do not accumulate. We can interleave hard jobs and easy jobs to prevent extended runs of hard jobs.

In manufacturing, this is done with production planning, where it is called mix leveling or *heijunka*. It is more difficult to do this in engineering because we do not know precisely how long it will take to accomplish individual tasks. Yet, we often have sufficient ability to use a similar approach by discriminating the difficult jobs from the easy ones. As mentioned in Principle V10, we can use the easy jobs to reduce queues by creating negative covariances in the workstream.

Scheduling tasks in the presence of uncertainty requires a bit more discussion. In Chapter 7, we will examine how approaches like round-robin scheduling permit us to do this.

B19: The Infrastructure Principle: Good infrastructure enables small batches.

Investments in infrastructure enable small batches. First, good infrastructure reduces transaction costs. The movement in software to daily build/test cycles is underpinned by test automation. As we automate our tests, we can use smaller test batches. This, in turn, creates a virtuous cycle. The smaller the batch, the more batches we must do; the more batches we do, the more we can justify investing in automation.

Second, good infrastructure permits different batches to be in different stages of completion. For example, if we wish to test subsystems before the entire system is ready, we need the testbeds to do this testing. This reduces dependency and coupling between batches. The infrastructure provides the scaffolding that permits subsystems to progress independently.

Why don't more companies have strong infrastructure? Primarily because infrastructure costs money. Companies like to test at the system level, because the system acts as its own testbed. Furthermore, system tests are inherently more comprehensive than subsystem tests. This combination of low investment and high validity creates the illusion that system tests are more economical than subsystem tests. This is actually not the case when we recognize that system tests occur on the critical path, which increases the cost of delay. Even worse, feedback from system tests occurs late in development, when the cost of making changes is high.

How do we break out of this trap? We need to justify investing in infrastructure using our economic framework. This will permit us to look at overall economic consequences, particularly the cycle time benefits.

B20: The Principle of Batch Content: Sequence first that which adds value most cheaply.

Shifting to smaller batch sizes in product development gives us the opportunity to use the work sequence to improve economics. We do this by carefully deciding which work content should go into each batch. In repetitive operations like manufacturing, this opportunity rarely exists. Nor does it exist in large batch development processes where all work is in the same batch and there is no degree of freedom associated with sequence. Only small batch development processes allow us to choose which work goes in each batch. We will call this the issue of "batch content."

Let us set the scene with a simple example to illustrate our economic logic. We are designing the first automobile to be powered by a perpetual motion device. The design of the perpetual motion device, Module 1, will cost $5 million and has a 5 percent chance of success. The design for the rest of the car, Module 2, will cost $100 million and has 100 percent chance of success. Which sequence for these two modules adds value most cheaply?

Effect of Sequencing

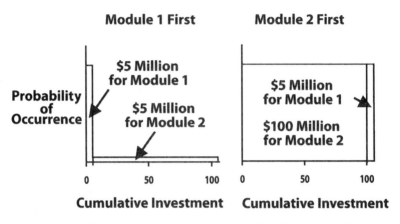

Note: All costs are expected values (probability weighted).

Figure 5-7 The most economic task sequence is a function of investment and risk. It is best to design an inexpensive but risky module as early as possible.

As Figure 5-7 indicates, if we do Module 1 first, we will incur an expected cost of $10 million. If we do Module 2 first, we will incur an expected cost of $105 million.[2] By sequencing the high-risk batch first, we reduce the amount of accumulated investment that is exposed to the risk of failure.

The general principle is that we should sequence first the activities that add the most value for the least cost.[3] This exposes the least investment to risk and allows us to make the minimum investment to create an acceptable product.

Let's look at a couple of examples of this logic in action. Consider a product where the dominant driver of value is the manufacturing cost of the design. We would want to refine the elements that control cost

---

[2] The expected cost of doing Module 1 first is 100 percent times the Module 1 cost and 5 percent times the Module 2 cost. We will only design Module 2 if Module 1 works, which occurs 5 percent of the time. The expected cost of Module 2 first is 100 percent times the Module 2 cost and 100 percent times the Module 1 cost. In this case, we always design Module 1 since Module 2 will always be successful.

[3] The individual activities that make up development each have a cost and benefit. By sequencing activities with high benefit to cost ratios first, we create a desirable convexity in the curve of cumulative benefit vs. cumulative cost.

first. For example, if the power supply was the most expensive component, and if this cost could be reduced by selecting a low-cost standard component, we should select this first. The rest of the design could follow this step.

We would choose a different sequence when cost of delay dominated. In such cases, we would want to minimize the length of the critical path, so we would start work first on components with the longest lead-time. For example, if the package lead-time dominated cycle time, we would design this component first. Other components could be selected later, without getting on the critical path.

The concept is simple. Sequence activities to create maximum value for minimum cost, and remember that removing risk from a project is a key way to increase the expected value of the project.

B21: The Batch Size First Principle: Reduce batch size before you attack bottlenecks.

Developers often ask if they should begin by changing capacity utilization or by reducing batch size. In theory, I could tell you to choose the approach that produces the most economic benefit for the least economic cost. However, the practical answer is much simpler: start with batch size. This is the great lesson of the Toyota Production System. The 100-fold improvement in manufacturing cycle times was *not* achieved by finding bottlenecks and adding capacity to the bottlenecks. It was achieved by reducing batch size.

Let us return to the example of the cafeteria that we discussed in Principle B2. We could have reduced queues by doubling the size of the cafeteria. This is attacking the bottleneck. Instead, we decided to stagger lunch hours, which reduced batch size. Reducing batch size reduces variability, and with lower variability, we may find our existing capacity is already sufficient.

Unfortunately, bottlenecks are terribly seductive. It is very easy to convince product developers that queues are caused by bottlenecks, because this explanation is much more intuitively appealing than blaming batch size. The average developer does not manage or even measure batch size. In contrast, a whole industry has emerged based on Goldratt's Theory of Constraints, convincing people that their first priority should be to find and fix bottlenecks.

In product development, bottlenecks are less of an opportunity than in manufacturing for two key reasons. First, the bottlenecks of product development are stochastic bottlenecks, not deterministic ones. They are temporally mobile. Sometimes they are there, sometimes they are not. For example, a random process operated at 80 percent utilization by definition does not have a bottleneck 20 percent of the time. When bottlenecks are ephemeral, it is hard to convince management that we have a bottleneck.

Second, bottlenecks in product development are also physically mobile, unlike the relatively stationary bottlenecks of manufacturing. Adding capacity at a temporary bottleneck may simply create extra cost where we don't need it.

Let us look at the engaging story in Goldratt's excellent book, *The Goal*, with our new insight into the importance of batch size. Goldratt suggested letting the slowest Boy Scout, Herbie, walk at the head of the line. In my years as a scout leader, we did not use this logical and conceptually appealing approach. You see, this approach contains the embedded assumption that the hiking group can only hike in one large batch. There are times when this assumption is correct, such as when you have a shortage of adult leaders. However, in practice, it is more common to break the hiking group into two smaller batches. The experienced and faster older scouts would blaze the trail. Some leaders and the younger scouts would form a second batch that moved slower. The integrity of these two smaller groups was maintained; no hikers were allowed to be out of sight of other hikers in their group. At key integration points, such as stream crossings and forks in the trail, the lead group would wait for the trailing group.

What was the advantage of using smaller batches? The advance group could stop to replenish water supplies while waiting for the rear group to catch up. The advance group could begin preparing the campsite as soon as it arrived. With modern technology, portable radios, we didn't even sacrifice communications. Reducing batch size avoids the least common denominator effects that large batch size frequently creates, as we discussed in Principle B10.

So, in practice, I always suggest reducing batch size before adding capacity at bottlenecks. Batch size reduction is cheaper than adding capacity, it is easy to sell to top management, and it massively reduces queues. It is always our weapon of choice for reducing queues.

B22: The Principle of Dynamic Batch Size: Adjust batch size dynamically to respond to changing economics.

As mentioned in Principle B10, the factors that lead to optimum batch size can be time-dependent. For example, the value of rapid feedback is high early in the project when risks are still high. During this stage, it makes sense to seek the fast feedback of small batch sizes. As we progress, the value of rapid feedback goes down and transaction costs can rise. At this point, it can make economic sense to move to a larger batch size.

People who are used to the relatively static batch sizes that are used in manufacturing are sometimes surprised by the use of variable batch size of product development. In manufacturing, batch size is a fairly static concept because the economic factors that drive EOQ do not change very quickly. In contrast, in product development, the economic factors that drive EOQ change continuously. Both holding costs and fixed costs vary with time. When this is the case, it makes sense to alter the batch size. Let's consider two examples.

One example is the effect of rising holding costs as we progress through the development cycle. This occurs commonly in pharmaceutical development, because the cost of delay rises near the end of the development process. In such cases, the batch size in which information should be processed should decrease near the end of the process. For example, the frequency of team meetings should increase in this stage of development in contrast to the less frequent meetings that might occur during preclinical trials.

A second example is batch size in testing. Early tests generate lots of valuable information, and we would like to obtain and react to this information quickly. As the rate at which defects are found drops, we can move to larger testing batch sizes because the holding cost of delaying feedback has decreased.

Round Up the Usual Suspects

Well, enough theory. You probably want to know where product development batch size problems typically occur. The good news is that they are all around us. The bad news is that it takes a little time to train yourself to see them. Let's look at a dozen typical examples.

Project Scope

One of the most dangerous of all batch size problems is the tendency to pack more innovation in a single project than is truly necessary. Excessive project scope easily leads to the self-reinforcing death spiral discussed in Principle B9. Long planning horizons lead to schedule slippage. When schedules slip, it changes the competitive environment that the product will confront, so marketing requests additional features. The additional features require extra effort, further extending planning horizons and increasing technical complexity. This regeneratively escalates slippage.

What is a small batch size approach? Don't overload the project with excessive scope. Some companies limit new products to three major improvements. This typically provides enough sizzle to make a product compelling, without dragging in all the extra features that add more complexity than value. We have less risk of total failure when we break a big project into a series of smaller projects, as explained in Principle V7.

Project Funding

Another common batch size error is the way projects are funded. The entire project is conceived and funded as a single large batch proposal. Since this large proposal requests a large investment, risk is high. To control this high risk, sensible managers demand thorough analysis and careful justification. This large transaction cost biases people towards minimizing the number of transactions and maximizing transaction size. Since it takes almost equal effort to ask for a big bag of money as a small one, people prefer to ask for big bags of money.

An attractive alternative is to permit smaller increments of funding using a streamlined process. These initial increments can be viewed as a way of buying information to create better plans for later stages. By funding in smaller increments, we make investment decisions at shorter time-horizons, with better information, and by putting less money at risk in each increment.

This, of course, is exactly the approach that venture capitalists use when funding risky new technologies. Initial funding rounds are small, because risk is high. After some risk is reduced, funding rounds become larger, but even then, they will be syndicated with other firms. Whereas typical corporate practice emphasizes controlling risk through careful analysis, venture capitalists excel at using funding batch size to control risk.

Project Phases

One of the most widespread and glaring examples of a batch size error is the use of gates to divide the development process into phases. Too often, companies establish rules requiring one phase to be completed before the next one begins.

What are the batch size implications of such a policy? The work product being transferred from one phase to another is 100 percent of the work product of the previous phase. This is maximum theoretical batch size and will result in maximum theoretical cycle time. It also leads to maximum possible delays in interphase feedback.

Interestingly, the practice of working in one phase at a time is so devoid of common sense that engineers seldom follow it, even when it is required by their procedures. Almost all companies that claim to work in one phase at a time actually have an underground process that works out of phase. In fact, my course surveys indicate that 95 percent of companies will admit that they have an underground process in which actual activities take place out of phase.

Some developers resist overlapping phases because they assume that gates are the only way to control project risks. In my experience, there are excellent ways to control risk without using large batch size gates. For example, if we don't want a team to spend a lot of money on long lead-time material before they complete design validation testing, we can set a limit on what they can spend. This is always better than blocking 100 percent of purchasing.

In general, whenever authority jumps from 0 to 100 percent at a single instant of time, we are transferring authority in maximum theoretical batch size. Instead, we should seek ways to grant limited authority, while still controlling risk.

Requirements Definition

Another classic batch size issue is the way we define requirements. Most product development processes attempt to define 100 percent of requirements at the very beginning of the process. They try to identify all design inputs before they begin design. This makes the batch size of the handoff between requirement definition and design equal to

100 percent of the work product. Again, maximum theoretical batch size results in maximum theoretical cycle time. It places requirement definition on the critical path for the maximum possible time.

Such an approach inherently leads to inferior designs because it breaks the feedback loop between design and specification. Design activities generate valuable information on the performance limits of our technologies and the cost impact of requested features. This information is vital for making optimal trade-offs between the cost and value of a feature. To get this information quickly, we must begin design before we finalize our specification.

A practical approach for implementing smaller batches is to progressively lock down requirements. Using this approach, some characteristics are frozen before others. In general, we freeze requirements that engineering needs first, before the ones that are needed later. We should never group all requirements into one large batch because this lets the slowest requirement hold up all of the work.

Project Planning

It is common for people to try to prepare a complete and detailed plan for the project at the beginning of the project. This forces planning to be done at a long time-horizon, where forecasting is very difficult. This, in turn, leads to frequent and massive plan revisions.

A better alternative is to do high-level planning for the entire project, but to limit detailed planning to a short time-horizon. High-level planning has lower variability, because grouped tasks benefit from the variability pooling effect, Principle V5. Detailed planning can only be done reliably when the time-horizon is short, benefiting from Principle V6.

Some observers describe this approach as, "walking down the road in the fog." We plan in detail what we can see clearly: the next several weeks. As we execute this plan, more of the road becomes visible. Now we can do more planning. Everything is done with a plan, but this is not a plan created in one large batch at the beginning of the project. It is plan created in small batches, with fresh information, and benefiting from knowledge acquired along the way.

Testing

Almost nowhere in product development have we seen a greater adoption of small batch sizes than in testing. Companies that used to test their product every 60 days are now testing daily. We discussed the benefits of this approach for software earlier in this chapter. It applies equally well to hardware.

For example, high-risk subsystems can be designed and prototyped before lower risk subsystems are even specified. This reduces the project risk without putting large amounts of development expense at risk.

Capital Spending

Like project funding, capital spending is carefully controlled by most companies. Detailed Capital Authorization Requests are submitted and screened through many levels of management. It takes a long time and a lot of paperwork to get capital, so people only like to do it once. Corporate environments encourage a single and comprehensive request. If you make multiple requests for the same project, you look either stupid or devious, neither of which is favored.

In contrast, some companies have learned to release capital in smaller batches. For example, one company permits its design teams to use up to 10 percent of its authorized capital budget before design verification is complete. This puts little capital at risk, but still gives teams enough capital to keep long lead-time items off the critical path.

Again, we can view the standard process as one that tries to control risk by using a large batch size. With large batches, the consequence of a mistake is high, so the probability of a mistake must be minimized. This leads to long delays in getting management approval. When companies release capital in smaller batches, the small batch size inherently limits the downside risk. As a result, they can accept a greater probability of failure, while still maintaining the same degree of financial control. Thus, small batch size is a highly effective risk control tool.

Drawing Release

Traditional drawing release processes release a drawing as a single unit. The drawing is either released or unreleased. If the drawing is released, we can trust everything on the drawing. If it is unreleased, we can trust nothing. When viewed from the perspective of batch size, this means that 100 percent of the information on the drawing is being released in a single batch. Since this is maximum theoretical batch size, it will lead to maximum theoretical cycle time.

A better way to handle drawing releases is to freeze the critical information necessary for downstream processes first. For example, one company did a tooling release on their drawings prior to the final machining release. The tooling release froze the dimensions critical to the toolmaker. Once these dimensions were stabilized, the tool could be designed without taking any risk.

Design Reviews

As previously discussed, many companies do design reviews by looking at many drawings in one large batch. If engineers are permitted to complete 200 drawings before they are reviewed, they embed the same bad assumptions in the last 180 drawings as they have in the first 20. By progressively reviewing drawings in smaller batches, we get the benefits of early feedback, and we avoid the inefficient review of 200 drawings at the same time.

Manufacturing Release

Like design reviews, many companies hold large batch manufacturing readiness reviews prior to releasing the product to manufacturing. They assume that by reviewing all 300 engineering drawings at the same time, they have a more inclusive view of the design. They are right, but they are ignoring a critical fact. If they release 100 percent of the project's drawings at the same time, they are using maximum theoretical batch size. This will result in maximum theoretical delay prior to drawing release. Furthermore, when the large batch of drawings arrives in the next process stage, it overloads its capacity and creates another queue.

A better approach is the one we described for design reviews. Conduct preliminary reviews in small batches, and then do a final comprehensive review to look at anything that has changed since the preliminary review. The small batches also allow beneficial feedback between manufacturing and engineering. As mentioned in Principle B6, small batch reviews are usually more efficient than large batch reviews

Market Research

Market research is often done in large batch sizes. A single comprehensive test is created that answers many questions at the same time. After all, this allows us to exploit scale economies in doing research. But, such comprehensive tests often generate information late in development when the cost of reacting to it is high.

What is a better way to do this? Decompose the market research into a series of events. Start with small-scale tests focused on high-risk questions. As you progress, make the tests less frequent, larger scale, and more comprehensive. This enables rapid reduction of risk and generates information when it is cheapest to react to it.

Postmortems

Project postmortems provide another example of a large batch size process. Companies review the entire project when it is complete. This extracts learning in one large batch at the very end of the project. Project members develop recommendations for other teams.

Contrast this with the small batch size approach. Every 90 days, the project takes a day to examine its methods and processes. It reflects on what is working and what is not working. It identifies how it wants to change methods going forward. The conclusions of the team are shared with other teams. Learning becomes available much earlier. Conclusions are more reliable since events are fresher in people's minds. Implementation rates are very high because the people recommending the changes are the same ones that will carry them out. Consider replacing the project postmortem with a periodic physical exam!

Conclusion

We opened this chapter by explaining the 10 principles that make small batch sizes desirable to product developers. I hope I have convinced you of the enormous opportunity associated with batch size reduction. Following this, we examined the economic trade-offs associated with batch size.

By now, you should recognize the enormous economic value of decreasing transaction cost. You've learned that by moving in small steps in the direction of smaller batch sizes, you will get more benefits than you anticipate.

Batch size is a tremendously useful tool for reducing queues. It is well proven in manufacturing as a path to shorter cycle times. It has even greater promise for product developers for two reasons. First, batch size reduction accelerates feedback and reduces risk. These effects are much more economically significant in product development than they are in manufacturing.

Second, batch size is a mature concept in manufacturing, where it has been used for almost a century. In contrast, today, product developers do not even recognize batch size as an issue. Instead, they have institutionalized large batch transfers in many areas of their processes. This makes it an area of great opportunity.

6

Applying WIP Constraints

It is easier to start work than it is to finish it.
It is easier to grow WIP than it is to reduce it.

How does Toyota maintain short cycle times in their factories? It uses WIP constraints to limit maximum inventory levels. How does the Internet enable the slowest personal computer to communicate reliably with the fastest supercomputer, even through a network of constantly and unpredictably varying capacity? It uses WIP constraints.

In the last chapter, we discussed batch size reduction, an approach that reduces queues for both predictable and random flows. While batch size reduction is a powerful tool, it does not fundamentally address the problem of random variations in flow.[1] We should not expect it to, because adjustments to batch size are too slow to respond to the short-period random variation in product development flow.

Yet, these short-period random variations are much more important than their magnitude would suggest. As we saw in Principle Q15, the diffusion principle, random variations can accumulate insidiously into large and expensive queues. We need a tool to respond to the accumulation of these short time-constant variations that are so common in development processes. We can do this with WIP constraints.

WIP constraints are widely used in manufacturing. In fact, they are central to the operation of the Toyota Production System (TPS). While we can learn much from manufacturing applications, we can learn even more from the way data communications networks use WIP constraints.

As we shall see later in this chapter, the flow control protocols used on the Internet have evolved further and far more quickly than the protocols used in manufacturing. They provide a rich source of advanced

---

[1] In fact, batch size reduction actually increases the variation *between* batches because large batches benefit from variability pooling, Principle V5. Nevertheless, the other disadvantages of large batches overwhelm the slight benefit created by variability pooling.

methods for the product developer, methods that fit precisely to the high variability flows found in product development processes.

Why can we learn so much from telecommunications networks? The WIP constraints of manufacturing are optimized for repetitive and homogeneous flows. They rarely deal with large amounts of variability, because manufacturers have systematically reduced variability to improve flow.

In contrast, the design of telecommunications networks assumes high variability as an inherent characteristic of the system. As a result, the Internet uses approaches that are robust in the presence of highly variable, nonhomogeneous flows. These approaches are particularly interesting to product developers because product developers share the same problem of nonrepetitive, nonhomogeneous flows.

The first section of this chapter will examine the economic logic behind WIP constraints. The next section will look at the interventions that can be made when WIP reaches its upper limit. The final section will cover practical details associated with WIP constraints and give you some examples of WIP constraints in action.

The Economic Logic of WIP Control

The First Queue Size Control Principle, Q13, provided a qualitative introduction to the concept of controlling queue size. Now we can treat this topic more quantitatively. Many product developers underestimate the mind-set shift required to begin focusing on controlling WIP rather than controlling cycle time. Today, 100 percent of product developers monitor the cycle time through their processes. Someday, I hope that 100 percent of product developers will monitor and control WIP.

As I mentioned in Chapter 3, we have a long way to go. Since 98 percent of product developers do not measure WIP today, we need a 50-fold increase. As Figure 6-1 shows, this requires shifting our focus from the horizontal axis of time to the vertical axis of queue size. As we explained in Principle Q14, controlling queue size has significant advantages over controlling cycle time.

In this section, we will start by explaining statistical and economic basis behind WIP constraints. Then, we will discuss how WIP

A Mind-Set Shift

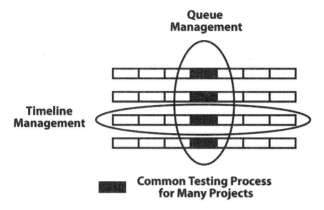

Figure 6-1 Today's processes focus on the horizontal axis of cycle time instead of the vertical axis of queues.

constraints force rate-matching. Next, we will examine the use of global and local constraints. Finally, we will learn how WIP ranges permit adjacent processes to use different batch sizes.

W1: The Principle of WIP Constraints: Constrain WIP to control cycle time and flow.

In Chapter 3, we discussed the time behavior of queues. We pointed out that high-queue states occur infrequently, yet, when they occur, they last a long time, and they do disproportionate economic damage. This naturally raises the question, what would happen if we prevented high-queue states? The simplest way to do this is to block arrivals when the queue becomes large. This type of queueing system is known as an M/M/1/k queueing system, where k represents the maximum limit on the number of items in the system. You may remember that the queueing system we described in Chapter 3 was called an M/M/1/∞ queueing system, a system where k equals infinity.

When we set a limit on WIP, we create one positive effect and two negative ones. The positive effect is to reduce average cycle time. The first negative effect is that we permanently reject potentially valuable demand. The second negative effect is that we ultimately reduce our capacity utilization, because we have permanently lost the demand that we rejected during periods of congestion.

The Effect of WIP Constraints

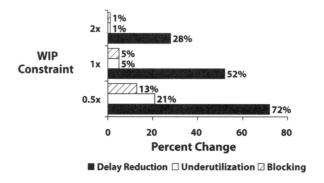

Note: Referenced to the average for M/M/1/∞ at 90% utilization.

Figure 6-2 WIP constraints affect delays, blocking, and utilization. When the WIP constraint is relatively light, cycle-time savings are much higher than the cost of underutilization and blocking.

Figure 6-2 shows what happens when we implement different levels of WIP constraints on a M/M/1/∞ queueing system. The WIP constraints are shown as multipliers of the average WIP level that would occur in the system without any WIP constraint. A relatively light WIP constraint, twice the average WIP level, produces a significant 28 percent cycle-time savings. Yet, it only causes a 1 percent penalty in the form of underutilization and blocking costs. In contrast, a heavy WIP constraint, half the average WIP level, creates large blocking and underutilization costs that counteract the cycle-time savings.

In Figure 6-3, we have done a sample cost-benefit analysis using a 2x average WIP constraint with quite conservative assumptions about delay cost, capacity cost, and the opportunity cost associated with blocked jobs. Even with a low ratio of delay cost to capacity cost, the benefits of the WIP constraint are about 10 times its economic costs.

W2: The Principle of Rate-Matching: WIP constraints force rate-matching.

WIP constraints produce another benefit. They are without question the easiest way to force rate-matching between adjacent processes. The average WIP pool that exists between two processes is determined by the average rate at which work flows in and out of this pool. By setting

Effect of WIP Constraint

	No WIP Constraint	WIP Constrained at 2x Average	Extra Cost/ (Savings)
Annual Cost of Capacity ($ Millions)	$2,000,000	$2,022,472	$22,472
Opportunity Cost of Blocked Jobs	$0	$25,000	$25,000
Cost of Delay	$1,643,836	$1,183,562	($460,274)

Note: Cost-of-delay savings is 9.7 times the added blocking and capacity costs.

Figure 6-3 A relatively light WIP constraint of twice average unconstrained WIP level produces less than $50,000 of blocking and underutilization costs in return for $460,000 of cost-of-delay savings.

an upper limit on the size of this pool, we inherently force the average rate of arrival into this pool to match the average rate of departure from the pool.

This rate-matching principle lies at the heart of modern data communications networks. In a packet-switching network, we set a limit on the number of unacknowledged packets that may be in flight between the sender and receiver at any moment. This simple WIP constraint forces the sender to slow its transmission rate to match the rate at which good packets arrive at the receiver. As a result, we can reliably interconnect computers with massive differences in operating speed (eight to nine orders of magnitude) through channels that continuously experience unpredictable changes in throughput.

W3: The Principle of Global Constraints: Use global constraints for predictable and permanent bottlenecks.

One popular approach for constraining WIP is known as Theory of Constraints (TOC). This concept was developed by Eli Goldratt in his book, *The Goal*. Goldratt suggests that we find the bottleneck in the process and release work into the system at the operating rate of the bottleneck. This acts to constrain the total pool of WIP that is upstream of the bottleneck. He suggests that the size of this global pool should only be large enough to ensure that the bottleneck is never starved for inventory.

This approach is simple and conceptually appealing. It is probably most useful for stable bottlenecks, like those of manufacturing, and less useful for the unpredictable, moving, and limited-duration bottlenecks of product development.

Because TOC does not attempt to control interprocess WIP pools, it only requires a single global target for all WIP forward of the bottleneck. This makes it a simple system to operate, but the absence of individual local WIP targets creates two disadvantages.

First, only the primary, stable bottleneck is being used for control purposes. A temporary bottleneck at another process will not generate any control signal until it causes WIP starvation at the primary bottleneck.

Second, when primary bottleneck capacity drops, WIP will tend to concentrate in front of this bottleneck. For example, imagine that the bottleneck dropped to zero throughput. No new work could be released into the system, but the work in the system would continue to flow downstream until it was blocked at this bottleneck. When capacity was regained at the bottleneck, the bottleneck would have a huge supply of WIP while the other upstream processes would be WIP-starved. As we shall see in the next section, the kanban system of Toyota has neither of these disadvantages.

W4: The Principle of Local Constraints: If possible, constrain local WIP pools.

The most popular and mature system of WIP constraints is the kanban system used in the Toyota Production System. While it is popularly called a pull system, it is more useful to recognize it as a system that constrains local WIP pools.

If a simple kanban system was trying to limit the WIP between two processes to 30 items, it might use six pallets that could each hold five parts as physical kanbans. The downstream process would take parts off a pallet and when it was empty, send it back to the upstream process. This empty pallet would signal the upstream process to make more parts. The upstream process is not allowed to make parts unless it has an empty pallet to put them on. This sets an upper limit on the amount of WIP between the two processes.

The system level effect of this approach is interesting. If all local WIP pools are constrained, then total WIP is constrained. If total WIP is constrained, by Little's Formula, Principle Q12, cycle time is also constrained. Thus, the kanban system uses WIP constraints to directly control the cycle time through a factory.

Moreover, the kanban system makes no assumption about the location of bottlenecks. Any emergent bottleneck will begin to send a control signal that throttles its upstream process. This throttling signal will propagate upstream, work center by work center. As soon as one work center has filled all its empty pallets, it can make no more parts, so it stops sending empty pallets to its predecessor process.

Thus, when a blockage occurs anywhere, the system stabilizes with each upstream process stopped and holding its maximum WIP. When capacity is regained, there are no WIP-starved processes and smooth flow begins immediately. Such a system is well-suited for the stochastic bottlenecks of product development.

The local constraints of the kanban system are also impressive in their feedback speed. These local control signals respond very quickly to variations in capacity. For example, if the kanban size is six and the *takt* time[2] is 1 minute, a control signal is generated on average within 3 minutes of a capacity change. Contrast this with a weekly MRP system that might take an average of 20 hours to achieve the same response. The kanban system is 400 times faster in responding to an emerging queue.

The feedback in a kanban system is also inherently faster than that of a TOC system. Consider what happens when a bottleneck increases its operating rate. In a kanban system, the upstream process is quickly signaled to increase its rate when the first empty pallet returns early. In the TOC system, the release rate of work into the system is increased, but this higher rate must propagate through the system to reach the process feeding the bottleneck. The feeding process will adjust to the higher rate, but since the time lag is long, this may no longer be the current operating rate of the bottleneck. In fact, control theory would suggest that under certain circumstances, such a system can be inherently unstable, swinging uncontrollably between high and low operating rates.[3]

---

[2] *Takt* time is the cadence of a manufacturing process. If one car comes off the assembly line every 60 seconds, the *takt* time of this line is 60 seconds.

[3] For example, consider what happens when restarting a blocked bottleneck. After it consumes the WIP pool that had accumulated in front of the bottleneck, it runs out of WIP as it waits for all the WIP-starved upstream processes to catch up. It is again blocked, so it stops any additional jobs from entering the system. Eventually, the jobs that had entered the system while the bottleneck was running will propagate to the bottleneck and start it running again. This will restart flow until these jobs are consumed and the bottleneck is again starved for WIP. Long time-constant feedback loops are inherently prone to instability.

Toyota further enhances the effectiveness of this WIP constraint by cross-training workers at adjacent work stations. When the WIP constraint throttles the upstream process, this frees up capacity that can easily assist the downstream process. As we shall see later in this chapter, this approach of combining WIP constraints and flexibility in adjacent resources can also be used in product development.

W5: The Batch Size Decoupling Principle: Use WIP ranges to decouple the batch sizes of adjacent processes.

If we fix the level of a WIP pool, we would inherently synchronize the arrival rate and the departure rate for this inventory pool. In such a system, each new arrival is blocked until a job departs from the WIP pool. Each departure "pulls" another arrival. This inherently forces the batch size and timing of the arrival process to match the batch size and timing of the departure process. However, this is not always desirable because these processes may have different economic lot sizes.

To avoid this problem, the kanban system permits interprocess WIP pools to cycle between an upper constraint and its natural lower limit of zero. By using a range of acceptable WIP levels, we can use different, and economically optimal, batch sizes in adjacent processes. Furthermore, we create the flexibility to desynchronize the timing of these batches.

Reacting to Emergent Queues

In fact, the real art of managing queues is not about monitoring them and setting limits, it lies in what we do when we reach the limits. In this section, we will provide you with nine possible ways to respond to WIP excursions. The first three are demand-focused. They involve blocking new demand, shedding existing projects, and shedding features.

The next five approaches are supply-focused. They involve pulling resources, using part-timers, using specialists, creating T-shaped resources, and cross-training workers at adjacent processes.

The final approach involves changing the job mix. With nine tools in our toolkit we have a variety of approaches for controlling WIP.

W6: The Principle of Demand Blocking: Block all demand when WIP reaches its upper limit.

The simplest way to use a WIP constraint is to block all demand when WIP reaches its upper limit. This is the method used in the kanban system. It is also the method used in a standard telephone system, which provides a busy signal to users when no lines are available.

We can accomplish this blocking in two ways. First, we can eject the arriving job from the system. This may seem like an extreme approach, but it enforces a true upper-limit on global WIP and cycle time. Remember that it takes a long time to correct a high-queue state, and the queue can do enormous damage during this high-queue period.

The second way to block demand is to hold back the job in an upstream queue. This does not actually reduce demand, it just shifts the location of the queue. Such an approach can actually generate economic benefits if different queues have different holding costs, as we shall see in Principle W21. This approach of queue shifting is actually used quite cleverly in the TPS. The TPS holds back work rather than ejecting it, but the amount of work in upstream queues is carefully controlled, because they also have WIP constraints.

W7: The Principle of WIP Purging: When WIP is high, purge low-value projects.

Whenever WIP is high, queues are high. When queues are high, jobs that are in process are generating high delay costs because of the multiplier effect described in Principle Q15. This means that the economics of holding WIP has changed. Therefore, we must ask whether jobs which were appropriate to hold in queue when costs were low are still appropriate to keep active with the new, higher, holding costs. It is logical to purge jobs of low value from the queue whenever there is a surplus of high-value jobs. This ensures that we will continue to generate open slots for the other high-value jobs that are constantly arriving.

By purging low-value jobs, we create the room to service high-value jobs. This improves the average value of the jobs we are working on. Think of it like a hospital moving noncritical patients from the limited number of emergency room beds so that critical patients can be served.

Of course, we must still evaluate WIP purging using our economic framework. Many companies have difficulty killing projects once they have started. If they used the sunk cost principle, Principle E17, they would recognize that they should only consider the incremental investment to finish the project compared to its return.

Instead of killing projects, many companies mistakenly starve them for resources, barely keeping them alive. This creates the legendary zombie projects—the unliving and the undead. They are not good enough to get sufficient resources, but they are not bad enough to kill. Zombie projects destroy flow. Kill the zombies!

W8: The Principle of Flexible Requirements: Control WIP by shedding requirements.

A smaller batch size approach to WIP purging is to shed requirements during periods of congestion. The underlying logic is that the economic cost of retaining a requirement rises during periods of congestion. This occurs because the delay cost generated by a requirement rises when it blocks a larger queue of waiting work. During such periods, it makes economic sense to drop requirements that have marginal economic benefits. We get a high payoff from such requirement relief, because we are already operating on the steep section of the queueing curve, where a small decrease in loading leads to a large savings in cycle time.

It is best to identify in advance which requirements we would consider eliminating or relaxing. We do this for two reasons. First, we can make a more well-reasoned decision before the pressure of a congestion crisis occurs. Second, if we preplan which requirements might be jettisoned, we can structure our product architecture to make it easy to jettison them. We do so by loosely coupling these elements to the rest of the system, so that we can cut them loose quickly.

In addition to relaxing performance goals by dropping features, we can relax our targets for unit cost at product introduction. For example, in many cases, our initial customer demand can be serviced with products manufactured using inefficient manufacturing processes. This is a particularly good strategy when production volumes are low early in product life.

When we relax cost targets, we can create variances that are painful for manufacturing. Obviously, this is a situation where the development team experiences the benefits of relaxing the goal, while the manufacturing organization feels the cost. As we explained in Principle E14, it is best when cost and benefit are both felt by the same decision maker.

What could we do differently? It often makes sense to change the way we account for variances during manufacturing ramp. A simple way to do this is for the development team to pay for variances during manufacturing ramp. Once the product has been in manufacturing for a fixed amount of time, responsibility for these variances can be transferred to manufacturing.

One of the biggest advantages of these three demand-focused approaches, demand blocking, WIP purging, and flexible requirements, is the speed with which they can be executed. In contrast, supply-focused approaches, which reduce WIP by adding capacity, often have longer response times.

W9: The Principle of Resource Pulling: Quickly apply extra resources to an emerging queue.

Supply-focused approaches apply additional resources at an emerging queue. To make these approaches effective, we must minimize the time between the onset of congestion and the application of added resources. At high levels of utilization, those which are typical in product development, we grow queues much faster than we can shrink them.

Think of what happens on a crowded freeway. If a single lane on a four-lane highway is blocked for 10 minutes at rush hour, we may create a 40-minute traffic jam. This happens because losing 25 percent of capacity generates a queue much faster than regaining capacity can shrink it.

How much extra resource do we have to apply to an emerging queue? Surprisingly little. Remember how steep the queueing curve is when congestion is present. Even small amounts of added resource lead to large reductions in queue size. Even an inefficient resource will improve the condition of a congested bottleneck. For example, an expert on the critical path can be supplemented with a resource that is 20 percent as productive, and it will still have a huge impact on the queue.

W10: The Principle of Part-Time Resources: Use part-time resources for high variability tasks.

One type of resource that is capable of responding quickly to an emerging queue is a part-time resource loaded to less-than-full utilization. Part-time resources are particularly valuable because we can shift their time allocation very quickly.

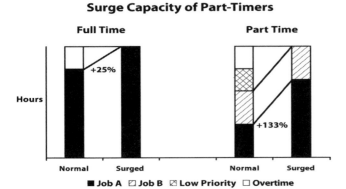

Figure 6-4 Part-time workers have significantly more surge capacity than full-time workers on the same project.

Figure 6-4 illustrates this with a typical example. Assume an engineer allocates 3 hours apiece to two programs and 2 hours to low-priority, low cost-of-delay activities. Assume this engineer is willing to work 2 hours of overtime during periods of congestion. If we allocate 8 hours of the engineer's time to a single program, our maximum surge capacity is 25 percent by using the 2 hours of overtime.

In contrast, if the engineer is assigned 3 hours per day on the high-priority program, he can use the overtime and he can steal time from the low-priority program. This increases time on the high-priority program by 4 hours, a 133 percent increase in capacity. Furthermore, if the engineer dropped everything to service the crisis program, he could raise his time allocation to 10 hours, a 233 percent increase in capacity.

Which project activities are most suited for part-time resources? Those that are most prone to expensive congestion. These are high-variability tasks on the critical path. Activities that are more predictable can be handled with full-time resources, since such activities experience less congestion.

Importantly, part-time resources can be applied without spending time on training and indoctrination; they are already working on the program. Other types of flexible resources often have longer start-up times. In the worst case, we may have to use the bottleneck resource to make its new assistants productive, a very undesirable condition.

W11: The Big Gun Principle: Pull high-powered experts to emerging bottlenecks.

When the Marines would make amphibious assaults during World War II, they relied on naval gunfire to reduce enemy strongpoints. The most valuable ships for doing this were the battleships with huge 16-inch guns. These big guns were scarce resources and their gunfire was allocated to strong points that could not be overcome by smaller guns of other ships.

Likewise, most development organizations have a handful of special people who seem to be able to overpower the most difficult problems. They are the 10 percent of the staff that handles 90 percent of the most difficult work. These people are typically highly experienced and very quick at coming up to speed on a new problem. They are often the ideal vehicle for breaking the back of an emerging queue.

If we wish to use such resources to destroy emerging queues, it is critical that we load them to less-than-full utilization. If they are heavily utilized, they will not be able to respond quickly.

Unfortunately, most organizations love to load these highly productive resources to very high utilization rates. We need to change this mind-set. The big guns are not most valuable as an efficient substitute for small guns, they are most valuable for handling situations that the small guns cannot handle.

W12: The Principle of T-Shaped Resources: Develop people who are deep in one area and broad in many.

What are the ideal resources for controlling emerging queues? Experts allow us to apply tremendous problem-solving power to a bottleneck. Generalists can be easily shifted to any place they are needed.

Is there a way to get both these benefits from the same person? Some organizations believe this is possible, and they characterize the people they are trying to create as T-shaped resources. By this, they mean people who can go deep within their chosen specialty while still being broad enough to go moderately deep in any other area.

These T-shaped resources are best created systematically. We start by hiring people who are interested in becoming T-shaped. We receive I-shaped engineers from universities. To convert them to T-shaped engineers, we must give them assignments that broaden their skill sets. We must invest in training them with new skills. We need to structure our incentive systems to reward this broadening process. The ideal resource is a jack-of-all-trades and a master-of-one.

W13: The Principle of Skill Overlap: Cross-train resources at adjacent processes.

We cannot instantly create T-shaped resources, since it takes a long time to create people who are broadly skilled in all aspects of engineering. To begin, we should recognize that the most valuable type of cross-training is cross-training people at adjacent resources. This is particularly useful because the adjacent upstream resource is the first node to receive a throttling signal from a downstream WIP constraint. If this adjacent resource is cross-trained, then the capacity that is freed up by throttling it can be immediately applied to the bottleneck process.

One software organization does this by cross-training some of their programmers to do testing. Whenever the testing queue gets large, these cross-trained programmers pick up testing tasks instead of programming tasks. They work down the queue, and then resume taking programming tasks.

We have discussed five supply-focused responses to emerging queues: pulling resources to the queue, using part-time resources, using high-powered experts, creating T-shaped resources, and cross-training. As mentioned earlier, supply-focused solutions usually take longer to implement than demand-focused solutions. It takes advanced planning to do cross-training and to create T-shaped resources. It takes discipline to load experts to less-than-full utilization. The decision to use part-timers must be made early. This leaves one final method, mix changing.

W14: The Mix Change Principle: Use upstream mix changes to regulate queue size.

One of the least obvious ways to control emergent queues is to selectively hold back work that will make the queue worse. This method is virtually never used in manufacturing, because manufacturing work is homogeneous. In manufacturing, holding back work simply creates another queue further upstream. In contrast, in engineering, we can selectively hold back work without creating an upstream queue.

Figure 6-5 shows how this can be done. For example, five different subsystems may place different loads on the adjacent processes of

Modulate Arrivals to Control Queues

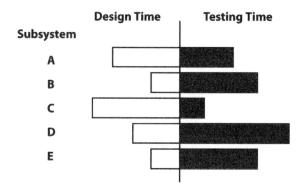

Figure 6-5 Different subsystems place unequal loads on adjacent processes. This can be exploited to reduce the variance of flow. When testing queues are growing, designers should work on subsystem C.

design and testing. If we monitor the size of the testing queue, we can selectively work on jobs in the design process that help manage the queues in testing. When queues are high, we should work on subsystems like subsystem C, which has high design-time and low testing-time. When queues are low, we work on subsystems like subsystems B and E, which have low design-time and high testing-time. We can implement this by making downstream queues visible and by creating a simple system to classify upstream jobs into rough categories depending on how they affect queues. For example, we can classify our subsystems as having high, moderate, and low testing demands.

You may recognize this as a use of Principle V10, the principle of negative covariance, to reduce queues. By making the input to the queue vary in a way that is negatively correlated with growth in queue size, we are reducing the random growth of queues.

Examples of WIP Constraints

Let's look at some typical examples of WIP constraints in product development. As mentioned earlier, one software company limits the amount of completed code that is awaiting testing. By limiting the size of the testing queue, programmers get testing feedback faster.

Another common constraint is to limit the amount of detailed planning to a 60-day horizon. Detailed planning is very perishable, and this perishability increases with the distance to the planning horizon. We can dramatically reduce the wasted effort in planning by limiting our detailed planning to a short time-horizon. At longer time-horizons, we do higher-level plans which aggregate many activities into higher-level milestones. These higher-level milestones become more reliable, because they benefit from the effect of variability pooling, Principle V5.

One of the most compelling WIP constraints in product development is limiting the number of active projects in the pipeline. When we limit active projects, we create a shorter flow time for the entire pipeline.

Figure 6-6 shows the effect of concentrating resources on two projects instead of four. Both cases have four projects completed at the end of the time interval. However, if we focus on two projects at a time project 1 and 2 will be delivered early, which creates cost-of-delay savings. At the same time projects 3 and 4 benefit for three reasons. First, they get the benefit of learning occurring on the earlier projects. Second, they define their requirements at shorter time-horizons, where the forecasting is more reliable. Third, they select technologies later, which reduces technology drift.

WIP Constraints in Practice

At this point, we will focus on eight practical principles for controlling WIP. These involve some slightly more subtle aspects of queue size control. Many of these more sophisticated strategies exploit the active queue management methods used on the Internet. We will begin by looking at aging analysis and escalation processes. Next, we will look at three sophisticated strategies used on the Internet. These are progressive throttling, differential service, and adaptive WIP constraints. Then, we will examine how we can prevent work from expanding and why certain queues are critical. Finally, we will discuss the cumulative effect of small WIP reductions and the importance of making WIP visible.

Limit the Number of Active Projects

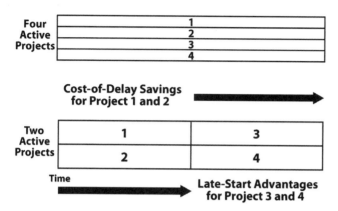

Figure 6-6 If we concentrate resources on two projects at a time, we get cost-of-delay savings on projects 1 and 2 and late-start advantages on projects 3 and 4.

W15: The Aging Principle: Watch the outliers.

Up to now, we have concentrated on the overall size of a WIP pool or queue. Because of Little's Formula, Principle Q12, average queue size determines average processing time. But, averages are deceiving. It is quite useful to know if our average processing time contains some jobs with very long processing times. We can assess this by monitoring the distribution of time-in-queue. We are particularly interested in the tail of jobs with very long queue times. This is called an aging analysis.

In business, we do this sort of analysis routinely for accounts receivable. We look at specific receivables that are more than 90 or 120 days past due. This is important because accounts that are very late at paying are often in financial trouble. As a result, receivables that are long past due have a disproportionate risk of being uncollectable. Likewise, engineering jobs that have been stuck in a WIP pool for a long time are likely to be experiencing unexpected problems. An aging analysis makes these problem jobs more visible.

W16: The Escalation Principle: Create a preplanned escalation process for outliers.

It is not enough to simply recognize outliers, we also need a process to bring them under control. We can do this in a variety of ways, such as by shedding requirements, following Principle W8, or by bringing in the big guns, following Principle W11. It is best to process outliers systematically, using an escalation process.

The simplest escalation process is to raise jobs to the attention of higher organizational levels when they pass a certain time limit in the queue. For example, drawings that have waited in the CAD queue for more than 7 days can be listed and reported to the manager of the department. With such an approach, we involve higher-level managers in managing exceptions.

Alternatively, we can create a process that automatically raises the priority class of a job depending on its age in the queue. This rule-based approach can be decentralized and automated. This approach is used in some computer operating systems which will raise the priority level of a job after it has spent a certain amount of time in a lower priority class.

Automated escalation inherently assumes that even low-priority jobs can be perishable. This is sensible since they can experience rising delay costs when they have been delayed excessively. We will discuss approach of adaptively escalating priority classes later in Chapter 9, Principle D3.

Of course, we must be careful when we prioritize jobs on anything other than economic criteria. Ultimately, our highest economic priority is always the job that generates the most cost-of-delay savings per unit of bottlenecked resource. For example, a high cost-of-delay job requiring very little resource should go ahead of a low cost-of-delay job requiring a lot of resource, no matter how long the low cost-of-delay job has waited in queue. If we truly believe that outliers have disproportionate delay costs, this should be reflected in economically-based priorities. We will explore this issue of sequencing in much greater detail in Chapter 7.

W17: The Principle of Progressive Throttling: Increase throttling as you approach the queue limit.

The throttling of demand at the upper WIP limit described in Principle W6 is the method used in the TPS. This method, known as a tail-dropping queue, was originally used on the Internet, but it had two limitations.

First, if we wait for buffers, which are the Internet equivalent of WIP pools, to fill before we throttle, the system will tend to gravitate to system states with buffers nearly full. This is bad because it leaves little safety margin to handle bursts of demand. Any heavy burst of traffic can cause buffers to overflow.

Second, because the control signal is either on or off, arrivals are either completely unrestricted or completely blocked. This creates jaggedness in flow, which is undesirable variability.

To overcome these disadvantages, the Internet uses more advanced schemes for throttling flow. These methods, known as Random Early Deletion (RED) and Random Early Marking (REM), begin throttling before a buffer is full. This causes smoother transitions in flow and permits the system to handle bursts of demand without overflowing buffers and experiencing congestion. It causes the system to spend more time in states that have sufficient reserve margin to handle bursts of demand.

We can use similar approaches in product development. For example, the approval criteria for initiating a new project can be made more demanding as congestion gets heavier. Rather than completely filling up our R&D portfolio and then blocking jobs, we can demand higher ROIs when we start approaching the limits of capacity.

We can also use progressive throttling for shared resources. One way to do this is to use congestion pricing to discourage projects from using resources during periods of congestion. This will progressively throttle demand and encourage projects to use resources when queues are lower.

W18: The Principle of Differential Service: Differentiate quality of service by workstream.

Now, let's consider another sophisticated approach for controlling the nonhomogeneous flows that we see in product development. Since our workstream has a wide range of delay costs, it can make economic sense to subdivide the workstream into categories with different quality of service goals. This allows us to achieve better service for the high cost-of-delay jobs.

We can do this by categorizing jobs in broad categories of high, medium, and low delay costs. We can then target a specific flow-through time for each category of work and use Little's Formula, Principle Q12, to determine its WIP limit. If we set both a WIP limit and a capacity allocation, this will control the flow-through time for that category.

Using a method like this, we can achieve different flow-through times for different categories of work, even when they are using a shared resource.

For example, at one software company, they permit one hot job in their software maintenance workstream. This hot job has head-of-the-line privileges in all queues, although it does not preempt work that is already underway at the resource. As a result, this job experiences no queue time and flows through the system very quickly.

Figure 6-7 provides an example of how we can allocate our resource pool and set WIP constraints to provide different target flow-through times. Many of our economic difficulties in controlling WIP come from treating it as a homogeneous flow. Since it is not homogeneous, it is usually better to break it into separate workstreams and use independent capacity allocations and WIP constraints for each workstream.

W19: The Principle of Adaptive WIP Constraints: Adjust WIP constraints as capacity changes.

The TPS uses relatively static WIP constraints. Kanban limits are set and changed very gradually. The Internet uses a very different approach because it must deal with enormous variability in demand and network throughput.

On the Internet, the WIP limit is called the window size. At any given moment, we permit a limited number of unacknowledged packets to be "live" in the system between the sender and the receiver.[4] The sender constantly probes system capacity by trying to increase its sending rate in linear steps. When it experiences congestion, which is signaled by dropped packets, it backs off on its sending rate. Then, it begins to probe capacity again by increasing its sending rate.

This method is called Additive Increase Multiplicative Decrease (AIMD) because of the algorithms that are used to raise and lower sending rates. These algorithms are specifically chosen to ensure stability of

---

[4] The Internet uses a method called Sliding Window Flow Control. A typical implementation ensures that the sender can never get more than a certain number of packets ahead of the *oldest* unacknowledged packet. While this window size creates an upper limit on the unacknowledged packets in flight, the lower limit can be a single unacknowledged packet, since a single, sufficiently late packet can stop flow until it is acknowledged.

Mixed Flow WIP Constraints

Work Category	Hours per Job	Jobs per Week	Weekly Load	Time Allocated	Percent of Total	Target Flow Time	WIP Constraint
Manufacturing Support	4.0	3	12.0	12	30%	1	3
Regulatory Questions	1.0	6	6.0	6	15%	0.5	3
Routine Engineering	2.0	11	22.0	22	55%	3	33
		Total	40.0	40	100%		

Figure 6-7 We can split the workstream into categories giving each category a percent of total resources and a WIP constraint. This sets cycle time for each workstream.

the system.[5] We don't want sudden congestion to cause everyone to completely stop sending, and then to reflood the system with traffic when they notice it is suddenly lightly loaded. Such behavior would cause unstable oscillations in flow.

We can use a similar adaptive approach in product development by permitting more WIP during periods when flow-through time is fast. For example, if the testing department is completing tests quickly, we can permit more active jobs in the system without jeopardizing cycle-time goals. When tests are completed slowly, we can lower the WIP constraint to ensure that cycle-time goals are maintained.[6]

W20: The Expansion Control Principle: Prevent uncontrolled expansion of work.

In product development, it is not sufficient to prevent uncontrolled arrivals; we must also control the expansion of work. Some work in product development can behave like the perfect gas of physics. It expands to fill the container, no matter what size of the container. For example, conceptual design can consume any amount of allocated time, no matter how long this time is. This inherent expandability is

---

[5] AIMD decreases its sending rate more rapidly than it increases it. This asymmetry is critical because increases in load trigger regenerative effects that can lead to severe congestion. If we find ourselves creeping up the queueing curve, we want to get back down very quickly.

[6] This is another application of Little's Formula, Principle Q12. We maintain a constant flow-through time by varying queue size when processing rate varies.

dangerous because it can lead to delays even when we carefully control the arrival rate of work.

We can take a lesson from computer operating systems on how to manage this problem. In a computer operating system, we accept certain jobs that have the potential to expand to infinite processing time. Unfortunately, we have no advance warning as to which jobs will fall into this category. We prevent these poorly behaved jobs from locking up the system by setting a limit on how long any job can run. This time-out limit ensures that one poorly behaved job cannot block all other jobs. In Chapter 7, Principle F19, we will discuss this method in more detail.

A second strategy for blocking task expansion is to terminate a task when we reach the point of diminishing returns. We can view this as establishing a minimum acceptable progress rate. As Figure 6-8 shows, this is the point at which further economic investment of time and resource is not resulting in sufficient incremental improvement in the value of the design. This is another application of the principle of marginal economics, Principle E16.

W21: The Principle of the Critical Queue: Constrain WIP in the section of the system where the queue is most expensive.

When we establish local WIP constraints, we should try to minimize the WIP in portions of the system where the queue is most expensive. Consider the approach that is used in an air traffic control system, which we discussed in Principle V16.

We recognize that destination airports can experience changes in their landing rates due to weather or other circumstances. We have several WIP pools: planes waiting to take off, planes in transit, and planes in holding patterns at the destination. Each of these locations has a different holding cost. It is most expensive to hold inventory by having planes circle at the destination in a holding pattern. It is least expensive to hold inventory on the ground at the departure airport. The air traffic control system limits the departure rate to congested destinations so that it can avoid expensive holding patterns. These adjustments are made dynamically to respond to changes in flow.

We can exploit the same principle in product development. For example, it is often better to hold new opportunities in a ready queue

Diminishing Returns

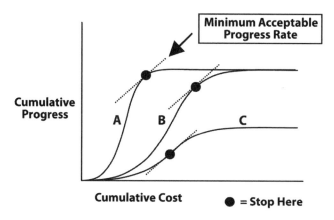

Figure 6-8 We can stop work on an activity when it reaches a minimum acceptable progress rate. This is the point where marginal cost begins to exceed marginal benefit.

ahead of the product development process instead of permitting these projects to enter the product development system. When the projects get into the system, they dilute resources, accrue costs, and increase overhead. Since they are perishable, their holding costs are quite high. We are better off holding these opportunities in a lower cost, upstream queue.

We see the same principle used in fixing bugs in software. As one manager from HP said, "We only want to work on fresh bugs." They limit the number of bugs that they are actively working on. This improves the flow-through time and ensures that they are always working on important problems.

W22: The Cumulative Reduction Principle: Small WIP reductions accumulate.

One of the most successful ways of achieving permanent WIP reductions is to create a sustained small excess in the departure rate of work over the arrival rate of work. If we consistently complete more work than we start, our queue will progressively become smaller. The cumulative effect can be enormous. One industrial R&D organization progressively tracked and reduced their WIP. Over a period of several years, they reduced the average cycle time for advanced R&D projects from 220 days to 30 days. This was done by making WIP visible and by slowly and relentlessly decreasing it.

W23: The Principle of Visual WIP: Make WIP continuously visible.

Inventory in product development is information, and information is usually invisible. To manage this information effectively, we must make it visible. We can do this by using physical artifacts as tokens to represent this invisible inventory.

The most common way to do this is to use white boards and yellow sticky notes. These notes are progressively moved from one section of a white board to another. With such a system, we can easily see how much work is in any stage of the process. We can also manage differential flows with this approach by using different color sticky notes for different classes of work.

Conclusion

Today, less than 1 percent of product development processes are managed with WIP constraints. Yet, once we recognize that queue size determines cycle time, we can easily use WIP constraints to control cycle time. This requires a basic shift in mind-set, a mind-set change that is very difficult for companies that believe a full pipeline is a good thing.

WIP constraints are powerful because they are inexpensive, incremental, and reversible. They enable gradual relentless improvement. Even light WIP constraints can produce significant cycle-time benefits. They prevent queues from reaching dangerously expensive levels of congestion.

Don't discount WIP constraints because they seem to be reactive. We need *both* proactive and reactive approaches to achieve flow. Consider the problem of maintaining traffic flow. Correct sizing of highways is important because this reduces congestion. This is a proactive long-term choice that must be made before the morning traffic jam occurs.

However, correct sizing of highways is not sufficient to maintain flow. Cars break down unpredictably, which reduces capacity and leads to congestion. It is not economical to provide highways with so much overcapacity that they can maintain flow despite unpredictable breakdowns. It is more cost-effective to clear breakdowns within a certain amount of time.

We use capacity planning to deal with the portion of the problem that is forecastable. Yet, we recognize that some aspects of the problem cannot be forecast. We need to react to them. In our next chapter, we will go deeper into the systems we use to maintain flow in the presence of uncertainty.

7

Controlling Flow Under Uncertainty

Anyone can be captain in a calm sea.

In the last chapter, we examined the use of WIP constraints. These constraints set upper limits on the amount of in-process inventory. We described several possible actions that could be taken upon reaching the upper WIP limit. They included limiting the admission of new work, reducing the work that was already in process, and adding resources to increase the clearance rate of work.

WIP constraints are powerful, but they do not solve all our problems. WIP constraints do not ensure we have selected a high-throughput operating point. WIP constraints do not prevent the gradual accumulation of variances in concatenated process steps. WIP constraints don't ensure we are processing work in the economically optimum sequence. We need additional tools to solve these problems, and I will introduce them in this chapter. In it, we will more carefully examine the problem of flow control.

This chapter is divided into five subsections. First, I will describe the problem of congestion and its effect on flow. Second, we will examine how a regular cadence works to improve flow. Third, we will discuss the use of synchronization. Fourth, we will look at methods of sequencing and routing work. In the fifth and final section, I will propose a network-based alternative to today's linear development processes.

Why propose an alternative to today's processes? Because today's processes are so vulnerable to variability that developers must spend inordinate time trying to reduce variability. I will suggest an alternative approach based on almost a century of careful analysis and experience in the telecommunications industry.

Telecommunications networks are based on fundamentally different assumptions than manufacturing processes. They assume variability is inherent to the problem and adopt flow control approaches

Traffic Flow

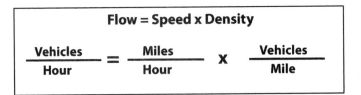

Figure 7-1 The flow of traffic on a highway is proportional to the speed of the traffic and the density of the vehicles.

that are robust in the presence of variability. These network-based approaches are well-suited to the natural variability of product development processes.

Congestion

To begin, we need to understand the technical phenomenon of congestion. Congestion is a system condition that combines high capacity utilization and low throughput. The onset of congestion can be gradual, but it is more likely to be sudden and catastrophic.

All of us are familiar with traffic on a crowded highway. The throughput, or flow, on a highway can be measured in vehicles per hour. As Figure 7-1 shows, this throughput can be decomposed into two factors: the traffic density (vehicles per mile) and the traffic speed (miles per hour). The product of these two factors is flow, or throughput.

Figure 7-2 shows how highway throughput behaves as a function of speed. The product of density and speed generates a parabolic curve for highway throughput. This occurs because density decreases linearly with speed. At higher speeds, drivers follow other vehicles at a greater distance to allow sufficient reaction time. This parabolic curve for throughput, originally observed by Bruce Greenshields in 1934, has interesting implications. It shows that throughput is low at both extremes: maximum density and maximum speed. If we wish to maximize throughput, we must operate at the top of the parabola.[1]

---

[1] Readers who have already grown fond of U-curves may wish to turn this figure, or themselves, upside down.

Highway Throughput

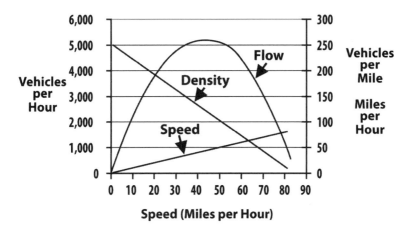

Figure 7-2 Throughput on a highway is a parabolic function of speed. It becomes very low at both low and high speeds.

This curve suggests that whenever throughput is below the peak, there are two distinct operating points that can generate a given amount of throughput, one on the left side of the parabola and one on the right. What is the difference between these two operating points? The left-side, low-speed operating point is inherently unstable, and the right-side, high-speed operating point is inherently stable.

The instability arises from the feedback loop between speed, throughput, and density, which is shown in Figure 7-3. On the left side, when density increases and speed drops, the flow decreases. This, in turn, increases density even more. With this regenerative feedback, the system operating point rapidly shifts to the left and ends in a state of heavy congestion. In fact, many empirical studies of highway flow have trouble gathering data on the left side of the curve because such states are inherently transitory.

In contrast, on the right side of the parabola, the feedback loop stabilizes the system. In this zone, when density increases and speed drops, it increases flow. This increased flow reduces density, counteracting the original density increase. Clearly, it is desirable to operate a highway on the stable right side of the parabola.

What can product developers learn from traffic flow? Product developers also experience drops in throughput during periods of

Feedback Loops

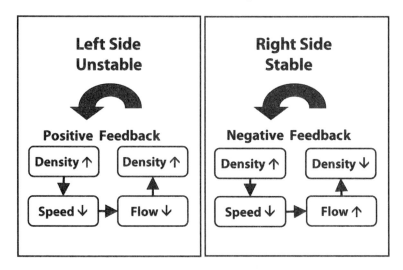

Figure 7-3 When density is too high, flow is inherently unstable since the feedback cycle is regenerative. In contrast, operating to the right of the throughput peak promotes stability because of a negative feedback effect.

congestion. When we cram too many projects into the product development pipeline, we create queues. These queues create a frictional drag on throughput as developers spend more time expediting and less time adding value. The added load reduces output instead of increasing it.

Product development flows also experience regenerative feedback that creates instability effects. As marketing becomes frustrated with delayed projects, they inject even more work into the system. Is the project going to be late? We'll need some additional features to compete effectively with a late launch. We'll also need to add a few extra projects to make up for the revenue shortfall. Falling throughput leads to increased load, which then drops throughput even faster. We can quickly slide down the left side of the throughput curve.

F1: The Principle of Congestion Collapse: When loading becomes too high, we will see a sudden and catastrophic drop in output.

Systems prone to congestion can experience a phenomenon called congestion collapse. This first occurred on the Internet in October 1986,

Congestion Collapse

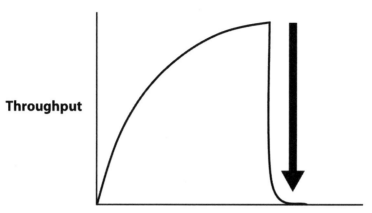

Throughput

System Utilization (Offered Load)

Figure 7-4 Congestion collapse is an abrupt drop in through-put at high levels of system utilization. It results in an unde-sirable state of high utilization and low throughput.

when the capacity of a fully utilized link to U.C. Berkeley suddenly dropped by a factor of 1,000.

When congestion collapse occurs, throughput vs. load displays the characteristics shown in Figure 7-4. In this figure, as system utilization increases, throughput increases by progressively smaller amounts. Then, when utilization reaches a certain critical level, there is a sharp and unexpected collapse in the throughput curve. Why does this happen?

When the Internet becomes congested, it takes longer to deliver packets. Senders wait a certain amount of time to receive an acknowledgement. If they do not receive an acknowledgement within this time period, they assume the packet was lost and resend it. At heavy loads, the number of resent packets increases, but this increases loads even more. The extra load causes router buffers to overflow, causing even more senders to lose packets. As ever increasing numbers of senders transmit extra packets, loads rise even higher. Eventually, the network is 100 percent utilized with zero throughput.

Congestion collapse creates a sharp discontinuity in the through-put curve. At one moment, everything is fine; at the next, the system is incapacitated. When congestion occurs, performance is no longer a simple extrapolation of throughput at lower loads.

Congestion collapse is not unique to highways and the Internet. It also occurs in other systems. For example, a factory with very high levels of utilization will have large queues and long cycle time. Large queues increase the incentive to expedite jobs. But, when we move one job ahead of another by expediting, we interrupt work and decrease our throughput. This lower throughput, in turn, further increases queues, cycle time, and expediting. We end up with a factory with both very high utilization and significant drops in output.

The throughput curve of systems with regenerative feedback behaves differently than those without feedback. In those without feedback, throughput will plateau with increasing load. In contrast, systems that have regenerative feedback loops can experience a sudden, unpredictable, and catastrophic congestion collapse. They are best operated safely below the point where throughput begins to plateau.

F2: The Peak Throughput Principle: Control occupancy to sustain high throughput in systems prone to congestion.

Whenever we have a system with a strong throughput peak, we have an incentive to operate near this point. For example, as shown in Figure 7-2, we could increase the throughput of a highway by a factor of five if we could change the average speed from 5 miles per hour to 45 miles per hour. This throughput change requires no change in either capacity or demand; it simply requires selecting the correct operating point for the system.

Of course, based on the discussion in the previous section, it would be best to operate slightly below peak throughput on the stable side of the curve. Since the curve is quite flat near its peak, the shift off peak costs very little throughput, but it gives us sufficient margin to absorb variability in flow without triggering the degenerative feedback that causes congestion collapse.

How can we maintain our system at this desirable operating point? In theory, we could choose either speed or occupancy as a control variable. (Occupancy is the more general term for density. It refers to the number of jobs occupying the system at a point in time.)

In practice, it is easiest to control occupancy. This is exactly what is done in well-managed highway systems. In Los Angeles during rush hour, stoplights control the rate at which cars enter the freeway. This maintains the correct traffic density, which enables the highway to operate near its peak throughput point. By controlling density, we control speed and throughput. We can use the same approach in product development by controlling the number of active projects as described in Chapter 6.

F3: The Principle of Visible Congestion: Use forecasts of expected flow time to make congestion visible.

We cannot control congestion if we do not know it is there. Since only 2 percent of product developers measure queues, most developers are only vaguely aware of congestion in their processes. We can rarely see queues when we walk through the engineering department because, as explained in Principle Q1, product development inventory is information, which is inherently invisible. We need to make high occupancy conditions visible.

How can we do this? One simple approach is to use tokens and artifacts that act as visible proxies for the invisible work, as discussed in Principle W23. We can use sticky notes to represent the work and whiteboards to hold the inventory pools of sticky notes. These whiteboards can be divided into sections with space for limited numbers of sticky notes. This acts as a WIP constraint. If we make the work content of the individual sticky notes approximately equal, the number of sticky notes will be roughly proportional to the total amount of work in a WIP pool.

Whiteboards and sticky notes are powerful, but queue size is still not the best way to inform users of congestion. It is better to provide the user with a forecast of expected flow time. Expected flow time can be calculated using Little's Formula, Principle Q12, by dividing the WIP by the current processing rate. Flow-time forecasts allow users to make informed choices.

For example, consider how Disneyland provides congestion information to its guests. Do they communicate queue size, telling guests that there are 500 people in line? No. Queue size doesn't help if you don't know the processing rate. Instead, Disneyland displays expected flow time, telling guests that it will take 30 minutes to get to the head of the line.

A well-managed highway system provides the same type of information to drivers. For example, the *Périphérique*, the ring road around

Paris, has displays that forecast driving time to the next several exits. This allows drivers to choose alternate routes when this makes sense. Contrast this with the less effective information systems found on some highways in America. These systems simply tell drivers there is a traffic jam 2 miles ahead. Forecasts of expected flow time are a useful way to make congestion visible.

F4: The Principle of Congestion Pricing: Use pricing to reduce demand during congested periods.

As we discussed in Principle E14, the first market principle, it is desirable to have decision makers experience both the cost and the benefits of their decisions. When a project places load on a resource, the overall economic cost of this load depends on the degree of congestion at the resource. We would like the decision maker to feel the extra cost of loading a congested process. The most elegant way to do this is to charge higher prices during periods of congestion.

For example, airfares and hotel rates vary with the time of the year. Certain customers, who have no flexibility, will pay high-season rates. Other customers who have flexibility will time-shift their demand to exploit lower off-season rates. Whenever we have *any* flexible customers, we can use pricing to reduce congestion. Because of the steepness of the queueing curve, even a small shift in demand can make a big difference in flow time.

As usual, I recommend starting with a simple approach. Premiums of 20 to 50 percent are sufficient to time-shift the demand of flexible customers. Does this require a massive change in our thinking patterns? I don't think so. Today, every project manager is already making deliberate choices to pay or not pay premiums for faster service from external resources. We simply have to extend these behaviors to congested internal resources.

Cadence

Cadence is the use of a regular, predictable rhythm within a process. This rhythm transforms unpredictable events into predictable events. It plays an important role in preventing variability from accumulating in a sequential process.

F5: The Principle of Periodic Resynchronization: Use a regular cadence to limit the accumulation of variance.

When I was young, I rode a bus to school in New York City. Waiting on a cold winter day for the bus, we often noticed that buses appeared to travel in pairs. There would be long periods without a bus, followed by two buses arriving in succession. Even when buses departed their origin at carefully timed intervals, the buses would eventually bunch up.

This occurred because the system design amplified the effects of variability. If the leading bus encountered more passengers at a particular stop, then it would take longer to load. This would delay it, which allowed even more passengers to build up at the stops ahead. The growing passenger load would increasingly slow it down.

Meanwhile, the following bus would encounter fewer and fewer passengers, because the previous bus had been running late. With fewer passengers, it was able to load and unload faster, speeding it up. With the leading bus coming later and the following bus coming earlier, it was inevitable that they would eventually bunch together. This bunching was caused by regenerative feedback, which made the slow bus slower and the fast bus faster.

How could we solve this problem? We could prevent the regenerative feedback by scheduling a specific departure time from each bus stop. If a bus arrived at a stop early, it would still have to wait for its scheduled departure time. This ensures that a fast bus will not run early, thereby creating an excessive passenger load for the next bus.

Why does this work? By constantly resynchronizing the buses to the cadence of their schedule, we prevent the variance of one bus from being coupled to subsequent buses. This isolates the variance to a single time interval, instead of letting it accumulate into a larger overall variance.

It is important to distinguish resynchronization from simply correcting an out-of-bounds condition. When we resynchronize, we restore conditions to the center of the control range—we do not simply bring them inside the control limit. I can illustrate this by returning to the coin-flipping problem that I used to illustrate the concept of diffusion in Principle Q15. There, we saw that cumulative random variables progressively accumulate to create large variances.

Consider what would happen in the coin-flipping problem if I started with 5 dollars and I lost a dollar each time tails came up. How could I prevent going bankrupt?

I should either exit the game or obtain more capital whenever I have lost 4 dollars.[2] But, how much more capital should I obtain? If I only replenish my capital by 1 dollar, there would be a 50 percent chance that I would need to replenish again on the next coin flip. In contrast, if I replenished my capital by 5 dollars, there would only be a 1 in 32 chance that I would need to intervene in the next five flips.

This is an important concept but a subtle one. We monitor the queue and intervene to restore it to the center of its target range, not to simply bring it back within bounds. This makes high-queue states much less probable. By periodically purging accumulated variances, we keep the system operating at a point that is robust enough to tolerate a burst of heavy demand. This makes congestion less likely.

The benefit of periodic resynchronization is a system-level effect. In our bus problem, if we choose to optimize the local performance of a single bus, we would let that bus travel ahead of schedule. After all, stopped buses do not accomplish the goal of moving passengers. However, doing so would let the fast bus desynchronize the entire system because of feedback effects. What is optimal for a subsystem is not always optimal for the system.

F6: The Cadence Capacity Margin Principle: Provide sufficient capacity margin to enable cadence.

It is important to recognize that we can only resynchronize to a regular cadence if we have sufficient capacity margin. This margin allows us to adhere to the cadence in the presence of variation.

Consider our bus system again. We must allow enough time margin in the schedule so that reasonable delays will not cause the bus to deviate from its schedule. This means we will need more buses to cover the route, so that some of them can spend time waiting at bus stops. Thus, shorter and predictable wait times for customers come at the expense of higher costs for the system operator.

The same principle applies in product development. If we wish to meet a regular product launch schedule, then we need enough capacity margin to absorb schedule delays at intermediate milestones. This is

---

[2] In the field of stochastic processes, this type of problem is known as a "gambler's ruin" problem.

an economic trade-off. We must compare the cost of the capacity margin to the economic damage done by the catastrophic accumulation of variances.

F7: The Cadence Reliability Principle: Use cadence to make waiting times predictable.

Cadence makes waiting times lower and more predictable. If buses depart their stops on the quarter hour, we can avoid waiting by synchronizing to this schedule. Our 10-minute bus ride will only take 10 minutes. If a bus system does not use cadence, we may have to wait up to 30 minutes for our bus to arrive. Our 10-minute bus trip could take from 10 to 40 minutes.

With a cadence, when we miss a bus, we know exactly how long we will wait for the next one. Without cadence, we cannot predict wait time; it could range from nothing to 30 minutes.

Does this happen in product development? Consider the difference between a product introduction cadence that reliably introduces products every 6 months with one that operates asynchronously. When there is a product launch every 6 months, if a good idea misses one launch window, the next product launch date is predictably 6 months later. The entire organization can plan around this cadence.

With an asynchronous process, we don't know when the next product will launch. If you get an idea for a new feature, you must choose between adding it to the current project or waiting for the next product. Since you cannot predict when the next product is coming, your only sensible choice is to fight to get your good idea into the current product. And this is exactly what happens. The current development program acts as a "feature magnet" attracting every good idea that anybody thinks of during its development.

How can we launch products on a regular cadence in a world with variation? We use variability substitution, Principle V14. We can drive out variability from the schedule by substituting variability in a cheaper variable, such as development expense, unit cost, or performance.

F8: The Cadence Batch Size Enabling Principle: Use a regular cadence to enable small batch sizes.

Cadence is also an important tool for enabling small batch sizes. It enforces small batch size by forcing work products to move forward on a fixed rhythm. If we review drawings every week, we automatically enforce a batch size of one week's worth of work. Thus, we can use cadence as a tool to keep batch sizes small.

But cadence also has an important effect on transaction costs. A regular cadence enables small batch sizes by reducing coordination overhead. For example, consider the difference between reviewing engineering drawings on a regular time-based cadence and doing this asynchronously at random times. If accumulated drawings are reviewed every Wednesday at 1:00 PM, there is no overhead associated with setting up this meeting. Everyone knows who will attend and when the meeting will occur. This reduces the fixed effort required to make the meeting occur. Now, with a lower fixed transaction cost, we can use smaller batch sizes, processing drawings at more frequent intervals. Cadence inherently makes activities automatic and routine. This lowers transaction overhead and makes it economical to use smaller batches.

F9: The Principle of Cadenced Meetings: Schedule frequent meetings using a predictable cadence.

Shorter, predictable, and frequent meetings give us all the advantages of small batch size that we discussed in Chapter 5. With more frequent opportunities for coordination and feedback, we simply can't get very far off track. In contrast, when we hold lengthy meetings at unpredictable times and at infrequent intervals, we lose urgency very quickly.

Of course, there is an economic lot size issue associated with meetings. Meeting once an hour may not make sense. We need to balance the transaction cost associated with holding a meeting against the cost of delaying decisions. When we reduce the transaction cost, we can cost-effectively hold meetings more frequently.

How do we reduce this transaction cost? The primary sources of transaction cost are noncolocated teams and asynchronous meeting timing. We will discuss the value of colocation in Chapter 8. Asynchronous meeting timing makes meeting times unpredictable. If meeting times are unpredictable, we will make a phone call or set up an ad hoc meeting. When we synchronize our meetings to a regular cadence, we can eliminate this unnecessary transaction overhead. When meetings take place at the same time every week or every day, coordination overhead is minimal.

We will get significant transaction cost savings with cadenced meetings. In our experience, teams that meet daily spend no more time in meetings than teams that meet weekly. Ideally, such daily meetings should be face-to-face using colocated teams. When this is not possible, some companies use daily conference calls to achieve the same goals.

We can even further structure meetings by using a subcadence inside a cadence. A 4-hour weekly meeting can be divided into rough time buckets to discuss specific issues. Attendees need only be present during the portion of the meeting that deals with their issues and for a short wrap-up session at the end. This wrap-up reviews conclusions and action items. This cadenced approach reduces the time investment in the meeting, which, in turn, leads to better attendance. Often people who can't devote 4 hours to a meeting can be in the room for the hour that covers the issues that are important to them.

Finally, I should correct a misconception. Many people assume that holding meetings on-demand will provide faster response time than holding them on a regular cadence. This would be true if everyone was just sitting idle, waiting to be called to a meeting. However, most organizations are loaded to high-utilization rates. It takes time to synchronize schedules for a meeting. This time adds an inherent delay, or latency, to the timing of an on-demand meeting.

For example, if it takes 3 days to gather project decision makers for an on-demand meeting, such meetings will respond to an emerging decision in 72 hours. In contrast, a cadenced daily meeting will respond to an emerging decision in less than 24 hours. Cadenced meetings can provide better response time than asynchronous "on-demand" meetings.

Imagine a rental car facility that was 10 minutes from the airport. If they wait for you to call them, it will take 10 minutes before their bus arrives. If their buses circulate on a regular cadence of every 10 minutes, it will take an average of 5 minutes between when you arrive at the pick-up point and when the bus arrives.

Cadence in Action

Now, let's look at 11 specific examples of cadence in product development processes.

Product Introduction Cadence

One of the most common examples of cadence is the cadence of product introduction. Many businesses in Hewlett-Packard introduce products at regular intervals. In some cases, these intervals are synchronized to major trade shows. In other cases, they are synchronized with semiannual training sessions for the field sales force. A regular cadence for product introduction prevents a delay in one product from cascading into other products. It also exploits economies of synchronization by allowing coordinated introduction of multiple associated products.

Testing Cadence

Another example of cadence is the use of daily build-test cycles. Programmers submit code that is ready to be compiled, integrated, and tested. The deadline for submitting code is fixed. If code is not ready, the programmer does not submit it. Because submission deadlines are frequent and predictable, the programmer knows exactly how long testing will be delayed. This cadence establishes a regular schedule for testing and eliminates timing uncertainty for the testing department. It exploits economies of synchronization by allowing multiple programmers to coordinate the completion of their work.

Prototyping Cycles

Prototyping is another area where companies are moving to cadence-based cycles. Some companies build a new prototype once or twice a month on a regular schedule. With a regular cadence, all subassembly designers know exactly when prototypes will be built months in advance. This is another example of variability substitution. The company chooses to accept variability in the content of the prototype to prevent variability in its timing. With predictable timing, there is lower transaction cost per prototype cycle, making it cost-effective to do more small prototyping cycles. With more small fast cycles, a feature that is displaced into a later cycle experiences very little time in waiting in queue. When buses leave every 5 minutes, missing a bus has very little schedule impact.

New Product Portfolio Screening

Most companies use a cadence-based approach to screen new product opportunities. In theory, they could review such opportunities whenever they accumulate a certain number of opportunities. However, since opportunities arrive at random, their reviews would also occur at random. Instead, they conduct these reviews on a regular cadence. In fact, such cadence-based review cycles are common in almost every operational aspect of business. Almost all companies conduct periodic operations reviews for their business and report business financial performance at regular time intervals.

Program Status

There are two basic approaches for reviewing program status. The dominant approach at most companies is to hold management reviews at gates which require specific program deliverables. We call this a scope-based approach.

The review date is scheduled in advance, but it is frequently rescheduled, when key deliverables are not ready on time. Rescheduling is very difficult because it occurs at the last minute when executive schedules are already packed. As a result, a small slip in a required deliverable expands into a large slip in the meeting date. Since the reviews depend on the simultaneous accomplishment of many uncertain activities, the probability that they will all be ready can be surprisingly low.

There is an alternative: scheduling reviews at regular time intervals. For example, Project A may be reviewed on the first Monday of every month. Whatever is available to be reviewed at this date is reviewed. The strength of this approach is that review dates can be predicted months in advance. Everyone knows precisely when the review will occur. If the program experiences a problem, the review occurs anyway. In contrast, with a scope-based approach, programs with slippage are reviewed less frequently than programs that are on time.

Resource Access

A more subtle example of cadence is using it to control access to resources. For example, in the semiconductor industry, paper designs are eventually turned into silicon in the form of test wafers. These wafers provide critical feedback to design teams. Some companies dedicate test wafers to specific projects and run them on demand. Each project bears the full cost of making its wafer. Since this cost is high, test wafers are run infrequently and at unpredictable time intervals.

But this is not the only possible approach. One semiconductor company schedules weekly test wafers that are shared across multiple programs. Since a large wafer can hold hundreds of chips, it can meet the needs of many programs at once. When 10 programs share the same wafer, each program gets 10 times as many opportunities to go to silicon.

These test wafers are run on a predictable cadence with a standardized protocol. This reduces transaction cost and enables smaller batch sizes. Programs get cheaper and more frequent opportunities for feedback. This leads to increased innovation because fast feedback enables teams to truncate an unproductive path quickly.

At another company, purchasing agents had to support multiple projects. There were not enough purchasing agents to give each team a dedicated buyer, so each team was given 10 percent of a buyer's time. Unfortunately, it was unpredictable when they would get this time.

They solved the problem by creating a purchasing desk in the team area. The buyer was told to be present in the team area every day from 8:00 AM to 9:00 AM. Since the buyer was now available at regular and predictable times, team members would only seek out the buyer if they had a problem that could not wait until 8:00 AM the next day.

A less obvious advantage of this approach was that team business was always top priority during this 1-hour window. The team could get their high-priority actions serviced within 24 hours. Under the old shared-resource approach, project business was combined in a FIFO queue with all other purchasing business. Since this was a 2-week queue, it would usually take 2 weeks to get a job serviced.

Project Meetings

As mentioned earlier, many projects hold meetings on a regular weekly or daily cadence. They coordinate telephone or videoconferences with dispersed sites on a regular monthly or weekly cadence. When these meetings have a regular cadence, they eliminate the overhead of trying to coordinate schedules between participants. Furthermore, with a cadence, we can predict exactly how long we will have to wait to access other decision makers.

Design Reviews

Some companies review designs in small batches at a regular cadence. For example, one aerospace contractor has major contractually required design reviews called Critical Design Reviews

(CDRs). Instead of waiting for all drawings to be ready before they are reviewed, they conduct a regular weekly review, processing any drawings completed during the previous week.

This small batch approach provides fast feedback to designers. It prevents a bad assumption from being embedded in dozens of drawings before it is detected in the CDR. This approach also results in a higher-quality review, because more attention can be focused on an individual drawing. The final CDR now focuses on integration issues instead of drawing-level details.

Prototype Part Production

One computer company allowed prototype parts to be run for 1 hour per day on its production line. This created a virtual factory within their factory. During this 1-hour time window, prototype parts had the highest priority. Since this time window was predictable, engineers knew exactly when they could access this resource.

Supplier Visits

Some companies visit their suppliers periodically. As anyone who has been visited this way realizes, there is a rush of activity in the final several days before the visit. The project gets high priority in all queues. When these visits are performed on a regular cadence, they become predictable.

Coffee Breaks

For many years, Hewlett-Packard had morning and afternoon coffee breaks. Engineers would emerge from their cubicles at the same time every day as a coffee cart rolled through the development lab. This enabled informal information exchange between teams. If an engineer was working on a tough power-supply design issue immediately before the break, and he saw another engineer that was an expert on power supplies, the conversation would turn to power supplies. The coffee break cross-pollinated knowledge across teams.

Sadly, as Hewlett-Packard became "professionalized," this coffee break disappeared. To save the cost of a coffee cart attendant, they put coffee stations at the ends of the floors. Finally, they stopped giving free coffee and made it available in the cafeteria. These changes made the coffee breaks asynchronous, eliminating their predictable cadence. This is an interesting case where the heirs of a brilliantly designed system failed to understand the underlying logic of the system. What HP was doing was much less important than why they were doing it.

Hopefully, these examples provide some evidence that time-based cadences are already present in product development.

Synchronization

We can treat synchronization as a separate issue from cadence. Cadence causes events to happen at regular time intervals. Synchronization causes multiple events to happen at the same time. We can synchronize activities with or without a regular cadence.

For example, we have integration points in a development process which synchronize the integration of many subsystems. These integration points can occur at regular time intervals, or they can occur randomly whenever a predefined set of subsystems is ready to be tested.

Synchronization is valuable when we gain economic advantages from processing multiple items at the same time. These advantages may arise from cost advantages, such as scale economies in processing, or from the situations where there is higher value in processing multiple items simultaneously.

For example, we may be able to reduce testing costs by testing several subsystems at the same time, or we may be able to do a higher fidelity test because we are exercising more system-level interactions. As we shall see in Principle F13, one of the more interesting properties of synchronization is that it permits us to reduce queues without reducing capacity utilization or decreasing batch size.

Synchronization is used routinely in electronic circuits. These circuits change state quickly, but not instantaneously. As pulses propagate on different paths through a system, they diverge from their original timing. We can design electronic circuits to be synchronous or asynchronous.

In a synchronous circuit, we use a clock pulse to ensure all gates change state at the same time. This prevents timing errors from accumulating. In an asynchronous circuit, we pass the signal to the next gate as soon as it arrives. This reduces delays, but it permits timing errors to accumulate. In general, asynchronous circuits are faster, but synchronous circuits are more stable.

F10: The Synchronization Capacity Margin Principle: To enable synchronization, provide sufficient capacity margin.

In Principle F5, I pointed out that cadence requires capacity margin. The same is true for synchronization. If we are trying to coordinate the simultaneous processing of multiple items, then our schedule will be determined by the arrival of the most limiting item. We need sufficient schedule margin to ensure this item does not delay the entire group.

Think of an airline with multiple commuter flights feeding a larger long-haul flight. Since some of the commuter flights may arrive late, we must allow a safety margin for passengers to connect to the long-haul flight. The more feeding flights we are trying to support, the more margin we need.

F11: The Principle of Multiproject Synchronization: Exploit scale economies by synchronizing work from multiple projects.

Synchronization can enable us to combine the scale economies of large batches with the cycle-time benefits of small batch sizes. Let's illustrate this with two examples.

First, recall the semiconductor test wafer example earlier in this chapter. Producing an individual test wafer has very high transaction costs. These wafers require multiple expensive masks for their fabrication. Companies that dedicate test wafers to individual programs must aggregate a lot of design content in a single batch to take advantage of scale economies.

However, there is another way to achieve these scale economies. We can combine the work from multiple projects on a shared test wafer. This gives us scale economies in making the wafer, but it exploits the advantages of small batch size at the project level.

Let's look at another example: project reviews. One company wanted to move to smaller, more frequent project reviews. Instead of reviewing projects every 8 weeks, they wanted to review them every 2 weeks. They were worried that this would increase overhead since it quadrupled the number of reviews. They prevented this by reviewing four projects in the same session, as shown in Figure 7-5. Instead of conducting a 4-hour review of each project once every 8 weeks, they conducted a 1-hour review for each of four projects every 2 weeks. They preserved the scale economies of their meetings by combining work from multiple

Synchronous Reviews

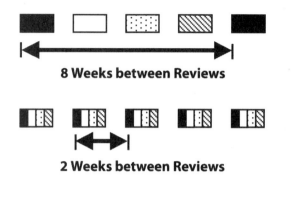

8 Weeks between Reviews

2 Weeks between Reviews

■ **Project 1** ☐ **Project 2** ▢ **Project 3** ▨ **Project 4**

Figure 7-5 When there are scale economies associated with reviews, we can achieve these scale economies by combining the reviews of multiple programs in a single session.

projects. At the same time, they increased the meeting frequency and the speed of feedback.

F12: The Principle of Cross-Functional Synchronization: Use synchronized events to facilitate cross function trade-offs.

Synchronization can be a powerful tool to enable better cross-functional trade-offs. One company adopted an asynchronous software-supported process to handle engineering changes. They expected this system would prevent engineering changes from getting lost in in-boxes and permit people to review changes at their own convenience.

Figure 7-6 shows what really happened. Each stage of the review cycle had the ability to reject a change. When the needs of one functional department were met, the change would travel to another function for review, only to be rejected for a different reason. Now the planned change followed a slow and tortuous path through the approval process. Even worse, each reviewer worked independently. There were no group meetings, which would have allowed decision makers to quickly reconcile their different needs and to craft an optimal compromise.

Asynchronous Processing

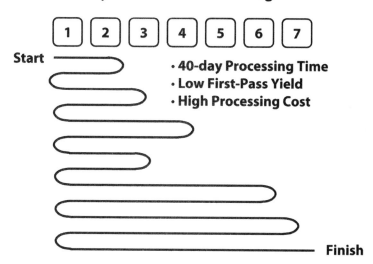

Figure 7-6 Asynchronous processing can cause a work product to travel a long path before it satisfies all seven reviewers. Each sequential review has the potential to send the work product back to the originator.

Aware of these problems, the company implemented a synchronous review process. All reviewers met at the same time and the originator of the change only had to respond to a single review. To reduce transaction overhead, these reviews were done weekly, at a predictable time. This combined the predictability and low overhead of cadence with the scale economies of synchronization. As a result, the average processing time dropped from 40 days to 5 days. At the same time, the cost of processing changes dropped, and the first-pass yield increased.

F13: The Synchronization Queueing Principle: To reduce queues, synchronize the batch size and timing of adjacent processes.

If we synchronize both the batch size and the timing of adjacent processes, we can make capacity available at the moment the demand arrives. This leads to a dramatic reduction in queues. The effect of synchronizing adjacent processes can be shown on a cumulative flow diagram in Figures 7-7 and 7-8. When batch sizes and timing are asynchronous, the minimum inventory between two processes is proportional to the average of the two batch sizes. When

Unsynchronized Batches

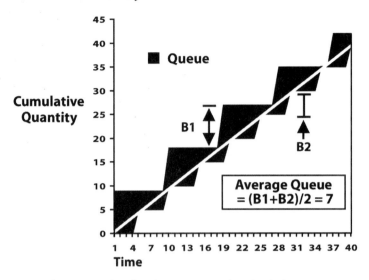

Figure 7-7 When batches are unsynchronized, the average queue is proportional to the average of the two adjacent batch sizes.

we synchronize both batch size and timing, we can get much lower inventory.

In the example shown, we achieve a 7 times reduction without altering either capacity utilization or batch size. This strategy is implemented in some traffic systems where green lights are synchronized to create a moving wave of cars flowing down a major street.

At first, this reduction of queue size may seem to violate queueing equations, but we must remember the queueing equations of Chapter 3 are based on the completely random arrivals of memoryless processes. When we synchronize arrivals to capacity, we are no longer dealing with random processes. This enables us to reduce the queue.

F14: The Harmonic Principle: Make nested cadences harmonic multiples.

In many cases, we must coordinate processes that have fundamentally different cadences. The best way to do this is nest these processes hierarchically as harmonic multiples of each other. For example, a daily module-testing process can be nested inside a weekly higher-level test.

Synchronized Batches

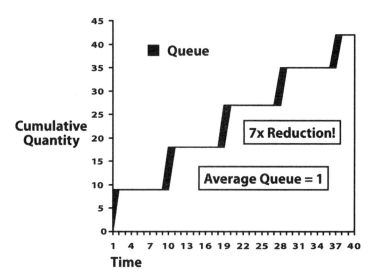

Figure 7-8 When batch sizes and cadence are synchronized, queue size can decrease dramatically.

This nesting process creates similar benefits to those we get by synchronizing batch sizes and timing. This is a well-established practice in financial reporting, where we nest monthly, quarterly, and annual reporting cycles.

Sequencing Work

A third dimension of flow control is how we sequence work. In manufacturing systems, like the Toyota Production System, work is processed on a first-in-first-out (FIFO) basis. This is a perfect approach when the work items have similar task durations and similar costs of delay. Manufacturing processes rarely exploit queueing discipline because queueing discipline creates no economic payoff when task durations and delay costs are homogeneous.

However, our situation is quite different in product development. Both delay costs and task durations vary between projects. We will examine a number of strategies for sequencing work as it flows thorough the development process. We will begin with strategies that work when we have reliable estimates of delay cost and task duration.

Then, we will progress to strategies that work when task durations are unpredictable.

I should stress two points. First, companies often create complex prioritization algorithms that produce precise priorities based on very imprecise input data. I prefer the simple approach. To select between two almost equivalent choices creates great difficulty and little payoff. Instead, we should try to prevent the big, stupid mistakes. This does not require precision.

Second, remember that sequencing matters most when queues are large. This is when head-of-the-line privileges save the most cycle time. By operating with small queues, we minimize the payoff of sequencing and, thus, the need to do it.

A good mental model for thinking about sequencing issues is a hospital emergency room. Hospital emergency rooms perform tasks with nonhomogeneous durations and nonhomogeneous costs of delay. They must deal with random arrivals. Their work flow has more in common with product development than the repetitive homogeneous flows found in a factory.

For example, consider the point made in the last paragraph, that queueing discipline provides little payoff when queues are small. When emergency rooms are heavily loaded, they practice triage, the classification of incoming work into priority categories. However, triage is not necessary when waiting lines are very short. Under such conditions, all cases will be serviced quickly, so very little prioritization is required.

F15: The SJF Scheduling Principle: When delay costs are homogeneous, do the shortest job first.

Figure 7-9 graphically depicts the economics of two different scheduling strategies. The top graph shows the effect of processing the shortest job first, a 1–2–3 sequence. The horizontal axis is time and the vertical axis is the cost of delay. Job 1 incurs no delay. Job 2 is delayed until Job 1 is complete, so the black area to the left of its box represents the delay cost for Job 2. Similarly, Job 3 is delayed until Job 1 and 2 are complete, so it has an even larger delay cost. The total black area represents the delay cost associated with this scheduling strategy.

The lower graph shows the effect of processing the longest job first, a 3–2–1 sequence. As you can see, this has a larger black area and, thus, a larger delay cost.

Shortest Job First (SJF)

Shortest First

Project	Duration	Cost of Delay
1	1	3
2	3	3
3	10	3

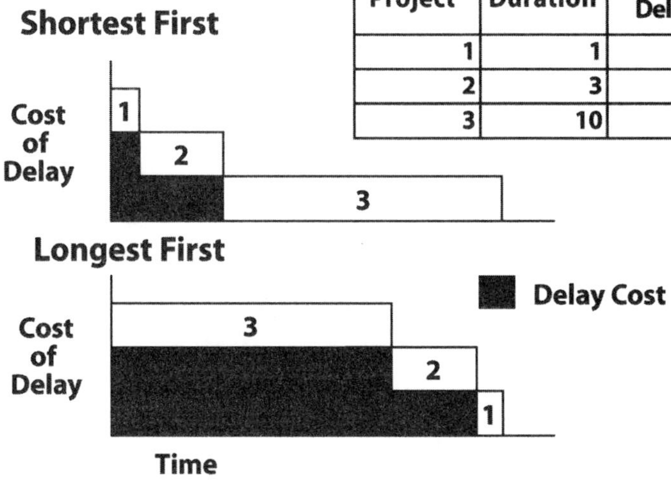

Figure 7-9 When all jobs have the same cost of delay, it is best to service the shortest job first. The black areas represent the total cost of delay associated with different sequencing strategies.

When all jobs have the same delay cost, the preferred scheduling strategy is to do the shortest job first (SJF). If we did the longest job first, it would delay many short jobs. This is often called the "convoy effect," since it resembles the way one slow car on a narrow road can delay all the cars behind it. The difference in the black areas on the two graphs is the savings produced by the optimum task sequence.

F16: The HDCF Scheduling Principle: When job durations are homogeneous, do the high cost-of-delay job first.

When all job durations are the same but delay costs differ, it is best to do the high delay cost first (HDCF). We delay the jobs with a low cost of delay so that we can service those with a high cost of delay. This is shown in Figure 7-10. Again, the incremental area between the two graphs shows the savings from the optimum task sequence.

F17: The WSJF Scheduling Principle: When job durations and delay costs are not homogeneous, use WSJF.

When both task durations and delay costs are different, we have both the most complex situation and the most common one. In

High Delay Cost First (HDCF)

High Delay Cost First

Project	Duration	Cost of Delay
1	3	10
2	3	3
3	3	1

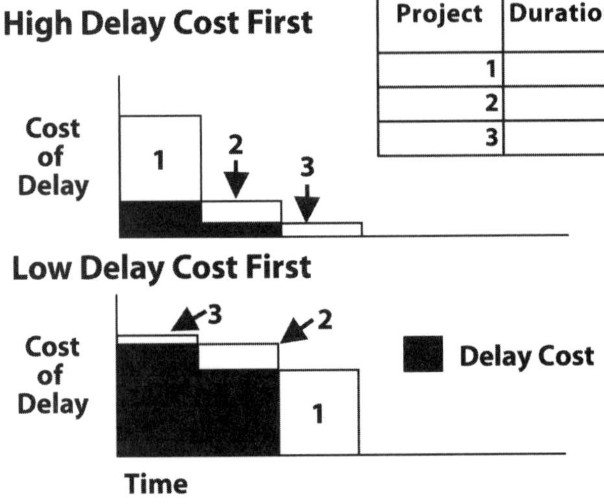

Cost of Delay

1 2 3

Low Delay Cost First

Cost of Delay

3 2

■ Delay Cost

1

Time

Figure 7-10 When job durations are the same, we should do the high delay cost job first. The black shaded area represents the delay cost for each sequencing strategy.

such cases, the best strategy is to do the weighted shortest job first (WSJF). In this case, we set priority based on a job's duration and its cost of delay. We base priority on delay cost divided by task duration. This is a useful scheduling metric because it uses data from a single job to determine the job's priority. Figure 7-11 shows this graphically.

How do these economically based approaches compare to the queueing disciplines used in today's product development processes? There are three common mistakes made in setting priorities. First, some companies prioritize jobs based on return on investment (ROI). They assume a high ROI project should have priority over one with a lower ROI. In fact, we should be more interested in how ROI is affected by sequence. The total profit of a high ROI project may be less sensitive to a schedule delay than that of a low ROI. In such a case, the low ROI project should go first. Overall portfolio ROI adjusted for delay cost is more important than individual project ROI.

Second, many companies handle jobs on a FIFO basis. This occurs when they have no quantitative information regarding delay costs or

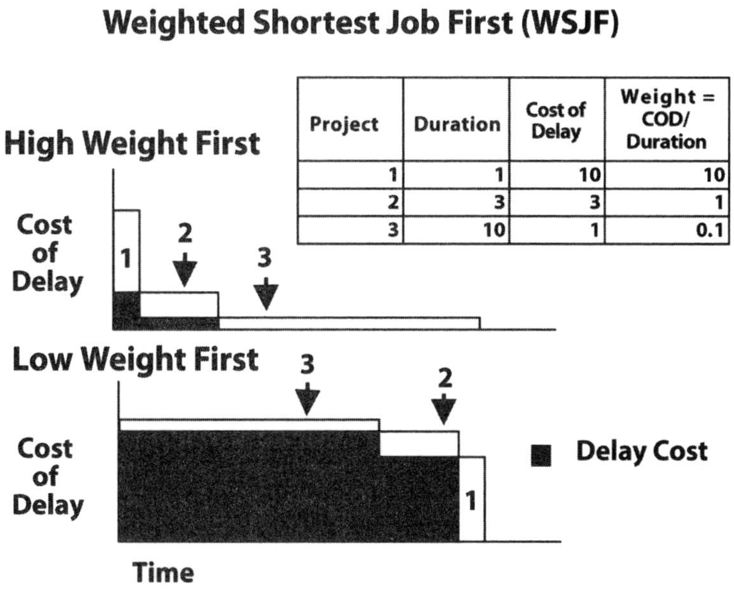

Weighted Shortest Job First (WSJF)

High Weight First

Project	Duration	Cost of Delay	Weight = COD/ Duration
1	1	10	10
2	3	3	1
3	10	1	0.1

Cost of Delay

Low Weight First

Cost of Delay

■ **Delay Cost**

Time

Figure 7-11 When both job durations and delay costs differ, we should prioritize by weighting the job durations. This is done by dividing the job's cost of delay by its duration.

job durations. While FIFO prioritization is simple, it is dangerous when jobs have different delay costs. Imagine a hospital emergency room that always prioritized their patients on a FIFO basis.

Third, some companies use an approach known as the Critical Chain. This approach allocates a certain amount of buffer time to each job and gives priority to the project with the smallest remaining buffer. In scheduling theory, this approach would be called minimum slack time first (MSTF). MSTF minimizes the percent of projects that miss their planned schedule and thus, the number of complaining customers. However, MSTF is not optimal when projects have different delay costs. For example, a project with low cost of delay and little remaining slack time should not get priority over a high cost-of-delay project that still has ample slack time.

It is critical to remember that we block a resource whenever we service a job. The benefit of giving immediate service to any job is its cost-of-delay savings, and the cost is the amount of time we block the resources. Both cost and benefit must enter into an economically correct sequencing.

F18: The Local Priority Principle: Priorities are inherently local.

There is a somewhat subtle implication of WSJF scheduling. Priority should be based on both delay cost, a global property, and remaining time required at a resource, a local property associated with the resource. This means that priorities at individual resources are local properties at those resources; they are not global properties of projects.

Many companies make the mistake of ranking their projects in priority order and telling the entire organization to support projects based on this ranking. This can lead to an unimportant task on a high-priority project displacing a high-priority task on a lower priority project. This local nature of priorities suggests that decentralized control might make sense. We shall explore this issue further in Chapter 9.

F19: The Round-Robin Principle: When task duration is unknown, time-share capacity.

Scheduling is relatively easy when job durations are predictable. We simply use a WSJF scheduling discipline. But what happens when we do not know task durations? In such cases, we cannot predict how long a task will block a resource. We would be vulnerable to the convoy effect, where a long job could block the resource for a long time.

But it could be even worse. What would happen if a task were impossible to complete? What if it took *infinite* time? This is not just a hypothetical problem. Many engineering tasks are difficult to forecast. Sometimes we unknowingly attempt to break the laws of physics, something that takes a very, very long time. How can we protect ourselves from such situations?

The good news is that we have solved this problem in computer operating system design. In scheduling computer processors, we don't always know how long it will take a program to run. Some programs may have infinite loops. If we let them run until they decide they are done, we could wait forever. How can we ensure fairness in prioritization when we have no idea how long individual jobs will last?

In operating system design, we solve this problem with a method known as round-robin (RR) scheduling. Instead of giving all of the capacity of a processor to a single job until that job is complete, we time-share the processor between multiple jobs. Each job is given a fixed time slice, known as a quantum, on the processor. At the end of this quantum of time, the job is placed back in queue and the next waiting job is serviced. This clever approach ensures that short jobs will always be completed faster than long jobs, even when we have no prior knowledge of the length of the jobs.

Deciding the size of the quantum is the key decision. If the size of a quantum is very large, the system behaves like a FIFO system. If the quantum size is very small, the system has high overhead due to context switching. One of the basic heuristics for RR scheduling is to ensure that 80 percent of jobs are cleared through the system in a single quantum of time. Only 20 percent of jobs will take multiple trips through the queue.

The careful reader will recognize RR scheduling as the approach we used when we had the purchasing agent work in the team area once a day at a predictable time. Using the classic RR heuristic, the purchasing agent should be in the team area long enough to complete 80 percent of incoming work in a single stay. If the average task duration is 30 minutes, it would be silly to have the purchasing agent support the team for 6 minutes every hour.

F20: The Preemption Principle: Only preempt when switching costs are low.

It is worth making a careful distinction between letting a project go to the head of the line in the ready queue and letting the project preempt a job that is currently being serviced. Preemption gives us the fastest possible cycle time, but it is usually a bad practice because it creates inefficiencies that reduce the effective capacity of a bottleneck resource.

Instead, it is usually sufficient to give head-of-the-line privileges. This will eliminate queue time, which is typically the largest component of cycle time. We will still have to wait for the previous job to clear the blocked server. The time it takes to do this is called the residual time, and it is usually quite small.

Residual time is rarely a big problem if you follow the principles of this book. Small batch sizes make residual time small, and round-robin scheduling makes residual time extremely predictable. There is seldom a good case for preemption.

When would we consider preemption? The gain from preemption is the difference between sequence-dependent COD savings and switching costs. Sequence-dependent COD savings arise from large differences in cost of delay and large differences in task duration. The only time we should consider preempting jobs is when switching costs are very low and when there are substantial sequence-dependent COD savings. For example, in our hospital emergency room, we will interrupt a doctor working on a patient with a cold to service a patient in cardiac arrest.

F21: The Principle of Work Matching: Use sequence to match jobs to appropriate resources.

When we route work through a product development network, we have certain specialized resources that are ideal for handling specific jobs. However, incoming jobs may not arrive in the same sequence as these specialists become available. This could cause us to dispatch work to inefficient resources. We can avoid this problem by maintaining a small pool of available work, the ready queue, and pulling work from this queue that fits the specialized resource.

For example, let's say we have a pool of designs awaiting mechanical analysis. Some of the jobs in this pool are routine stress analyses, and others are sophisticated vibration analyses that can only be done by one very smart Ph.D.

In such circumstances, we want to monitor the number of sophisticated vibration analyses in queue and the availability of our Ph.D. When there are no vibration analyses waiting, we can put the Ph.D. to work on routine stress analyses. When there are vibration analyses waiting, the Ph.D. should work on vibration analyses. If there is a vibration analysis due to arrive in the near future, it is better to briefly hold the Ph.D. idle, than it is to block this scarce resource with a routine stress analysis.

Let me make two key points. First, the nonhomogeneous work and nonhomogeneous resources in product development almost always create a matching opportunity. The simple FIFO sequencing that we use in manufacturing is virtually never optimal. Second, correct sequencing requires visibility into adjacent resources. We need information about both incoming work and likely resource availability times.

Managing the Development Network

What if we managed the resource network that we use to process product development tasks like we manage a data communications network? Why might we want to do this? Telecommunications networks are designed to be robust in the presence of variability. Customers send unpredictable amounts of traffic and the network still works. Circuits fail, and the network still works. Link throughput changes continuously, and the network still works. This robustness is not an accident, it is the result of careful design, testing, and constant refinement.

The Internet uses many concepts that are relevant to product developers. They suggest ways that we could design a product development process that could achieve high flow in the presence of variability.

Today's product development processes do not exploit these network-based concepts. Instead, they are much more sequential, linear, and rigid than telecommunications networks. Therein lies the opportunity.

F22: The Principle of Tailored Routing: Select and tailor the sequence of subprocesses to the task at hand.

The Internet tailors the route for each packet. Every packet does not have to visit every node in the network. It only visits the necessary nodes to reach its destination.

Contrast this with the rigid, least-common-denominator thinking typically found in product development processes. Too often companies create process maps that show all projects visiting all nodes in exactly the same sequence. This makes no economic sense. Projects should only visit nodes that add economic value. They should visit these nodes in the specific sequence that adds economic value most cost-effectively. Thus, the nodes traversed, and the sequence in which they are visited should always be an economic choice.

Let's illustrate this with an example. Consider a risky user interface concept. When should its test be sequenced? As early as possible. Otherwise, it may jeopardize investments in other activities. As a general rule, any inexpensive step that eliminates a lot of risk should occur early. When the greatest risk lies in different places on different programs, then the correct task sequence will differ.

Today, most product development processes are guilty of one-dimensional thinking. They use the mental model of a value stream. A raindrop falls down on the top of the mountain, and it flows towards the ocean sequentially, traversing every point between the two. It must leave one point to arrive at the next. This is a great model for physical objects, and a silly one for information. Information is the work content of product development.

Future product development processes are likely to recognize this. Instead of viewing product development as a linear sequence of steps, it will be viewed as a network. Projects will be broken into packets, and they will traverse this network in sequences that are appropriate for the particular packet.

For example, a mechanical subassembly with a long reliability test will be launched into the network early. This will permit it to start testing long before the rest of the system. In fact, this subassembly may begin testing before some other portions of the design are even specified.

What is the economic advantage of the network-centric approach? Existing sequential processes force a large number of low value-added activities to occur every project. Contrast this with a tailored process. One consumer product company created a modular process that permitted each project to tailor the modules they used. They have about 250 basic building blocks in their process, of which an average project uses 50 to 60 modules. This implies that 75 to 80 percent of the standard tasks were low value-added for any particular project.

This network-centric view has clear implications for development process design. It implies that it is incorrect to standardize the top-level process map; this is precisely where we need flexibility. Instead, we should standardize the modules, or nodes, that make up the development network. With standardized modules, we can easily select the specific modules that add value, and we can sequence them in the correct economic sequence.

F23: The Principle of Flexible Routing: Route work based on the current most economic route.

Telecommunications networks exploit alternate routes to obtain maximum economic efficiency. The packets that make up an Internet message are sent to a router that evaluates the optimum route to reach the receiver.

Since circuit conditions are constantly changing, the router needs to know the current condition of possible routes. This current condition is maintained in a routing table that is updated by adjacent nodes multiple times per minute. Whenever the router has to forward packets, it sends them to whichever adjacent node provides the "lowest-cost" path. The algorithm that selects the "lowest-cost" path has considerable sophistication. Among other things, it takes into account the instantaneous level of congestion on the network.[3]

As a result, the best path can change during the sending process. Although the packets in a message may travel different routes, they ultimately are reassembled at the destination into the original message, and the routing process is invisible to end-users.

It is important to recognize that the best route can *only* be selected at a short time-horizon. Congestion can rise and fall very quickly on a network. Sometimes congestion will make it attractive to route packets over a physically longer route simply because it is less congested. If routes were planned months, or even minutes, in advance, they would be unable to take into account the constantly changing congestion on the network.

Product development networks also experience congestion. They also need flexible routing. For example, when we start our project, we may plan to use our low-cost internal testing facility to test our design. However, as we approach the test date, we may discover that this node is congested. What can we do? If we have developed an alternate route, such as an external test facility, congestion at the internal facility can make this the new optimal route.

F24: The Principle of Alternate Routes: Develop and maintain alternate routes around points of congestion.

Flexibility in routing comes from having preplanned alternate routes. We need to consciously develop alternate routes around likely points of congestion. It is important to recognize that these alternate routes may be more expensive than the preferred route when congestion is low. They only become lower cost when congestion rises within the network.

These alternative routes must be maintained open and ready to use. A common mistake is to only use the alternate route for peak-shaving during periods of heavy demand. This creates an uneven flow to the alternate route. Instead, it is usually better to maintain a trickle flow of work through the alternate route, even when the primary route

---

[3] Some routing algorithms recognize the difference between traffic like videoconference streams, which like speedy delivery and tolerate missing packets, and traffic like binary file transfers, which requires all packets and tolerates delays.

is under-utilized.[4] This small flow should be viewed as an insurance premium that we pay in order to have a backup route available at short notice.

Do we need alternate routes for every link in our network? This would be overkill. In product development processes, the location of congestion is fairly predictable. It usually occurs at scarce or expensive resources for tasks that have high variability. For example, it is common to see congestion in testing departments. If we monitor queues in our development process, this tells us where congestion occurs, and thus where we would benefit from alternate routes.

F25: The Principle of Flexible Resources: Use flexible resources to absorb variation.

Flexible resources enable flexible routing. In Chapter 6, I stressed the value of flexible resources as a method to control WIP excursions. I explained how approaches like part-time team members, Principle W10, T-shaped people, Principle W12, and cross-training, Principle W13, give us the ability to cope with emerging queues. The principle of flexible resources is critical to creating robust networks.

The Internet has made many design choices that inherently lead to robustness. Among them is the choice to make resources interchangeable. This allows us to send demand through any open circuit. The Internet deliberately encapsulates the uniqueness of individual messages within standard protocols. This makes the handling of packets virtually independent of their contents.

Just as the post office does not care what language is used on the letter contained in an envelope as long as the external address conforms to its protocols, the Internet is capable of moving many types of information because this information is wrapped inside standard protocols.

F26: The Principle of Late Binding: The later we bind demand to resources, the smoother the flow.

Once we have a tailored task sequence for a project, we must decide when to allocate a task to a particular resource. If we do this allocation at a long time-horizon, we increase the accumulation of random variances.

---

[4] Internet routers actually practice load balancing, sending packet streams down multiple routes at the same time. If the path cost of these routes is identical, load is evenly balanced; otherwise, low-cost paths are weighted more heavily. This increases network utilization and efficiency.

Late Binding

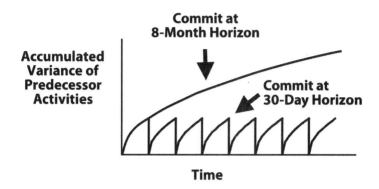

Note: Accumulated variance rises proportional to the square root of the time period.

Figure 7-12 If we bind tasks to resources at long time-horizons, we are affected by the cumulative variance of all preceding tasks. By committing at a short time-horizon, we can avoid this accumulation of variance.

Traditional circuit-switched telephone networks seize a trunk line for the entire duration of a call. They block the capacity from the beginning until the end of the call, even when the line is silent. Contrast this with packet-switching networks, like the Internet. In these networks, the packet seizes the resource at the precise time they are going to use it. We call this late binding between resources and demand.

There are clear advantages to a late-binding approach. It allows us to dispatch work when we know the actual conditions at the resource, instead of trying to forecast these conditions far in advance.

Figure 7-12 shows the statistical logic behind this approach. If we dispatch work early, there will be a lot of work committed to this node before our job arrives. That means the queue at the node will be affected by the accumulated random variance of all the preceding jobs. This cumulative random variance is proportional to the square root of the number of intervening tasks.[5]

---

[5] A large batch has a lower coefficient of variation (ratio of the standard deviation to the mean), but it has a higher absolute deviation than a smaller batch. In this case, the beneficial effect of variability pooling, Principle V5, is outweighed by the larger absolute deviation caused by large batch size. This absolute deviation increases with the square root of batch size.

In contrast, when we dispatch tasks late, we know the actual completion time of the previous tasks. If the cumulative effect of previous jobs has created a queue, we can allocate less work or use an alternative path. If the cumulative effect of previous jobs leaves plenty of capacity, we can allocate more work.

Early binding creates difficulties because it makes us dependent on our noisy forecast of the expected duration of an entire group of assigned tasks. This forecast is done at a long time-horizon, which makes it even noisier.

In contrast, late binding permits us to use the noise-free information from the tasks already completed to make our loading decision. This allows us to neutralize accumulated variance, and it creates much smoother flows.

F27: The Principle of Local Transparency: Make tasks and resources reciprocally visible at adjacent processes.

In classic queueing theory, jobs appear out of nowhere, and we have no prior knowledge of their precise size or arrival time. In product development, we can do much better than this. The curtain between adjacent processes does not have to be completely opaque. As work nears completion, we should make its character visible to downstream resources. As downstream resources are about to become available, we should make this availability known to upstream processes. This enables us to better match demand to resources, as explained in the principle of work matching, Principle F21.

For example, if we have a single expert on an Internet protocol like TCP/IP, we should make her aware of when the next "perfect match" job will arrive. If there will be a slot opening in her schedule, we should make upstream processes aware of this. We don't need to make all work in the entire process visible, just work flowing to and from adjacent processes.

As mentioned earlier, a common way to do this is with whiteboards and sticky notes. Workflow is managed in a daily stand-up, face-to-face meeting at this whiteboard. The whiteboard is partitioned with zones for the ready queue of work, and zones for work that has been dispatched to the specialized resources. Decisions are made at a synchronous, cadenced meeting where people from adjacent processes can easily interact. They can accelerate upstream work for an underutilized resource, or de-emphasize work for an overloaded resource. Companies inevitably feel they can computerize this whiteboard, however, they almost always create a more elegant but less useful system.

As simple as the whiteboard is, it makes WIP continuously visible, it enforces WIP constraints, it creates synchronized daily interaction, and it promotes interactive problem solving. Furthermore, teams evolve methods of using whiteboards continuously, and they have high ownership in their solution. In theory, all this can be replicated by a computer system. In practice, I have not yet seen an automated system the replicates the simple elegance and flexibility of a manual system.

F28: The Principle of Preplanned Flexibility: For fast responses, preplan and invest in flexibility.

Flexibility is not simply a frame of mind that enables us to react to emerging circumstances. Flexibility is the result of advance choices and planning. If we plan to jettison requirements to hold schedules, we should decide which requirements are nonessential in advance. If we plan to pull resources to emerging queues, we should invest in making these resources productive on short notice.

For example, some companies identify product requirements as mandatory, important, and optional, at the very beginning of their development process. This makes it possible to jettison low-value requirements quickly. Furthermore, it allows system architects to couple these optional requirements loosely to the rest of the architecture.

We can also improve the response time of backup resources by investing in keeping them informed on the program. Invite them to team meetings. Send them copies of meeting minutes and action item lists. A small investment in keeping up with the program leads to much faster response times. Flexible requirements and flexible resources are best planned in advance.

A useful analogy is the doctrine used by the navy to fight shipboard fires. A typical naval ship does not have a permanent fire-fighting force waiting at shipboard fire stations. Fires occur too infrequently to justify resources that would be idle most of the time.

However, fires do occur, and they must be addressed quickly. This is done using a hierarchical approach. The watchstander, who has limited resources, first reports the fire, and then fights it. The report triggers the response of the damage control party, a group of people assigned to quickly come to the scene. The third level of response is from the shipwide resources, allocated by the watch quarter and station bill.

Naval ships use a preplanned system, and they constantly drill to improve the response time of this system. The fire-fighting teams are assigned in advance and equipment is pre-positioned in strategic locations. Sailors do not fight fire by randomly swarming a fire with everyone who is available, the way 5-year-olds swarm a soccer ball.

Correcting Two Misconceptions

Let me close this chapter by correcting two common misconceptions. First, many product developers assume that it is always preferable to decentralize all resources to dedicated project teams. I will explain why it is better to centralize certain resources.

Second, many developers assume that the queueing delays at a bottleneck are solely determined by the characteristics of bottleneck, such as its loading and processing variability. In fact, the process *before* the bottleneck also has an important influence on the delays at the bottleneck.

F29: The Principle of Resource Centralization: Correctly managed, centralized resources can reduce queues.

Many companies misunderstand the important role of centralized resources. They assume decentralized resources will always lead to faster response time. This is often the case, but we must remember that decentralized resources fail to exploit the principle of variability pooling, Principle V5. We can service random demand with less queueing if we aggregate this demand and serve it with a shared resource. The greater the variation in the demand, the more useful this approach.

Figure 7-13 illustrates this phenomenon. It shows three projects that individually have variable demand. When this variability is combined, total demand has less variability than its components. In this situation, the same amount of resources can achieve more throughput and faster flow time when it is centralized. A centralized resource is often more effective at handling variable demand than a decentralized one.

Centralized Resources

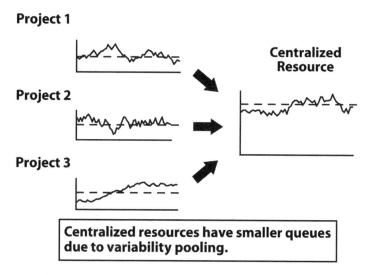

Project 1

Centralized Resource

Project 2

Project 3

Centralized resources have smaller queues due to variability pooling.

Figure 7-13 When we combine multiple demand streams with uncorrelated variability, the combined variability is reduced. This leads to lower queues from a centralized resource.

In Chapter 9, we will explore the decentralized control philosophy of the Marine Corps. The U.S. Marines are an organization that intensely emphasizes initiative and decentralization. Yet, the Marines recognize that certain resources should be controlled centrally. When they are trying to break through enemy lines, they combine the effect of ground troops, close air support, and artillery to produce concentrated fire at the point of vulnerability. This concentration of fire is critical to success. It is achieved by combining both centralized and decentralized resources. The locally controlled resources of the attacking unit are supplemented with centralized heavy artillery and centralized close air support. If these centralized resources were dispersed to individual units, it would be much harder to achieve the concentration of fire necessary for success.

In product development, centralized resources are also a tool to combat unanticipated queues. Many product developers complain that centralized resources are inherently unresponsive. This poor response time does not arise from centralization, but from the way we measure and manage these resources.

If we load centralized resources to high levels of capacity utilization, they will have queues and slow response times. If we measure centralized resources on their efficiency, they will operate at high levels of capacity utilization. Never assume that centralized resources *automatically* lead to poor response time. Instead, find out which incentives and policies are causing poor response time and correct them.

F30: The Principle of Flow Conditioning: Reduce variability before a bottleneck.

Many developers believe that bottlenecks control system performance. After all, it is intuitively appealing that a system should not be able to operate any faster than its slowest element.

While this is true, we need a bit more sophistication when dealing with the stochastic bottlenecks of product development. Optimizing the economics of a process is very different than maximizing its throughput. The economics of a bottleneck process are usually dominated by the size of its queue. However, the size of this queue is affected by more than the operating rate of the bottleneck.

In Principle Q5, I pointed out that queue time at a bottleneck is determined by four factors, the average operating rate of the bottleneck, its capacity utilization, the variability in processing time, and the variability in arrival rate. In particular, the variability in the arrival rate of work is determined by the variability of the process *upstream* of the bottleneck.

This means that we can affect the size of the queue without changing throughput. We can reduce the size and cost of a queue by reducing the variability of the process immediately upstream of the bottleneck. The term we use for reducing the variability in the upstream process is flow conditioning.

We discussed a few examples of flow conditioning when we discussed Principle Q8, but let me give you a physical analogy. In fluid mechanics, we get minimum resistance when we achieve smooth flow, which is known as laminar flow. If we have a bottleneck in a piping system, we try to create laminar flow upstream of the bottleneck. This is done by preventing upstream turbulence. By conditioning flow upstream of a bottleneck, we reduce its variability, which increases the throughput of the bottleneck.

Conclusion

I've packed this chapter with 30 principles. I began by explaining congestion, the concept of a peak throughput point, and methods for maintaining this operating point. Then, we progressed to discussing the advantages of a time-based cadence and how to achieve it. We followed this with a discussion of synchronization. This is an underutilized tool which can reduce queues without changing either batch size or capacity utilization.

The ideas of cadence and synchronization should be familiar to readers knowledgeable in lean manufacturing. In contrast, the ideas regarding sequencing go considerably beyond the standard FIFO discipline that is used in manufacturing. We have borrowed important concepts from the domain of computer operating system design since it shares the issues of nonhomogeneous task durations, nonhomogeneous costs of delay, and unpredictability.

Finally, we examined what I consider to be a likely future: network-based development processes. I feel these are a much better fit with our needs than the linear processes that are common today. In the next chapter, we will discuss the importance of feedback loops, another powerful tool for creating flow.

8

Using Fast Feedback

A little rudder early is better than a lot of rudder late.

In this chapter, we will examine the use of feedback loops and control systems. This material combines ideas from economics and control systems engineering. The principles of control system engineering are commonly applied to managing the physical parameters of engineered systems. However, lessons learned in designing closed-loop control systems are quite relevant to those of us who want to control economic performance. In particular, the engineering approach forces us to deal with issues of dynamic response and stability, which we might otherwise ignore.

Readers with a manufacturing or quality control background will have to make a significant mental shift in digesting this material. They will be more accustomed to feedback loops with static goals and to economic contexts in which variation *always* hurts economic performance. They may also underestimate the economic importance of feedback, since it is always much less important in repetitive manufacturing processes.

Their views are shaped by the economics of manufacturing, where payoff-functions have the inverted U-curve shape as shown in Figure 8-1.[1] In the presence of such payoff-functions, it is appropriate to use feedback to reduce variation, since we make more money by staying near the top of the inverted U-curve.

However, product development has very different economics. Our goals are dynamic, not static, and our payoff-functions are asymmetric, as explained in Principle V2. As you shall see in this chapter, this fundamentally changes our approach to control. In fact, because

---

[1] In manufacturing, this curve is called the Taguchi Loss Function. It measures losses rather than payoff, which inverts the y-axis. Thus, the U-curve is inverted. We draw it as a payoff-function to be consistent with our approach in Chapter 4.

Manufacturing Payoff-Function

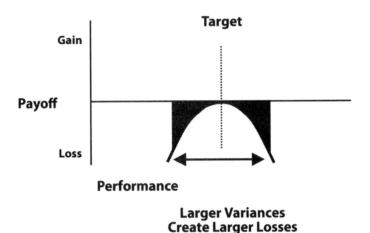

**Larger Variances
Create Larger Losses**

Figure 8-1 In manufacturing, variance above or below the target creates losses. Under these conditions, it is desirable to minimize variation.

asymmetries can increase the economic value created by variability, we are very interested in increasing the degree of economic asymmetry. How might we do this? Fast feedback loops are key, because they affect both sides of the payoff-function.

As shown in Figure 8-2, fast feedback can lower the expected loss on the left side of the payoff-function by truncating unproductive paths more quickly. On the right side of the payoff-function, fast feedback permits us to raise the expected gain because we can exploit an emergent opportunity by rapidly redirecting resources. Obviously, using feedback to increase payoff asymmetries is quite different from using it to reduce variation.

This chapter is divided into five subsections. First, we will discuss feedback and control from an economic perspective. Second, we will examine some of the more subtle benefits of fast feedback in development processes. Third, we will incorporate a number of ideas from control system engineering. Fourth, we will examine the human factor, what happens when we introduce a human being into the control loop. Finally, we will apply all of this to the practical problem of selecting metrics for product development.

Product Development Payoff-Function

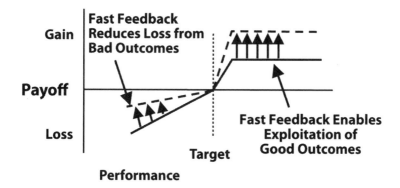

Figure 8-2 In product development, fast feedback is capable of altering our economic payoff-function. This changes the economics of variability.

The Economic View of Control

Let's begin by looking at control from an economic perspective. We cannot design a control system unless we know the purpose of this control system. The purpose of controlling product development is to efficiently influence overall economic outcomes. How can we do this? We need to find proxy variables that have strong transfer functions to overall economic results. Then, we need to find a way to efficiently influence these proxy variables. In some cases we can influence the proxy variable directly. In other cases, we must do this indirectly through an intermediate control variable.

As Figure 8-3 shows, it is the combination of economic influence and efficiency of control that makes a control variable attractive. For example, compare the attractiveness of controlling development expense, queue size, and cycle time. Queue size and cycle time both have higher economic influence than development expense. This makes them better proxy variables to control. While queue size and cycle time both have high influence, queue size is more efficient because it is a leading indicator whereas cycle time is a lagging indicator. It is the combination of economic influence and efficiency that makes queue size the most attractive of these three control variables.

Seeking Efficient Economic Influence

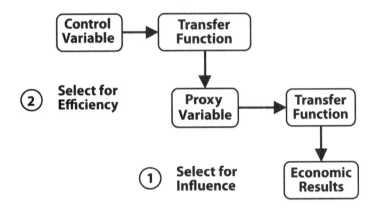

Figure 8-3 From an economic perspective, the best control variables are efficient at influencing the proxy variables which have the strongest influence over economic results. Queue size fits these criteria.

This economic view of control is too often absent in many companies, and it distinguishes our approach to this issue.

Taking this economic view, we will examine four issues. First, how to find good control variables. Second, how to deal with multiple economic objectives. Third, we will explore the difference between static and dynamic goals. Finally, we will take a more careful look at the issue of deviations.

FF1: The Principle of Maximum Economic Influence: Focus control on project and process parameters with the highest economic influence.

We want to control measures of performance that have strong influence on economic success. We can identify these parameters using the economic framework discussed in Chapter 3. If a 10 percent increase in project expenses reduces profits by 1 percent, and a 10 percent increase in unit cost reduces profits by 50 percent, we should focus our attention on controlling unit cost, not project expenses.

FF2: The Principle of Efficient Control: Control parameters that are both influential and efficient.

Just because a parameter has strong economic influence doesn't mean that we can control it efficiently. For example, average sales price almost always has a strong influence on life cycle economics, but it is very hard to control market pricing directly.[2] In contrast, unit cost has almost as much influence, and it is more directly controllable.

We find good control variables by looking for the intersection of economic influence and efficiency. We do our sensitivity analysis to determine which proxy variables have economic influence, then we rank these control variables on their control efficiency. This tells us which control variables are most attractive.

FF3: The Principle of Leading Indicators: Select control variables that predict future system behavior.

One of the shortcuts for finding efficient control variables is to look for leading indicators. Leading indicators are useful because they enable us to make early interventions. Early interventions are economically attractive because the cost of intervention rises exponentially as we progress through development and the value of early intervention is exponentially higher. These two effects can combine to make early interventions very efficient economically.

Let's look at an example. A very experienced manager once told me that he paid more attention to task start times than task completion times. What was his logic?

He said that in his organization, there was a very high correlation between having the correct person start a task on time and completing this task on time.[3] There was also a very high correlation between a task starting late, or with the wrong resources, and that task finishing late. He exploited this correlation by using task start times as a reliable leading indicator of task completion times. In this case, the manager

---

[2] It is often hard to change the price of our own product without experiencing reduced demand due to an effect called price elasticity.

[3] In other words, if the task had started on time with the right resources, the conditional probability that a task would complete on time was very high. This high conditional probability meant that the condition itself could reliably predict the outcome.

explained that if he focused on task completion times, the task would already be late by the time he tried to control it. By then, his intervention would be very inefficient.

In contrast, if he discovered a task had not started on time, he had many options. He could assign new resources, shift priorities, or alter constraints on the project. He believed that early interventions were much more economically efficient.

These two favorable conditions, strongly predictive leading indicators and high leverage early interventions, will not always be present. When they are not, the payoff of using leading indicators can disappear or even reverse.

FF4: The Principle of Balanced Set Points: Set tripwires at points of equal economic impact.

In Principle FF1, we suggest controlling high influence parameters. Does this mean that we can safely ignore all parameters with low economic influence? Unfortunately, a large deviation in a parameter with low economic influence can still be expensive. We need to prioritize our interventions based on the economic impact of a deviation. This economic impact is determined by the economic influence of the parameter times the size of the deviation.

It is surprisingly easy to base control on economic impact. We simply identify the magnitude of economic deviation that is worth controlling and determine the amount of change in each proxy variable that will create this economic impact.

As Figure 8-4 shows, we can structure set points so that they trigger interventions for deviations of equal economic significance. Although Project A and B have different economic sensitivities and multiple measures of performance, we consistently react to any problem that will cost more than $50,000.

Unfortunately, this simple but sensible approach is rarely used today. Instead, companies typically make three critical mistakes. First, they focus on controlling proxy variables instead of controlling economic impact. By disconnecting the concept of control from economics, they can expend control effort on variables with little economic influence.

Second, they often rank these proxy variables in order of priority. This is a subtle but significant mistake. Consider a typical prioritization, "The highest priority on this program is schedule, followed

Balanced Set Points

		Sensitivity Factor	Economic Limit	Control Set Point	
Project A	1% Expense	$ 50,000	$ 50,000	1.00	Percent
	1% Unit Cost	$ 250,000	$ 50,000	0.20	Percent
	1% Product Performance	$ 200,000	$ 50,000	0.25	Percent
	1-Month Delay	$ 500,000	$ 50,000	0.10	Months
Project B	1% Expense	$ 100,000	$ 50,000	0.50	Percent
	1% Unit Cost	$ 50,000	$ 50,000	1.00	Percent
	1% Product Performance	$ 200,000	$ 50,000	0.25	Percent
	1-Month Delay	$ 50,000	$ 50,000	1.00	Months

Select Control Set Points for Equal Economic Deviations

Figure 8-4 When we select out-of-bounds conditions for our control variables, we should use set points that cause us to react to events of equal economic significance. Projects with different economics require different set points.

by unit cost." This prioritization implies that the smallest deviation in schedule is more important than the largest deviation in unit cost. This makes no economic sense. Project performance parameters almost never have priorities; they have transfer functions.[4]

Third, companies often establish control set points based on absolute changes in proxy variables, instead of basing them on the economic impact of these changes. For example, one company moved any project to the hot list if it deviated from the planned schedule by more than 4 weeks. Since the cost of delay on different programs can easily vary by an order of magnitude, this could cause them to react to a $10,000 problem on a low cost-of-delay program, while they ignored a $100,000 slip on a high cost-of-delay program. All three of these mistakes are easily corrected by using our economic framework to set consistent, economically based, out-of-bounds criteria for all projects.

---

[4] There is a small class of binary parameters that can be either present or absent. It is appropriate to prioritize these parameters. For example, FDA approval can usually be viewed as a binary state. However, a binary parameter can only be prioritized relative to another binary parameter, not compared to an "analog" parameter with a transfer function.

FF5: The Moving Target Principle: Know when to pursue a dynamic goal.

Many companies create economically destructive control systems because they don't appreciate the difference between static and dynamic goals. In fact, it is quite common for product developers to assume their goal is to correct deviations from a static plan. They assume that the plan is correct, and a deviation is always bad. Therefore, they try to close the gap between the two by making results closer to the plan. They often discover it is cheaper to prevent deviations than it is to correct them, so they also emphasize preventing deviations.

Consider the typical practitioners of Six Sigma, striving to reduce nonconformances below 3.4 defects per million opportunities. They try to prevent deviations from a static plan, and to close any gaps that they can't prevent. Thus, they are closing gaps between a stable goal and varying actual performance.

This approach is commendable in the repetitive world of manufacturing, but it is very dangerous in product development, where our original goal is based on noisy assumptions. In product development, we continually get better information, information that makes it desirable to reevaluate and shift our goals. When goals are dynamic, we need different control systems. If we have stable goals, we try to prevent deviations, often by increasing inertia and avoiding risk. If we have dynamic goals, we try to quickly correct deviations, often by decreasing inertia.

We see this distinction clearly in military fire control systems. Such systems deal with two extremely different problems. Some targets are geographically stable. If we are trying to blow up a building, we use a missile that is relatively slow, heavy, and one that goes precisely where it is told to go. This approach works because there is no uncertainty in the future position of the building.

Other targets move. We cannot accurately predict the future position of a maneuvering jet fighter. To shoot it down, we use a heat-seeking missile like an AIM-9 Sidewinder. This missile is lightweight, fast, and not very precise. It simply relentlessly follows the target, continuously reducing the gap between its position and the target position.

Adaptive control systems designed to track dynamic goals are different than those designed to conform to static goals. Because product development has inherently high variability, it is critical to recognize situations where our goals should be dynamic. In such cases, we should strive to constantly reduce the gap between our current state and the economically optimal state, even when this economically optimal state is constantly changing. For example, this is commonly done in consumer marketing, where continuous preference-testing is used to detect market shifts that take place during development.

FF6: The Exploitation Principle: Exploit unplanned economic opportunities.

The handicap of thinking in terms of static goals is that it leads most product developers to view all deviations from plan as negative. As result, they try to reduce deviations. They focus all their attention on unfavorable deviations. If they encounter an unplanned obstacle, they exert heroic efforts to adhere to their original plan. If something conforms to plan, there is no deviation and they take no action.

Yet, in Chapter 4, Principle V2, we stressed that product development has asymmetric economic payoff-functions. Not all deviations have negative economic consequences. Because product developers encounter unexpected opportunities, conformance to plan may not represent the best economic choice. Our control system must enable us to exploit unexpected opportunities by *increasing the deviation from the original plan* whenever this creates economic value.

We would stress that the choice to expend scarce resources, either by correcting performance shortfalls or by responding to emergent opportunities, is another question of marginal economics, as described in Principle E16. For example, car manufacturers were years late introducing MP3 compatibility into automobile sound systems. Yet, adding a jack to accept the input of an MP3 player is trivially easy. Aftermarket suppliers introduced these products long before car manufacturers did. The car manufacturers seemed more concerned with adhering to their original plan than exploiting a new opportunity. As a result, they missed a low-cost opportunity to differentiate their products from competitors.

Thus, we should remember that our control system can add economic value in two ways. It can help us to reduce negative deviations from the plan, and it can attract effort to emergent opportunities, thereby increasing positive deviations from plan.

The Benefits of Fast Feedback

So far, we've only looked at the more obvious economic benefits of fast feedback. Fast feedback also creates some more subtle benefits. It enables our development process to operate with smaller queues, and it enables us to generate information more efficiently.

FF7: The Queue Reduction Principle of Feedback: Fast feedback enables smaller queues.

One of the more subtle effects of fast feedback is its ability to shrink queues. Fast feedback loops enable a process to operate with less WIP. Consider the design of the Internet. The Internet uses end-to-end flow control in which the receiver tells the sender to slow down when it is sending too fast. However, the speed of this end-to-end feedback loop cannot be faster than the time it takes for a message to travel from the sender to the receiver and back. This time is called the round-trip time or RTT.

Round-trip time sets a lower limit on the closure time of the feedback loop from receiver to sender. How do we compensate for any variability that accumulates before this feedback signal takes effect? We insert buffers in the path to absorb the variability that builds up before the primary feedback control loop can be closed. These buffers should only be large enough to handle the variability that accumulates in less than one round-trip time. We actually hurt performance if we make the buffers too large, because large buffers will increase round-trip time, and longer round-trip times permit more variance to accumulate.

This means that fast feedback loops do not simply provide feedback; they also reduce the WIP we need in our systems. This is very important because WIP itself intrinsically creates delays. By accelerating feedback, we can design processes with less WIP, thereby lowering delay times. This is a regenerative cycle, as shown in Figure 8-5. Less WIP leads to lower delay times. Lower delay times lead to faster feedback. Faster feedback leads to even less WIP.

FF8: The Fast-Learning Principle: Use fast feedback to make learning faster and more efficient.

It should be obvious that fast feedback improves the speed of learning. What may be less obvious is that fast feedback also increases the

A Reinforcing Cycle

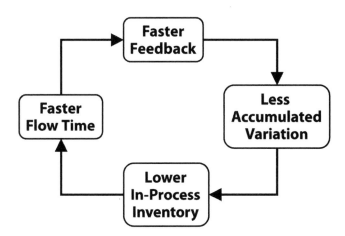

Figure 8-5 Fast feedback loops prevent the accumulation of variance. This means we can operate with less WIP. With less WIP, flow times are faster. This acts regeneratively to produce even faster feedback.

efficiency with which we generate information and learn new things. It does this by compressing the time between cause and effect. When this time is short, there are fewer extraneous signals that can introduce noise into our experiment.

Team New Zealand designed the yacht that won the America's Cup. When they tested improvements in keel designs, they used two virtually identical boats. The unimproved boat would sail against the improved boat to determine the effect of a design change. By sailing one boat against the other, they were able to discriminate small changes in performance very quickly.

In contrast, the competing American design team used a single boat supplemented by computer models and NASA wind tunnels. The Americans could never do comparison runs under truly identical conditions because the runs were separated in time. This made it both harder to detect improvement and slower to obtain information. Fast feedback accelerates learning in design processes.

Team New Zealand completed many more cycles of learning, and they generated more information in each cycle. This ultimately enabled them to triumph over a much better funded American team.

It is worth noting that Team New Zealand explicitly invested in a second boat to create this superior test environment. It is common that we must invest in creating a superior development environment in order to extract the smaller signals that come with fast feedback.

Control System Design

Now, let's look at some technical details of how we should design our control systems. It is worth making a careful distinction between a metric and a control system. A metric is only the measurement portion of a control system. If we focus on measurement alone, we ignore some of the most important characteristics of control systems, such as their dynamic response and inherent stability.

FF9: The Principle of Useless Measurement: What gets measured may not get done.

When I went to business school, one of my professors profoundly stated, "What gets measured gets done." I carefully wrote this down. The compelling sensibility of this observation prevented me from ever questioning it. However, I eventually began to pay attention to what actually happens. As anyone who has ever purchased a bathroom scale as a method of losing weight is aware, what gets measured does not necessarily get done. A metric is only a piece of a control system. Selecting metrics is part of control system design, but it is only a part.

FF10: The First Agility Principle: We don't need long planning horizons when we have a short turning radius.

One way to make a control system more effective is to reduce the work it must do. We can do this by making our system more agile. Let's illustrate this with an analogy.

Supertankers begin slowing down miles before they arrive at their destination, because it takes them a long time to maneuver. When they maneuver in the fog, they must comply with the Nautical Rules of the Road, which require ships to proceed at a speed that will allow them to stop within half the distance of visibility. This rule ensures that vessels meeting in the fog will not collide. A supertanker must proceed very slowly in the fog.[5] Contrast this with a speedboat operating under the same conditions. It can proceed much faster because it is more maneuverable.

Whenever we have a short turning radius and a quick reaction time, we can proceed safely at a higher speed. We can refer to this property as agility: the ability to quickly change direction while traveling at a high speed. We can use the physical analogy of changing the direction of a moving object. The time it takes to change the momentum of an object is proportional to the mass of the object and inversely proportional to the applied force. If you wish to quickly change the direction of motion of an object, pick a small object and apply a large force.

The same logic applies in product development. We need less massive programs and sufficient resources to redirect them. Megaprojects are difficult to redirect because they are so massive.

The U.S. military continued to develop the B-1 bomber long after the improved altitude capability of Russian surface-to-air missiles made it obsolete. Rather than terminating the project, the government decided to redefine the plane's mission. They decided to use the B-1, a plane with aerodynamics optimized for high-altitude flight, to fly missions 50 feet off the ground. You can probably guess how well that worked out.

In product development, we need to quickly apply adequate resources to redirect programs. Organizations operating at 100 percent capacity utilization usually apply too little resources, too late, to get a quick change in direction.

We can shorten our turning radius by reducing the size of the task and increasing the speed with which we can bring meaningful resources to bear on this task. This permits us to operate at higher speeds in an uncertain environment, and reduces the magnitude of our control problem.

FF11: The Batch Size Principle of Feedback: Small batches yield fast feedback.

One of the recurring themes of this book is the importance of reducing batch size. Chapter 5 was devoted to this issue, and it also applies to

---

[5] For purposes of this analogy, we will ignore the existence of radar, since there is no equivalent technology that allows us to see through the fog of product development with similar precision.

control system design. At any given processing rate, small batches will reach downstream processes faster, and they will trigger faster feedback. Reducing batch size accelerates feedback.

In fact, for many companies, fast feedback can be the biggest single benefit of reducing batch size in product development. These feedback effects are orders of magnitude more important in product development than they are in manufacturing, where work is highly repetitive.

Product development processes cannot innovate without taking risks. Fast feedback truncates unsuccessful paths quickly, and thereby reduces the cost of failure associated with risk-taking. Thus, as mentioned earlier, fast feedback is an attractive way to favorably alter the asymmetry of our economic payoff-function.

FF12: The Signal to Noise Principle: To detect a smaller signal, reduce the noise.

Reducing batch size increases the speed of feedback, but small batch sizes can introduce a new problem in a noisy environment. When we cut the batch size in half, the signal is cut in half, but the noise is only cut by the square root of two. Therefore, the coefficient of variation[6] actually increases by the square root of two when we cut the batch size in half. As we reduce our step size, we reach a point where the steps get so small that we have trouble distinguishing what is signal and what is noise.

For example, say we are doing an experiment to determine whether a coin is fair. We would expect a fair coin to come up heads and tails with equal probability. We can run an experiment by flipping the coin. As the run length of this experiment shortens, the experiment becomes less and less reliable at detecting an unfair coin. When we flip a coin 10 times, a run of 10 heads or 10 tails is quite improbable, and thus, a strong signal that the coin is not fair. When we flip a coin two times, it is very hard to judge whether the coin is fair or not, because a string of two heads or two tails will occur half the time, even with a perfectly fair coin.

Therefore, if we want to reduce batch size in an information generating process, we need to reduce noise. This enables us to detect the weak signals generated by small steps.

---

[6] The coefficient of variation is the ratio of the standard deviation of a probability distribution to its mean.

One way to reduce noise is to systematically reduce external sources of noise. For example, when Team New Zealand designed the yacht that won the America's Cup, they needed to detect small changes in the performance of their design. In addition to racing two boats at the same time, they deliberately chose a test course with consistent steady winds. By reducing the external noise sources, they were able to reliably detect smaller performance changes in their design.

FF13: The Second Decision Rule Principle: Control the economic logic behind a decision, not the entire decision.
We can make control systems both faster and more efficient by controlling decisions without participating in them. We can do this by controlling the underlying economic logic behind the decision. This controls outcomes without delaying decisions. It can be done easily using the economic decision rules introduced in Chapter 2.

Let's return the example of the Boeing 777 discussed in Principle E13. The weight of a new commercial aircraft is a critical performance variable. Aircraft designers provide weight guarantees that can cost millions of dollars if they are breached. Since weight is a key success factor, does this mean that the program manager should get involved in all weight decisions? No, he simply must control the economic logic used in making these decisions.

For example, if every engineer knows that the program manager is willing to sacrifice up to $300 of unit cost to save a pound of weight, thousands of engineers can make the correct weight decisions. This provides full economic control without requiring higher levels of management to participate in each decision. And if we can get control without participation, this saves a great deal of time for management.

Using decision rules brings another more subtle benefit. When management focuses on communicating and articulating the economic logic behind decisions, they develop the organization's capacity to make sound economic decisions. In contrast, consider what happens when only management knows the logic behind decisions. Engineers are told, "This seemingly bizarre decision is actually best for the company due to mysterious and sophisticated reasons that are too esoteric to articulate." This develops a culture of magical decision making, where everybody feels they can make great decisions unencumbered by either analysis or facts.

FF14: The Locality Principle of Feedback: Whenever possible, make feedback local.

Local feedback loops are inherently faster than global feedback loops. It simply takes longer for a control signal to propagate through a larger system. As mentioned earlier, when feedback loops have long closure times, more confounding factors can come into play. Furthermore, there is a greater chance of instability. Let us look at both of these issues.

Consider the difference between the local WIP constraints of the kanban system and the global WIP constraints of the TOC system. If a brief bottleneck occurs in a TOC system, this reduces the start rate at the system input. This reduction in flow then propagates from work center to work center until finally, the work center immediately upstream of the bottleneck is adjusted to the new bottleneck rate. The control loop closure time is equal to the flow time between the entry of the system and the bottleneck. Because of the long time lag of this loop, the bottleneck may now be operating at a completely different rate.

In contrast, a kanban system throttles the operating rate of the process immediately upstream of the bottleneck. This throttling signal occurs within minutes, as soon as the first empty kanban is delayed in reaching the upstream process. The throttling only propagates sufficiently far upstream to compensate for the flow excursion, then it automatically readjusts when capacity recovers.

Because the kanban system uses local WIP constraints, its control signals operate very quickly, and the perturbation in flow is limited to adjacent work centers. In the TOC system, the perturbation is guaranteed to affect the flow of every process between the input of the system and the bottleneck.

Thus, fast local feedback loops prevent the accumulation of variance. This effect of variance accumulation is very important, and it commonly occurs when we concatentate a series of operations. We discussed the underlying mathematics behind this effect in the principle of late binding, Principle F26.

But variance accumulation is not the only problem. Long feedback loops can lead to instability. When I was an 18-year-old sailor in the navy, I had a chance to steer an aircraft carrier. This was a much greater challenge than steering a smaller vessel because of the long lag time between when you apply the rudder and when you observe the course change.

It is quite common for a new helmsman to zigzag the ship across the ocean. He applies the rudder to change course and waits to see the effect of the rudder. When he observes the ship changing course, he removes the rudder. By this time, the rudder has been on so long that the ship continues to change course. Time lags in feedback loops can be deadly to system stability. Fast local feedback loops provide better control and higher stability.

FF15: The Relief Valve Principle: Have a clear, predetermined relief valve.

A key part of control system design is selecting the action that will be taken in response to the control signal. As we discussed in Principle V14, we can reduce the economic effect of variability by substituting variability in a cheap measure of performance for variability in an expensive measure of performance.

It is useful to think of the inexpensive measure of performance as a relief valve for the process. In mechanical systems, a relief valve releases excessive pressure in the system to prevent us from doing things like blowing up boilers. In a similar way, a relief valve for a project is a predetermined outlet for variability.

A mechanical relief valve opens at a certain pressure. This pressure is chosen to avoid overstressing the system that is being protected. The relief valve recloses at a certain pressure, since it is undesirable to completely depressurize a system. If the pressure range between the opening and closing point of this valve is too small, the valve will cycle open and shut many times, an undesirable condition. If the pressure range is too large, it may excessively depressurize the system.

When we establish a relief valve for a project, we worry about similar details. For example, consider the case of using the feature set as a relief valve for schedule variation. This entails dropping features when we deviate from the planned schedule. We need to decide how large a deviation will trigger dropping features, who will make the decision, which features can be dropped, and how much total work content should be dropped.

It is important to drop sufficient work content to return the project to the center of its control range, as discussed in the principle of periodic resynchronization, Principle F5. It is insufficient to simply return the system to slightly below its upper limit because this is an inherently unstable operating point. We want to jettison features once, not repeatedly. It is like taking a hot air balloon over a mountain. If we need to drop ballast, we should do it early and aggressively. If we wait to drop ballast late, we have wasted the energy necessary to lift the ballast that we eventually drop.

The same is true of product features. If we hover near the upper control limit by cutting the feature set in many small increments, we increase the wasteful investment that we make in the dropped features. If we aggressively restore the program to its optimum operating point, we will have more margin to keep the surviving features under control.

FF16: The Principle of Multiple Control Loops: Embed fast control loops inside slow loops.

A feedback loop that has a long time-constant can only smooth variation that has an equally long time-constant. This means that we often need to embed fast time-constant feedback loops inside the slow ones. These fast time-constant feedback loops do not need a large dynamic range because cumulative variation is roughly proportional to the square root of time. Thus, it takes less resource margin to maintain control for fast feedback loops.

We use this strategy when sailing a boat. A small gust of wind is absorbed by easing off the helm, slacking the sails, and shifting weight of the crew. A sustained increase in wind requires that we reduce the amount of sail exposed to the wind. This can be done by reefing the sails or putting up a storm sail, actions that take more time and effort. Fortunately, we typically have enough time to adapt because winds usually do not change from 0 to 60 knots instantaneously. Nevertheless, we do need to plan ahead because it is difficult to change sails in strong winds. Seasoned sailors observe that, "The time to prepare for bad weather is before bad weather is upon you."

In product development, we need to combine long time-constant and short time-constant control loops. At a short time-horizon, we want to adapt to the random variation of the process. At a long time-horizon, we want to improve process characteristics that we consider causal to success.

For example, every 24 hours, we may choose to pull flexible resources to an emerging queue. At a longer time-horizon, for example, every

12 months, we want to look at our pool of flexible resources and determine if we have invested sufficiently in developing this capability. The short time-constant loop responds to random variation. It filters out the variation for the long time-constant loop. This enables the long time-constant loop to respond to overall trends. Both loops, working together, provide a better solution than either one would working alone.

FF17: The Principle of Controlled Excursions: Keep deviations within the control range.

When we design control systems, we determine the range in which we will achieve control. Within this range, the control system behavior is predictable; outside of this range, it can often become unstable. Effective control usually depends on preventing excursions into this region of instability. This also applies to product development control systems.

For example, consider what happens as testing queues grow. If we keep the size of the testing queue small, it will provide adequate response time for most projects. However, when the testing queue reaches a certain critical size, the queue can become regeneratively unstable. Engineers will start requesting extra tests, just to be sure they don't have to get in line again. This extra testing makes the queue even larger and causes other engineers to increase their testing requests. Regenerative feedback quickly drives the process into the state of congestion collapse.

We can avoid this regenerative instability by keeping queue excursions within a controlled range. We do this with WIP constraints, as discussed in Chapter 6.

FF18: The Feedforward Principle: Provide advance notice of heavy arrival rates to minimize queues.

Our feedback systems do not just have to flow information back to upstream processes. We can usefully flow information forward to downstream processes. This will reduce queues, because it reduces the inherent randomness of the arrival rate. Early warning information permits us to counteract variability with negative covariances as discussed in Principle V10.

For example, if we know a large amount of work is going to arrive in testing, we can anticipate the imminent growth of an expensive queue. Under such circumstances, it would make sense for the testing manager to use overtime to work his queue down to the low end of the range immediately prior to this heavy arrival period.

A fast-food restaurant prepares food to specific customer orders for most of the day. However, prior to lunch hour, it anticipates demand and builds extra inventory. If it did not do this, the heavy demand at lunch hour would overload the kitchen capacity and create queues.

What information should we feed to downstream processes? The information with the greatest economic impact. In processes prone to congestion, it is useful to give early warning on the arrival rate of work. It is also helpful to feed forward information that can lead to a large reduction in uncertainty.

For example, if we have mechanical drawings for 100 parts, only 10 of these parts may be extremely challenging to manufacture. On these 10 parts, only a handful of critical attributes may be the source of greatest difficulty. This is the small subset of information that should be delivered first, so that manufacturing can develop process capability before it is needed. Remember, information should flow in both directions.

The Human Side of Feedback

The principles that we have discussed up to now apply to all systems, whether or not they contain a human element. However, there are other principles that come into play when one of the elements of our system is a human being. In such cases, human behavior affects the overall behavior of the system. The effect of this human element can be anticipated and managed.

FF19: The Principle of Colocation: Colocation improves almost all aspects of communication.

What is the simplest thing we can do to create fast feedback in a group of humans? Increase face-to-face communications. Face-to-face communication is inherently real-time and combines both verbal and nonverbal information. What is the simplest way to increase face-to-face communication? Colocate the team. Not only does colocation accelerate feedback, but it has many beneficial side effects.

We discussed the value of physical proximity in connection with the proximity Principle B17. Physical proximity enables small transport batches. This is as true with human systems as it is with manufacturing and engineering systems. When we put people at adjacent desks, it takes less effort to communicate. As this transaction cost drops, people communicate in many small and frequent batches instead of in a few large batches. People address issues immediately instead of queueing them up for a weekly meeting. This accelerates feedback.

But communications speed is only one of the benefits of colocation. As the effort to communicate decreases, we see large increases in interpersonal communications, communications that have nothing to do with the work content of the project. People learn about each other's families, backgrounds, and outside interests. Why is this important?

Psychologists know that we have a general bias to interpret the behavior of other people negatively. This tendency is reduced when we get to know others as complex human beings, much like ourselves. Task-related communications by itself is not enough to create an appreciation of this complexity. Non-task-related interpersonal communications that comes from colocation is key to developing cohesive teams.

Over the last 20 years, I have asked thousands of developers whether they have ever worked on a team that had marketing, engineering, and manufacturing located within 50 feet of one another. Of those who have, I ask a second question, "Would you do it again if development speed was important?" Only one developer ever said no. He said, "The other team members knew too much about what I was doing."

Sadly, most developers and most managers have never worked in a colocated environment. As a result, too many development teams fail to exploit one of the simplest and most powerful methods of improving performance. If you ever have an opportunity to colocate a team, do it. If you don't, fight hard to get it, and you will be glad you did.

FF20: The Empowerment Principle of Feedback: Fast feedback gives a sense of control.

The human brain makes attributions of causality when there is a short elapsed time between cause and effect. If we push a button and a light goes on quickly, we assume that pushing the button made the light go on.[7] If we push a button and it takes 5 seconds for the light to go on, we assume that the button did not turn on the light. Fast feedback causes people to perceive the cause and effect relationships in their actions.

When people see that their actions cause consequences, it changes their behavior. They feel a sense of control, and this causes them to take even more control of the system. Instead of being the victim of a vast monolithic system, they become aware of a subdomain where they have power and influence.

Victims often can remain victims because they assume they have no control over outcomes. They have the steering wheel in their hands, but they don't turn it. When people begin to believe that the steering wheel they are holding can actually turn the car, they start steering the car. Thus, the human effects of fast feedback loops are regenerative. Fast feedback gives people a sense of control; they use it, see results, and this further reinforces their sense of control.

FF21: The Hurry-Up-and-Wait Principle: Large queues make it hard to create urgency.

Slow feedback produces the opposite effect, and large queues create slow feedback. When queues are large, it is very hard to create urgency. There is simply too long a time lag between when we arrive in the queue and when our job is serviced. With a long time lag, we only see a weak relationship between our completion of work and the start of the next activity.

This becomes even worse when large queues lead to expediting. Under such circumstances, jobs approaching their deadline get shoved to the head of the line. Since an imminent deadline appears to be the primary prerequisite for priority service, there seems to be little payoff in completing a job early. After all, we can complete our job late and we will be pulled to the head of the line as soon as our deadline approaches.

In contrast, when queues become small, work can often be processed in strict FIFO sequence. This causes a short time between arrival and processing, so the relationship between early arrival and early service is reinforced. With this rapid consequence, it is much easier to promote an atmosphere of urgency.

---

[7] We tend to automatically assume A causes B if the time lag between A and B is less than about 500 milliseconds.

FF22: The Amplification Principle: The human element tends to amplify large excursions.

Homeostasis is the tendency of a system to maintain its current state. When we introduce the human element into a system, it makes the system homeostatic for small deviations and destabilizes it for large deviations. Small deviations can motivate people to conform to plan. This is why realistic stretch goals often promote higher performance. In contrast, large deviations can have the opposite effect. Large deviations can promote disengagement rather than motivation, particularly when these deviations are large enough to cause us to question the basic feasibility of the plan.

Take the example of an engineer assigned to three programs. One program is extremely challenging and has fallen severely behind schedule. The two other programs are only slightly behind schedule. How will this engineer allocate his time? Will he increase the time allocation for the program that is severely behind?

Our years of experience suggest this is unlikely. It is much more likely that he will allocate less time to the delayed project and apply this time to projects that have a better chance of success.

The reason for this choice is psychological rather than economic. If more time is allocated to the problem project, it is likely that all three projects will be late. When every project that an engineer works on is late, the engineer is likely to be considered a bad engineer. If time is allocated to the nonproblem projects, then only the problem project will be late. If only one project is late, people are more likely to blame the project than the engineer. Human psychology encourages disengagement from problem projects.

Again, this illustrates the wisdom of preventing large excursions from the optimum operating point. Large excursions can lead to regenerative destabilizing feedback, which fattens the tail of our performance distributions. It is best to keep our system operating within a controlled range.

FF23: The Principle of Overlapping Measurement: To align behaviors, reward people for the work of others.

Some companies believe in creating crisp organizational boundaries so that each person or organizational unit has unambiguous responsibilities. It appears quite sensible to select metrics that are mutually exclusive and collectively exhaustive. But while this is mathematically elegant, it is bad psychology. In human systems, there are advantages to giving people credit for results that appear to be out of their control.

For example, one large professional service firm compensates its partners on the basis of personal results, local office results, and overall firm results. This produces a highly supportive structure because each partner benefits when other partners succeed.

The correct amount of overlap is a delicate decision. Place little weight on individual performance and people can lose their focus on the things that are within their primary control. Place too much weight on individual performance and they will focus myopically on their personal goal.

FF24: The Attention Principle: Time counts more than money.

Although this book has a strong economic focus, I personally do not believe that money is the scarcest or most valuable resource. The scarcest resource is always time. Our organization decodes what is important to us by how we spend our time. Allocating personal time to a program or project is the single most effective way to communicate its importance. This is as true in business as it is in raising a child.

If we want to communicate the importance of an issue, we need to allocate time to it. If an issue is the first item discussed at every staff meeting, the organization decodes it as being important. If the issue is the last item and it is sometimes displaced to the next meeting, it will be decoded as unimportant.

Metrics for Flow-Based Development

Now let's take these principles and put them to work. Which metrics will help developers follow the principles of this book? Our goal is to influence economic outcomes. We have provided you with a model of the causal relationships that will lead to economic success. In particular, this book has stressed the central importance of queues and their effect on economics. We've also identified the underlying root causes of queues. Now, we can select metrics that are consistent with these causal relationships.

In the past, you may have been told that the key to economic success is efficiency. If you believe this, you will focus on metrics like

Metrics for Flow-Based Product Development

Queues
- Design-in-Process Inventory
- Queue Size
- Trends in Queue Size
- Cost of Queues
- Aging of Items in Queue

Batch Size
- Batch Size
- Trends in Batch Size
- Transaction Cost per Batch
- Trends in Transaction Cost

Cadence
- Processes Using Cadence
- Trends in Cadence

Capacity Utilization
- Capacity Utilization Rate

Feedback
- Feedback Speed
- Decision Cycle Time
- Aging of Problems

Flexibility
- Breadth of Skill Sets
- Number of Multipurpose Resources
- Number of Processes with Alternate Routes

Flow
- Efficiency of Flow
- DIP Turns

Figure 8-6 Since Flow-Based Product Development identifies different causes for success, it follows that it emphasizes different metrics.

capacity utilization, operating your development process at high rates of utilization. In the past, you may have been told that the key to economic success is conformance to plan. If you believe this, you will focus on preventing and correcting deviations from plan. You would spend heavily to overcome unexpected obstacles and ignore emergent opportunities.

I would suggest that both of these popular beliefs are fundamentally wrong. I believe that the key to economic success is making good economic choices with the freshest possible information. When this information changes, the correct choice may also change.

Our beliefs about causality clearly drive the metrics we recommend. If we believe that evil spirits cause malaria, we will try to appease evil spirits rather than trying to control mosquitoes. If we believe that product development inventory is nonexistent or unimportant, we will not try to control it.

But since we actually believe that in-process inventory, caused by queues, is centrally important to economic performance, we emphasize the importance of measuring queues and the factors that cause them. Figure 8-6 summarizes the metrics that follow logically from the principles of this book.

Flow

The overall efficiency of flow within a development process can be measured in terms of DIP turns.[8] This is the ratio of DIP to revenue. It answers the question, "How much ongoing development work do I need to support a given level of revenue?"

As we improve the flow time of our process, we will need less DIP to support the revenue. This metric is similar to traditional financial metrics such as accounts receivable turns, inventory turns, and fixed asset turns.

It is worth remembering that DIP turns behave differently during steady state and dynamic conditions. Under steady state conditions, this metric will remain stable. Under dynamic conditions, we need to pay attention to the timing of the revenue associated with the inventory. When revenue is growing rapidly, we may need more DIP to support this growth. The same thing happens with manufacturing inventory when a business is growing. We need more raw materials and WIP to support higher levels of future sales.

Another useful metric of flow is average flow time. We can compute this by dividing the time period by the inventory turns. For example, if we turn our DIP inventory twice per year, then our flow-through time is 365 days divided by 2, or 183 days. This is analogous to measuring days receivable outstanding for accounts receivable.

If we adopt a differential service approach in which we target different flow times for different workstreams, then we must evaluate DIP turns and flow-through times for each of these workstreams.

We can also apply these two metrics to individual process stages by calculating the WIP turns and flow times for subprocesses. This will highlight specific areas of congestion.

Inventory and Queues

To improve DIP turns and flow-through times, we need to control inventory and queues. Therefore, it is useful to measure both queues and trends in queues. When companies begin measuring queues, clever engineers quickly realize that big queues are bad. Sometimes these clever engineers decide to eliminate queues using the magical

---

[8] Design-in-process inventory (DIP) refers to cumulative investment in partially completed designs. The most practical way to measure this is to sum project cost-to-date for all viable active projects.

power of reclassification. They simply claim that nothing is waiting in queue and that everything is being worked on.

In our experience, the easiest way to deal with this is to measure total DIP rather than only measuring the portion of DIP that is in queue. Trends in total DIP will automatically include what is typically its largest component, the work that is in queue.

In-process inventory is an extremely useful metric in its own right, not simply a poor substitute for measuring queues. As mentioned previously, we have seen companies get 5 times to 8 times reductions in cycle time by simply measuring and driving down total DIP.

We can measure queue size in terms of the number of items in queue, which is easy, or by trying to estimate the amount of work in queue, which is difficult. I normally recommend that you start with the easy metric, the number of items in queue. This is astonishingly effective even though most people assume it could not be.

For example, software developers have measured the queue of open bugs for decades. Measuring the number of bugs works extraordinarily well, even though software bugs take radically different amounts of time to fix. In fact, if you ask software managers why they don't classify bugs by the amount of work required to fix them and use this to compute the total amount of work in the queue, they will make two interesting comments.

First, they will say it takes almost as much effort to create a moderately reliable estimate of the work content of a bug as it does to fix the bug itself. They would rather use scarce programming resources to fix bugs than to estimate work content.

Second, they will comment that they actually do classify bugs, but not by the amount of work required to fix the bug. They classify bugs based on the criticality of the bug. Priority 1 bugs must be fixed immediately, whereas Priority 5 bugs may never get fixed. They can more easily and reliably estimate the value of fixing a bug than the effort required to fix it. This value alone is sufficient to set good economic priorities.

Nevertheless, some readers will feel compelled to ignore my advice and will insist on estimating the specific work content in the queue. If so, I recommend the following approach. Classify the jobs in the queue into three or four simple categories. For example, one company estimated the queue in their CAD area by classifying drawings into

Estimated Work in CAD Area

Drawing Type	In Process FEB 1	Standard Hours	In Process FEB 14	Standard Hours
Easy	10	10	5	5
Moderate	13	52	15	60
Difficult	2	32	1	16
Total Standard Hours		94		81

Drawing Type	Standard Hours
Easy	1 hours
Moderate	4 hours
Difficult	16 hours

Figure 8-7 We can approximate the overall work in a queue by classifying it into categories with different average work content. This is much faster than estimating the work content of each individual job.

rough categories of work as shown in Figure 8-7. This simple method will give you a good rough sense of what is happening to the work in your queue.

It can also be quite useful to measure the queues associated with particular processes. This will provide process owners with visibility on their performance. Furthermore, when we combine knowledge of the processing rate with queue size, we can calculate the forecast flow time of a process by using Principle Q12, Little's Formula.

Both the queue size and the flow time will have trends that can be usefully monitored. When monitoring both cycle time and queue size, remember that cycle time is a lagging indicator, so focus on queue size. As a reminder, the single most useful tool for tracking trends in queue size is the cumulative flow diagram (CFD), discussed in Principle Q11.

It can also be quite useful to do an aging analysis on items within a queue. There is often a nonlinear relationship between time in queue and economic damage. An aging analysis determines if there is a fat tail on our processing time distribution. This was discussed in the aging principle, Principle W15.

Cost of Queue

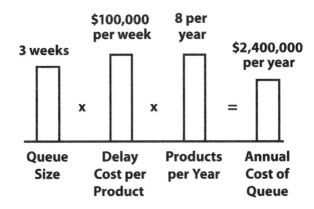

Note: This queue is on critical path for all 8 products.

Figure 8-8 We can estimate the total cost of a queue by considering the delay cost, the queue time, and the number of products. The queue time for individual products may vary with the queueing discipline.

Finally, I always like to attach a financial value to queues. We do this by multiplying queue time by cost of delay as shown in Figure 8-8.[9]

Batch Size

Since large batch sizes are one of the primary causes of queues, we want to measure the batch sizes that we use in our process and the trends in batch size. Because we enable smaller batch sizes by reducing transaction costs, we should also measure transaction costs and trends in transaction costs.

Cadence

Companies can often drive batch size reduction by accelerating the cadence of a process. If you use this tool, you should monitor the number of processes using cadence and trends in conformance to cadence.

Capacity Utilization

Any discussion of metrics should include a mention of capacity utilization. Despite the clear role of capacity utilization as a cause of queues,

---

[9] This simple calculation is not accounting for differences in costs of delay or queueing discipline. However, it is quite simple to use a spreadsheet to account for this.

I don't feel this is a good metric for practical day-to-day control. We simply cannot estimate work content and server productivity accurately enough to forecast capacity utilization. We discussed this issue in Principles Q3 and Q13. This does not mean that there is no role for capacity utilization as metric. It is simply a better metric for long-term planning than for day-to-day control.

Feedback Speed

There are additional metrics for measuring feedback speed. For example, we can measure average decision cycle time and the outliers that comprise this average. An aging analysis on unresolved problems is also useful.

Flexibility

Finally, we can measure the flexibility of our resources. Indicators of this are the breadth of skill sets that we have created. For example, on a factory floor, we track the number of people who are qualified to handle any station on the production line. We can also look at the number of multipurpose resources and the number of congested processes that have alternate routes.

Conclusion

Our goal in managing product development is to influence economic outcomes. We design control systems to help us achieve this goal. These control systems must deal with multiple objectives and moving targets.

We began this chapter by examining the problem of control from an economic perspective. We discussed the concepts of leading indicators and balanced set points. Our control systems must go beyond a simple focus on conformance, because our goals will evolve with emerging information. Product development presents us with unplanned economic opportunities, opportunities that we should exploit.

In the second section of this chapter, we discussed how fast feedback reduces queues and accelerates learning. Then, in the third section, we examined a number of technical issues of control system design. We learned that small batches accelerate feedback and that we can design control systems to handle small batches of information. We discussed the importance of decentralizing control and how we could do this with decision rules.

In fourth section of this chapter, we explored the human side of feedback. Slow feedback undermines urgency in product development and leaves workers feeling like the victims of a monolithic machine. When we accelerate feedback loops, we improve efficiency and generate urgency. Feedback is several orders of magnitude more important in product development than it is in manufacturing. Tight feedback loops can become an explicit organizational focus.

In the fifth section, we discussed a variety of metrics that support Flow-based Product Development. These metrics enable us to drive many of the key changes required by this approach.

In this chapter, we have stressed the importance of fast local feedback loops. These loops work best when we decentralize control. This will be the topic of the next chapter. In it, we will explore the value of decentralized control and how we can maintain alignment in the presence of this decentralization.

9

Achieving Decentralized Control

In this chapter, we will introduce information from a new domain. We will examine what we can learn from military doctrine. Why might this be useful? The military has spent centuries wrestling with the balance between centralized and decentralized control. They have thought carefully about both the advantages and disadvantages of decentralized control. They have tested their ideas in battle, against other smart and motivated thinkers. If their ideas do not work, they die.

As a result, sophisticated military organizations can provide very advanced models of centrally coordinated, decentralized control. Readers without military experience may find this surprising, since both Hollywood and academia consistently depict the military as a centrally controlled, highly hierarchical structure, where orders flow downward from the generals to the privates. They create the impression that the military seeks robotic compliance from subordinates to the orders of superiors.

In reality, the modern military relies upon the initiative of subordinates. It focuses on responding to a fluid battlefield, rather than executing a predetermined plan. It views war as a domain of inherent uncertainty, where the side that can best exploit uncertainty will win.

An exemplary model of this modern view of warfare is the U.S. Marine Corps. I was first exposed to Marine Corps doctrine as a midshipman at the Amphibious Warfare School in Little Creek, Virginia, and again, much later, when I took courses at the Naval War College.

Why do I believe Marine Corps doctrine contains potential lessons for product developers? Let me begin with one simple example. Marines, like product developers, prepare plans for their activities. Product developers track deviations from their plans and invest effort to correct these deviations. They assume that all deviations are bad and seek to conform to the original plan.

In contrast, Marines believe that warfare constantly presents unforeseen obstacles and unexpected opportunities. They do not believe they can anticipate all opportunities in their plans. They do not believe that all obstacles should be overpowered. Instead, they frequently bypass obstacles by leaving behind a small force to contain them. They plan to quickly exploit unforeseen opportunities and hold sufficient forces in reserve to do this.

The Marines believe that their original plan was based on the imperfect data that was available when the plan was prepared. It was only the best possible plan at that precise moment. They believe that the enemy will actively change its behavior in response to the unfolding battle, and that new information constantly emerges during battle. They recognize that this emerging information is visible first to the people who are closest to the front lines of the battle. Since advantages are created by reacting quickly, they push control down to the level of these frontline troops, and they select and train frontline troops to fight this way. They would be baffled by the way product developers try to cope with uncertainty by using ever more detailed plans and ever more centralized control.

I will begin this chapter with a brief discussion of warfare. Next, we will examine the need to balance centralization and decentralization. Then, we will discuss lessons that have been learned by the military. Finally, we will describe decentralization from a technical and a human perspective.

How Warfare Works

In battles, one side attacks and the other defends. Outcomes depend on the ability to concentrate overpowering forces at the right place and time. The military believes that attack and defense require different organizational approaches. An old military adage states that one should centralize control for offense and decentralize it for defense. Why? A military rule of thumb is that for an attacker to succeed, he should outnumber defenders by 3 to 1. This is possible, even when the attacker has inferior strength, because the attacker can concentrate his forces at one key point. In contrast, the defender does not know where the attack will come, so he must allocate forces to his entire perimeter. The attacker achieves this locally superior strength with centralized control. This ensures the highest possible concentration of attacking forces at the precise time of the attack.

Defenders can cope with this in various ways. One approach is to harden the perimeter at the most logical places for an attack. This was done in World War II when the French built the Maginot Line to stop the Germans. Unfortunately, as is common in the history of warfare, the Germans chose not to make a frontal assault on the Maginot Line.

A better approach is to respond to an attack by quickly massing nearby forces to counteract the local superiority of the attacker. If this is done fast enough, the defenders can turn back the attack. How can we do this quickly? With decentralized control.

An important variant of this approach is called defense in-depth. Defense in-depth creates an outer perimeter that is strong enough to slow attacking forces, but not strong enough to completely stop them. Slowing the attack creates time for more defending forces to be moved to the area of the attack. The faster we can move large concentrations of defenders to the point of penetration, the more likely we will reverse it.

Of course, attackers anticipate this behavior. They use tactics that make it hard for the enemy to anticipate the exact point of attack, and they try to delay the organization of an effective defense. For example, rather than attacking at a single location, they simultaneously attack in multiple areas. Then, the attackers respond to the actual flow of the battle and exploit weakness wherever it is found. They may also shift focus quickly to keep defenders off guard. Attackers will also try to delay the organization of an effective defense by sealing off the battlefield and interdicting the flow of supplies and reinforcements.

The use of surprise and movement in warfare is called maneuver warfare. It is most commonly contrasted with attrition warfare, also known as positional warfare, which is exemplified by the trench warfare of World War I.

The U.S. Marine Corps provides an ideal example of the modern practice of maneuver warfare. Their entire military doctrine is based on the belief that they will face superior forces, who have heavier equipment, and that the Marines will initially have to fight with limited support.

Marines are brave, but they do not succeed simply because they are brave. They have thought long and hard about how to fight wars and combine carefully developed doctrine with intense training to defeat equally brave opponents.

Balancing Centralization and Decentralization

In this chapter, I will emphasize the importance of decentralized control. I push you in this direction because most product development organizations are moving in the opposite direction, towards centralization.

This does not mean that 100 percent decentralization is the solution. The military skillfully avoids the simplistic idea that they must choose between 100 percent centralized and 100 percent decentralized approaches. Instead, they focus on decentralized execution supported by centralized coordination.

Let us start by looking at a number of principles that should convince you why it is useful to combine the advantages of decentralization and centralization.

D1: The Second Perishability Principle: Decentralize control for problems and opportunities that age poorly.

Certain problems and opportunities are perishable. By this, I mean that they are best dealt with quickly. An example of a problem that ages poorly is a fire. It is best to put out fires quickly, when they are small, because small fires can turn into big fires.

In contrast, some other types of problems are inherently self-limiting. For example, if you invest $1,000 in a bad stock, and it loses 90 percent of its value, you needn't worry that this magnitude of loss will continue. Even if the stock continues its decline, you can lose no more than $100. Our control strategy should focus on reacting most quickly to problems that age poorly.

Opportunities may also be perishable. For example, in many markets, the first entrant sets the standard for the rest of the industry. IBM defined the standards for 8-inch and 5¼-inch floppy disks. However, IBM was late to introduce their next standard, the 4-inch floppy disk. Instead, Sony and HP beat them by introducing the 3½-inch floppy disk, and the 4-inch floppy disk has been forgotten.

How can we quickly solve problems that age poorly? How can we seize opportunities that are fleeting? We need to decentralize control. And decentralizing control does not simply mean decentralizing responsibility. We need to decentralize the authority to act, and pre-position sufficient resources to make this action meaningful.

Think of it like fighting fires. We put fire extinguishers where fires are likely to break out, and we train people to use them. People do not have to request permission to put out a fire, nor do they have to run to the corporate fire extinguisher storeroom to sign out a fire extinguisher.

D2: The Scale Principle: Centralize control for problems that are infrequent, large, or that have significant economies of scale.

Not all problems and opportunities are perishable. There is another class of problems and opportunities that truly benefit from large-scale responses. Big fires are best handled by fire trucks, not by individuals with garden hoses and fire extinguishers. When we encounter problems that require mass, we need a method to bring sufficient mass to bear. We do not park a tiny fire truck in front of every home. Instead, we centralize this resource by providing a few big fire trucks that we can move to the location of serious fires.

Of course, centralizing resources increases response time. How do we ensure that fire trucks can reach a rapidly growing fire quickly? We recognize that fire trucks have a high cost of delay, and we give them priority over other traffic. We would need many more fire trucks if they traveled our streets at the same speed as regular vehicles.

It is appropriate to use centralized resources in similar ways in product development. Rather than putting a regulatory affairs expert on every program, we centralize this resource. By pooling the variable demand of many projects, as explained in Principle F29, we can provide faster response times to all projects. Moreover, we get the added benefit of consistency between projects.

Whenever we have infrequent but large excursions in demand, we use centralized resources. This is even more attractive if these central resources have scale economies.

For example, purchasing agents have specialized expertise and vendor relationships. Managed properly, a centralized purchasing organization can outperform the same resources deployed to individual teams. Too often, it does not, because it is measured on the wrong criteria: purchasing efficiency instead of response time.

In contrast, frequent, small-excursion, low-variability demand, with limited scale economies, should be serviced with decentralized resources.

D3: The Principle of Layered Control: Adapt the control approach to emerging information about the problem.

What happens when you are not really sure whether the approach to a problem should be centralized or decentralized? There are two basic possible approaches, depending on your ability to judge the severity of the problem at the time of its arrival.

The first approach is triage. This approach is used in hospitals and for mass casualties. When medical resources are insufficient to treat everyone, we try to provide the maximum benefit to the maximum number of people. We do this by making tough sorting decisions at the intake point. Some of the wounded will die no matter what we do. They get no resources. Some of the wounded will live no matter what we do. They get no resources. Instead, scarce resources are concentrated on the third group of wounded, those for whom medical care determines whether they will survive. Triage works whenever we have sufficient information to make good judgments at the intake point.

We must use a different approach when we cannot judge the severity of a problem when it first arrives. Computer operating systems deal with such problems and provide us with useful methods.

In a computer operating system, we may not know which job will take the most time to run. Under such conditions, we use the round-robin approach discussed in Principle F19. We allocate a quantum of time to each job. Any job that is not completed at the end of its quantum is put back into the work queue. This guarantees that short jobs will not be blocked by long jobs, even when we have no idea which job is shortest.

Sometimes operating systems divide jobs into priority classes and service the jobs in order of priority. However, this creates a risk that a job in a low-priority class may never get resources. How do we prevent this from happening? We automatically escalate the priority of a job when it has waited too long in queue.

We can use the same approach for problem solving. Problems that are not resolved within a certain time are moved to a higher level. This works because most small problems turn into medium-size

Multilevel Queues with Escalation

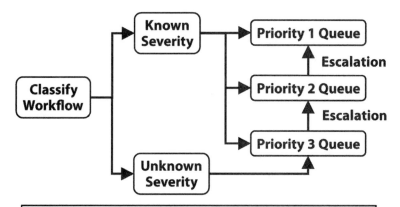

1. Each queue is allocated a portion of capacity.
2. Use round-robin scheduling within each queue.
3. Jobs stuck in queue move to a higher priority queue.

Figure 9-1 Jobs with known severity can be allocated to queues based on their priority. Jobs with unknown severity start in the lowest-priority queue and escalate if they exceed a certain time limit in the queue.

problems on the way to becoming big problems. If we establish clear out-of-bounds conditions, we can quickly escalate problems that are too severe for decentralized resources. A good escalation process prevents us from elevating all problems to centralized resources. At the same time, it prevents important problems from getting stuck at low levels in the organization.

We can even combine triage and escalation, as shown in Figure 9-1. A quick triage can set priorities for most jobs. These jobs can be serviced in prioritized queues. Jobs that cannot be classified can start in the lowest-priority queue. If they remain in this queue too long, they can be escalated to a higher-priority queue.

D4: The Opportunistic Principle: Adjust the plan for unplanned obstacles and opportunities.

In Principle FF5, we made a distinction between static goals and dynamic goals. We focus on conformance when we have static goals. When we have dynamic goals, we continuously adapt. We try to make the best possible choices based on emerging information.

Attrition warfare emphasizes conformance, while maneuver warfare emphasizes adaptation. In fact, a classic military saying observes that, "No war plan survives the first shot of battle."

The modern military does not create plans for the purpose of measuring conformance; they plan as a tool for maintaining alignment. The plan forms a baseline that synchronizes complex changes. If we decide to move up the invasion by 1 day, the thousands of activities required to make this happen, each of which may have different lead times, can all be quickly realigned.

Opportunism also adds enormous value in product development. As we progress, we may discover that a feature is valued by 10 times fewer customers and that it will require 10 times more effort to execute. A good process will recognize that this feature no longer makes economic sense. Rather than battering down this obstacle, we will bypass it.

Similarly, we may discover a feature is easier to implement and more highly valued than we originally thought. In such circumstances, we should consider exceeding our original goal, even if it requires jettisoning other marginal requirements. It is quite difficult to do this in today's conformance-oriented processes.

D5: The Principle of Virtual Centralization: Be able to quickly reorganize decentralized resources to create centralized power.

In some cases, it is not cost-effective to leave centralized resources idle, while waiting for infrequent large demands. To avoid inefficiency, we often use these resources for background activities and mobilize them as needed to create the centralized power needed to deal with a big problem. If we do this quickly enough, we can get the combined benefits of having both centralized and decentralized resources.

For example, navy ships use this approach to fight fires, as discussed in Principle F28. Fires occur infrequently, but when they occur, they are very dangerous and must be fought quickly. It is not cost-effective to have specialized firefighters who do nothing when there is no fire to fight.

Instead, we train all sailors to fight fires, but these sailors do other jobs until a fire breaks out. Then, they are formed into damage control parties, bringing substantial resources to bear on the fire. This entire system is planned in advance. Equipment is located in damage control lockers, sailors are trained in firefighting schools, and they are constantly drilled on their responsibilities. We get the effect of a large, centralized resource without the cost.

Civilian firefighting organizations also create virtual centralized capacity. Fire departments in adjacent communities provide mutual support. This permits a community to cope with infrequent large fires without having a large fire department.

We can also use this approach in product development. Some development organizations use "tiger teams" that are assembled from experienced and highly productive people. These teams are brought to bear when a program gets in unexpected and severe trouble. Yet, when there is no crisis, these team members do not sit idle; they work at their normal day jobs. Such resources can be brought to bear quite quickly if this is planned in advance.

D6: The Inefficiency Principle: The inefficiency of decentralization can cost less than the value of faster response time.

In many cases, we are willing to pay the price of inefficient, decentralized resources simply to provide responsiveness. We do this when response time is very valuable. For example, most people trained to do CPR will never use this skill. Why do we invest in training them? For response time.

The average response time of the Emergency Medical System is about 9 minutes, but brain damage occurs when a person has no blood flow for 4 to 6 minutes. Even when CPR does not restart the heart, it can provide enough blood flow to improve outcomes.

So don't assume the goal of efficiency should be given higher priority than response time. Instead, use your economic framework to make this choice.

Military Lessons on Maintaining Alignment

The dark side of decentralized control is misalignment. If all local actors make locally optimum choices, the system level outcome may still be a disaster. Is there a way to achieve alignment without centralized control?

This is the sophisticated heart of maneuver warfare. How do the Marines achieve alignment in the presence of uncertainty? How do they opportunistically shift their focus without losing alignment? They do not use elaborately detailed plans and micromanagement. Instead, they use tools like mission orders, doctrine, and lateral communications to combine initiative and alignment. We will examine these principles in the following section.

D7: The Principle of Alignment: There is more value created with overall alignment than local excellence.

To begin, let's examine the logic behind alignment. It has been said that one barbarian could defeat one Roman soldier in combat, but that 1,000 Roman soldiers could always defeat 1,000 barbarians. The strength of the Roman army lay in its ability to coordinate and align its combat power.

This ability to achieve alignment is enshrined in the principles of war, two of which are *mass* and *economy of force*. Mass refers to the ability to concentrate force in one area. Economy of force refers to the ability to allocate minimum resources to all other activities.

Thus, when military force is being focused, we subordinate all other activities to the main objective. This is simply a recognition that combat effects are not linearly proportional to effort. We exploit this nonlinearity by distributing our resources unequally.

The same applies in product development. Economic leverage does not come from slightly exceeding parity across the entire range of features. One percent excess over parity on 15 features creates no excitement, but a 15 percent advantage on a key attribute may shift customer preference.

Sometimes we won't know where the greatest leverage will lie until development is underway. Therefore, we need to dynamically reallocate resources to produce a compelling advantage on a handful of key attributes, not a modest advantage in all areas. As in warfare, alignment in product development produces disproportionate effects. But, how do we create and maintain such alignment?

D8: The Principle of Mission: Specify the end state, its purpose, and the minimal possible constraints.

In maneuver warfare, a key tool for creating alignment is a mission, and this mission is communicated using "mission orders."

Observers unfamiliar with maneuver warfare might think that a mission would tell a unit what to do, when to do it by, what resources it should use, and by what concept of operations this mission should be accomplished. All this seems quite logical, but it is the polar opposite of how mission orders actually work.

Mission orders focus on the intent of the operation, rather than constraining how the mission is to be accomplished. The mission is the end state that is trying to be created by the battle. It is always a goal that is larger than the battle itself. It communicates the "why" of the operation, not the "what" or "how."

In maneuver warfare, the mission is commonly described in the section of an operation plan called the "Commander's Intent." The Marines believe orders are incomplete without this information. They believe that intent needs to be understood deeply through the organization. They believe that when intent is clear, Marines will be able to select the right course of action. This is particularly true when Marines have to deal with an emerging obstacle or opportunity. In many ways, intent is simply a robust and compact way of providing direction.

In the same sense, the mission statement for a project can be a powerful way of maintaining coordination. Again, the most important part of this mission is the "why," not the "what" or "how."

D9: The Principle of Boundaries: Establish clear roles and boundaries.

The military does not approach warfare the way five-year-olds approach soccer. To five-year-olds, swarming around the ball seems to make a lot of sense. After all, the objective is to kick the ball, and you can't kick the ball unless you are near it. Unfortunately, the next step of the process doesn't go nearly as well. If everyone is near the ball, once it is kicked, there is nobody anywhere else to receive it.

The military is quite rigorous in defining specific roles for individual units and establishing clear responsibilities for adjacent units. This is a life-and-death matter, since on a fluid battlefield there is a constant danger of attacking your own troops, what is known as a "blue-on-blue" attack. With decentralized control, the discipline of roles and boundaries becomes especially important. Both excessive overlap and gaps are dangerous.

Clear role definition is equally important on product development teams. Poorly defined roles increase the need for communications and increase the time spent in meetings. What happens when only two people on the team decide on the color of the product? Information on this issue needs to be sent to two people, and meetings to make this decision only require two people. What happens when everyone on a 20-person team gets to vote on color? The information must be sent to all 20 people, and the only time the decision can be made is when all 20 people are present. Well-defined roles make teams much more efficient.

Of course, we need to be alert for white space between roles, gaps that nobody feels responsible for. One of the best slogans I have encountered to describe the desired state came from a team that said, "If you are going to worry about it, I won't."

D10: The Main Effort Principle: Designate a main effort and subordinate other activities.

In executing a mission, the Marines designate one point of action as the main effort. This is where maximum possible effort is focused. Forces in other areas are reduced to create maximum strength at this focal point.

Obviously, alignment requires that all forces know the location of the main effort. It is most desirable if the main effort is aimed at a point of weakness, since it is desirable to concentrate strength against weakness. However, sometimes the main effort will be directed at a strong point. This is often referred to as the enemy's center of gravity, the heart of their ability to fight. Since the enemy realizes they are vulnerable to an attack at this point, it will be well defended. However, this does not rule it out as a focus for the main effort. The choice of main effort depends on assessing both the cost and the benefit of attacking a particular point.

In much the same way, it is useful for product developers to designate a main effort for their projects. In many years of doing market research, I have consistently found that only a small set of product attributes truly drive success. While the customer may be able to identify 200 features and articulately explain what they want, only four to six of these features are actually capable of shifting preference from one brand to another. It is critical for the entire team to focus on these preference-shifting features on their project. The other 195 features can be subordinated to achieving performance on these critical features.

D11: The Principle of Dynamic Alignment: The main effort may shift quickly when conditions change.

Even more important than the idea of having a main effort is the concept that the main effort may shift in the course of battle. In maneuver warfare, the main effort is a fluid concept. At one instant, one unit may be the main effort. All supporting resources are devoted to making this main effort successful.

But battlefield conditions may change. When the defenders attempt to oppose the main effort, they may create weakness in another area. If so, it may be attractive to designate a different location as the main effort.

We've made the same argument for product development many times in this book. As we progress through a project, new information becomes available. We want to make the best economic choice using this new information. If this choice involves shifting our focus, we must be able to do this easily and quickly.

D12: The Second Agility Principle: Develop the ability to quickly shift focus.

We previously discussed the idea of agility in the first agility principle, Principle FF10. Maneuver warfare also places great emphasis on the ability to make fast transitions. The Marines believe that it is not sufficient to quickly decide to change focus; one must execute this change quickly. They have been heavily influenced by the concepts of Colonel John Boyd of the Air Force, who developed the concept of the OODA loop.

Col. Boyd analyzed Air Force performance during the Korean War and tried to determine the reason for the 10 to 1 kill ratio achieved by the F-86 Sabre jet against the MiG-15. Although the MiG-15 could outclimb and out-accelerate the F-86, and it had skilled pilots, the F-86 virtually always won in air combat.

Boyd discovered that the F-86 pilots were able to more quickly orient themselves to the tactical situation because their cockpits extended further out from the fuselage. They were able to more easily conduct an extended series of maneuvers because they had hydraulic flight controls compared to the MiG's manual controls.[1]

---

[1] The F-86 had some other key advantages. Its pilots had G suits which enabled them to tolerate maneuvers better. The F-86 had the APG-30 radar-guided gunsight, enabling accurate gunnery while maneuvering. And its six 50-caliber machine guns had a higher rate of fire and more ammunition capacity than the cannons on the MiG-15.

The OODA Loop

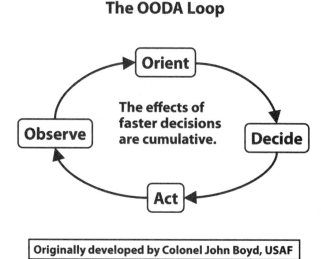

Originally developed by Colonel John Boyd, USAF

Figure 9-2 Colonel John Boyd, USAF, originally developed the concept of the OODA loop to explain patterns of success in air combat. Victory came from completing time-competitive cycles of action faster than the enemy. Slight differences in speed accumulated to a decisive advantage.

Boyd developed the concept of the OODA loop, show in Figure 9-2, in which a pilot observes the tactical situation, orients himself, decides what to do, and then takes action. He asserted that air combat consists of time-competitive decision cycles, and that the side that could close this decision loop most quickly would progressively gain an increasingly superior position. Ultimately, they would attain a firing position from which they could kill the other plane.

The Marines were the first military service to recognize the relevance of Boyd's ideas to ground combat. Marines believe that they should begin their next action before the enemy has had time to react to the previous one. They believe that they need the capability to make quick transitions, and that this capability comes from constant practice.

In product development, we can change direction more quickly when we have a small team of highly skilled people instead of a large team. We can change direction more quickly when we have a product with a streamlined feature set, instead of one that is bloated with minor features. We can change direction more quickly when we have reserve capacity in our resources. It is very difficult to apply an extra burst of effort when people are already working 100 hours per week.

We can also exploit architecture as an enabler of rapid changes. We do this by partitioning our architecture to gracefully absorb change. For example, we might segregate uncertainty into one zone of the design and couple this zone loosely to the rest of the system.

For example, some of Nokia's cellular handsets have colored faceplates. This permits them to change colors very late in the design process. In fact, the color of the phone can even be changed after the phone is in the hands of the customer. They do not permit the uncertainty of color preference to permeate the entire design.

D13: The Principle of Peer-Level Coordination: Tactical coordination should be local.

Maintaining alignment is easy with centralized control. It is much more difficult when we decentralize control and emphasize local initiative.

The Marines solve this problem with peer-to-peer communications. They achieve this with both explicit and implicit lateral communications. The explicit communications are achieved with face-to-face and voice communications. The implicit communications are achieved with doctrine and training. Marines can predict how other Marines will act in similar situations with a surprising degree of accuracy. They can make this prediction because they have common beliefs about the best way to fight, and they have trained extensively with their peers.

This focus on very effective lateral communications is a surprise to people unfamiliar with the military. In fact, academics constantly use the military as the prototypical example of strict hierarchical communications. However, the Marine Corps places much more emphasis on lateral communications since this leads to rapid realignment of adjacent units. Virtually all areas of the military that have to respond quickly to rapidly changing conditions have short peer-to-peer communications links. For example, a flight of fighters does not coordinate their actions by sending requests up the chain of command and waiting for instructions. Instead, they communicate directly with one another.

This maneuver warfare approach is quite different from that of many product development organizations. Such organizations typically try to achieve control by creating detailed plans and project management offices to manage these plans. The continuous peer-to-peer communications of a colocated team is far more effective at responding to uncertainty than a centralized project management organization.

D14: The Principle of Flexible Plans: Use simple modular plans.

Some readers assume that responding to the flow of battle leads to an absence of planning. This is not the case. Everything that can be forecast reasonably well in advance is carefully planned.

For example, Marines do not wait until the battle starts to decide how to communicate. They carefully plan their communication nets, primary and secondary frequencies, the traffic that will flow on each net, and who will be net control and alternate net control. The Marines also carefully plan the sequence in which material is loaded on their amphibious ships so that the correct supplies are unloaded from these ships in the correct sequence.

However, this does not tell the entire story. Since the Marines expect plans to change, they focus on simple, modular, and flexible plans. Simplicity leads to fast adaptation. Modularity solves the problem of adaptation because different modules can be configured many different ways. Flexibility is achieved by preplanning "branches" and "sequels." Branches are points where different paths can be selected depending on existing conditions. Sequels are preplanned follow-on actions. This approach to planning increases the chance that we can maintain alignment when conditions change.

D15: The Principle of Tactical Reserves: Decentralize a portion of reserves.

There is a final method that makes quick realignment possible in maneuver warfare. It is the pre-positioning of reserves at different organizational levels. If response time were not an issue, it would be best to consolidate reserves. This would allow a smaller overall reserve force to meet needs over a large area. Such centralized reserves, under the control of generals, were common in the days of attrition warfare.

In maneuver warfare, reserves are held at every organizational level. This gives every level of the organization enough reserve capacity to deal instantly with a certain range of contingency. For example, assume one of three infantry companies is held back in reserve and then used to supplement the offensive or defensive action of another company. This can double the strength of the supported company at a critical moment.

By holding reserves at each organizational level, ever larger supplementary forces can be brought to bear, albeit with longer delays. This allows us to apply force at the right time and place, instead of making guesses prior to the battle. Depending on the nature of the military operation, from one-third to one-half of the force will be held in reserve.

The product development equivalent of tactical reserves is capacity margin pre-positioned at various levels within the project organizational structure. This approach is fundamentally different from the common approach of having the project manager control a single program-level reserve. This tactical margin can exist in the form of both human resources and budgetary capacity. Likewise, we can provide safety margin in key processes. This permits support groups to absorb variation locally, instead of having to elevate the issue to higher organizational levels.

Computer engineers may recognize this layered approach as being similar to the way we structure memory hierarchies to design fast but cost-effective computer systems. The microprocessor has a small cache memory on the chip which is fast but expensive. The motherboard has much more memory, known as DRAM. DRAM is higher capacity and cheaper than cache memory but slower. The largest and cheapest storage capacity in the system is the disk drive, and it is also the slowest. Data that is used very frequently is kept in cache memory, whereas data that is used very infrequently is stored on the hard drive.

The combined functioning of these three layers of memory produces performance that approaches the speed of the fastest layer at the cost of the cheapest layer. This is the same reason we layer reserves; we can achieve the speed of local reserves with the efficiency of centralized reserves.

D16: The Principle of Early Contact: Make early and meaningful contact with the problem.

Finally, I would like to mention a method that is not strictly a technique of maintaining alignment, but is a key element of the Marine approach to fighting wars. In offensive operations, the Marines believe in making early contact with opposing forces. They do this to reduce uncertainty with regard to the composition and disposition of enemy forces. This early contact goes beyond simple observation or light contact; it includes substantial actions that allow the Marines to more accurately judge the opposition. Contact with the enemy resolves a great deal of uncertainty, and it prevents it from generating.[2]

In product development, our opposing forces are the market and technical risks that must be overcome during the project. To dispose of these risks, projects must do more than assess them. Projects must apply meaningful effort to judge how severe the risks are and whether they can be overcome. There is no substitute for moving to a quick proof-of-concept. There is no substitute for early market feedback. It is critical to focus these early efforts on zones of high technical or market risk.

This focused approach is very different from doing a systematic top-down design of the entire system. Such top-down approaches appear logical, but they rarely resolve risks rapidly enough.

The Technology of Decentralization

At this point, we should discuss four technical factors that help make decentralized control work. First, if we want to decentralize control, we must decentralize information. Second, we need to accelerate decision making if we wish to get the full benefit from decentralized control. Third, if we believe response time is critical, we should measure it. Finally, we should consider using internal and external markets to decentralize control.

D17: The Principle of Decentralized Information: For decentralized decisions, disseminate key information widely.

Decentralizing control requires decentralizing both the authority to make decisions and the information required to make these decisions correctly. In the Marine Corps, the minimum standard is to understand the intentions of commanders two levels higher in the organization.

In contrast, many companies compartmentalize information, insisting that important information be closely held. This approach is dangerous because it undermines the ability of decentralized actors to support

---

[2] Since ground military units move in two dimensions, the uncertainty in their position is proportional to time squared. It is much harder to find an enemy unit if it has been a long time since the last contact.

the overall mission. If the locus of control is decentralized, then decision-making information must be available at the decision-making point.

This does not mean that all information should be collected in isolated local pools. For example, the cost vs. weight decision rule used on the Boeing 777 was calculated at the overall system level. This system-level optimum trade-off rule was then dispersed to the level of the individual engineer, enabling thousands of small decisions to be made quickly and correctly.

D18: The Frequency Response Principle: We can't respond faster than our frequency response.

Electronic circuits cannot respond to signals that exceed their frequency response. To get a control system to respond to rapidly changing signals, we must increase its high-frequency response. The same approach applies to our response to emerging queues. If we adjust quickly, we can reduce the effect of the queue. As we discussed in Principle Q16, queues do more damage if we respond to them slowly.

In product development, we need to accelerate decision-making speed. This is done by involving fewer people and fewer layers of management. We need to avoid overloading the limited bandwidth at high management levels by ensuring the majority of decisions can be made correctly at low levels of the organization.

To enable lower organizational levels to make decisions, we need to give them authority, information, and practice. Without practice and the freedom to fail upon occasion, they will not take control of these decisions. A general principle in control theory is that the speed with which we can respond to a transient ultimately tells us how fast we can respond to any other signal.

D19: The Quality of Service Principle: When response time is important, measure response time.

Although this principle is trivially simple, it is too often violated. If time on the critical path is worth a lot of money and a support group is on the critical path, this support group should be measured on response time, not efficiency.

For example, at a medical device company, the tooling shop was constantly getting on the critical path. The shop manager was measured on efficiency, so he kept his shop heavily utilized and he used no overtime. When his metric was changed to how long tooling was on the critical path of projects, his behavior changed completely.

If response times drive economics, then measurements and incentives for support groups should be aligned to response time. A straightforward way of moving in this direction is to create a quality of service agreement that spells out the response time that users can expect from the department. This can specify mean response time and the portion of jobs that are permitted to exceed an upper bound.

D20: The Second Market Principle: Use internal and external markets to decentralize control.

The final principle of this section is really a forecast of the future. In Principle E14, we commented that pricing allows markets to balance supply and demand more effectively than centralized control. When different service levels are priced differently, the user of the service can make self-serving decisions to buy premium service when this premium service is most valuable. For example, this is done millions of times a day when people choose to pay premiums for express delivery of goods or documents.

Today, most product development organizations only permit pricing to play a role when using external services. There is no additional price for premium service from internal support groups, so all users request premium service. This creates infinite demand for premium service and forces us to allocate this service. To deconflict projects, we elevate the decision to a management level above that of the project. Thus, our lack of pricing mechanisms pushes decisions up to high management levels and adds delays.

Differential pricing is a superb way to solve this problem. It decentralizes control and ensures people make good economic choices. And what happens if all our users are willing to pay for premium service? This is the market telling us we have made the wrong balance between capacity and queue size.

One interesting variant of this is to allow users to buy premium service with a limited number of tokens rather than money. This happened quite by coincidence at one computer company. They allowed each project to have a limited number of coffee cups decorated with the project logo. Their support groups had large queues and it was difficult to get head-of-the-line privileges.

One project manager explained how these limited edition coffee cups were used to buy priority in the queues. He would go to a support group and explain how important the task was to his project. The support group manager would reply, "I understand this task is important, but it is important enough to give me a project coffee cup for expediting it?" Offering a limited number of tokens is like controlling the money supply. The tokens can be exchanged for valuable services.

The Human Side of Decentralization

Finally, we should mention three human dimensions of decentralized control. First, initiative is self-reinforcing. Second, the easiest way to build the cohesive groups that enable decentralized control is to use colocated groups that can engage in face-to-face communications. Third, cohesion will be highest when there is a high level of trust in the organization.

D21: The Principle of Regenerative Initiative: Cultivating initiative enables us to use initiative.

The Marine Corps does not view initiative as one of many virtues that could be present in a leader. They view it as the most critical quality. They are very sensitive to the risk created by stifling initiative. As a result, they consider inaction and lack of decisiveness to be much more dangerous than making a bad decision. An imperfect decision executed rapidly is far better than a perfect decision that is implemented late. They believe that one of the biggest mistakes a leader could make is to stifle initiative.

The more we encourage initiative, the more chance we have to provide positive reinforcement for this initiative. The more chances people have to use initiative, the more they will feel this is not a risky thing to do.

D22: The Principle of Face-to-Face Communication: Exploit the speed and bandwidth of face-to-face communications.

As mentioned in Principle D13, the Marines maintain alignment with lateral communications. They place great emphasis on face-to-face communications rather than elegantly worded messages. They believe that face-to-face communications is the best way to communicate, and the voice communications is the best substitute when this is not possible.

As an engineer, I would observe that both of these methods have much higher bandwidth than textual alternatives like written messages. A picture may be worth 1,000 words, but a spoken word is worth much more than a written word. The Marines also value the real-time nature of face-to-face communication and radio communications. This shortens the feedback loop, which is valuable for all the reasons noted in Chapter 8.

One of the best ways to achieve this fast communication is with colocated teams, discussed in Principle FF19. Colocation can be implemented in varying degrees. Even when we can't colocate the entire team for the full duration of the project, we have many options for partial colocation. Partial colocation occurs when we colocate either part of the team or part of the time.

For example, in Chapter 7, we provided examples of using a regular cadence to make resources like a purchasing agent available in the team work area. This allows us to exploit face-to-face communications without demanding a continuous presence.

Even if we can't colocate team members, we can emphasize phone conversations instead of email. Verbal communications are simply much more effective in generating rapid feedback than email. When we can't colocate the team for the full duration of their activities, we can colocate them at frequent predictable intervals. When we can't colocate certain members, we can communicate with them using phone conversations instead of email.

D23: The Trust Principle: Trust is built through experience.

Decentralized control is based on trust. This trust must be present both hierarchically and laterally. Subordinates must trust their superiors, and superiors must trust their subordinates. Peers must trust their peers and the other groups they rely upon.

What builds trust? We trust someone when we feel we can predict their behavior under difficult conditions. Marines do not move forward into machine-gun fire because they think that this would make their President happy. They do it because they know their buddies would do the same for them. How do they know this? Through experience. The

Marines, and all other elite organizations, maintain continuity in their organizational units. They train them together, and they fight them together.

Psychologists use the term *social expectancy theory* to refer to the ability to predict the behavior of other members of our social group. They point out that we can work effectively with people when we can predict their behavior. We actually do not need others to have similar attitudes and values to ours; we just need to predict how they will act. The Marines have high confidence that they can predict how other members of their unit will behave.

In product development, we have similar opportunities to create trust throughout the organization. Since trust is primarily based on experience, it follows that we can increase trust by maintaining continuity in our teams. Furthermore, as we move to small batch size activities, we expose team members to more cycles of learning. With each cycle of learning, we are better equipped to predict the behavior of other organizational members.

Contrast the development organization that introduces one big product every 5 years, and the one that introduces one product each year five times in a row. Small batch sizes build trust, and trust enables the decentralized control that enables us to work with small batch sizes.

Conclusion

In this chapter, I have stressed how decentralized control permits us to adapt to uncertainty. I have emphasized decentralization because many development organizations are moving in the opposite direction towards centralized control. This is not to suggest that pure decentralization is optimal. Instead, we should recognize that we do not have to make a binary choice between centralization and decentralization. We can design robust systems that combine both methods.

Centralized control works well for problems that are infrequent, large, or those with scale economies. In contrast, decentralization works well for problems and opportunities that are perishable. We examined methods for combining centralized and decentralized control, including layered control and virtual centralization.

Then, we explored what the military has learned over centuries dealing with this problem. I have used the U.S. Marine Corps as a model of an organization that exemplifies a careful balance between centralized and decentralized control. If you think that decentralized control is always associated with lack of discipline, you would be wise to test this assumption.

Finally, I must stress that decentralized control is not simply a philosophy; it is a set of technical skills that can be developed and practiced. It is supported by a set of management choices that enable lateral communications and the creation of cohesive teams.

This book is still missing one chapter. It is the chapter that *you* will be writing, the one on implementation. My goal was to provide you with a solid foundation for challenging the current orthodoxy. I hope I have done this. The path ahead will not be easy, but it should be quite rewarding. Of course, if it were easy, it would only create a temporary advantage. Good luck!

Selected Bibliography

For readers who wish to acquire a deeper understanding of the science underlying this book, I recommend the following references. Most of these books are textbooks and will require slow, methodical reading.

Computer Operating Systems

Silberschatz, Abraham, Peter Baer Galvin, and Greg Gagne. *Operating Systems Concepts*. New York: John Wiley & Sons, 2008.

Tanenbaum, Andrew S. *Modern Operating Systems*. Englewood Cliffs, NJ: Prentice Hall, 2007.

Control Engineering

Nise, Norman S. *Control Systems Engineering*. New York: John Wiley & Sons, 2004.

Ogata, Katsuhiko. *Modern Control Engineering*. Englewood Cliffs, NJ: Prentice-Hall, 2001.

Data Communications Networks

Comer, Douglas E. *Internetworking with TCP/IP Volume I: Principles, Protocols and Architectures*. Upper Saddle River, NJ: Prentice Hall, 2005.

Kurose, James F., and Keith W. Ross. *Computer Networking: A Top-Down Approach*. Boston: Addison-Wesley Publishing Co., 2008.

Peterson, Larry L., and Bruce S. Davie. *Computer Networks: A Systems Approach*. New York: Elsevier, 2007.

Finance and Economics

Luenberger, David G. *Investment Science*. New York: Oxford University Press, 1998.

Information Theory

Pierce, John R. *An Introduction to Information Theory: Symbols, Signals & Noise.* New York: Dover, 1980.

Shannon, Claude E., and Warren Weaver. *The Mathematical Theory of Communications.* University of Illinois Press, 1963.

Maneuver Warfare

Coram, Robert. *Boyd: The Fighter Pilot Who Changed the Art of War.* New York: Little Brown & Co., 2002.

Isely, Jeter A., and Philip A. Crowl. *The U.S. Marines and Amphibious War: Its Theory and Its Practice in the Pacific.* Princeton: Princeton University Press, 1951.

Lind, William S. *Maneuver Warfare Handbook.* Boulder: Westview Press, 1985.

Marine Corps Doctrinal Publication 1, *Warfighting.* Secretary of the Navy, 1996.

Marine Corps Doctrinal Publication 1–3, *Tactics.* Secretary of the Navy, 1997.

Marine Corps Doctrinal Publication 6, *Command and Control.* Secretary of the Navy, 1997.

Manufacturing

Hopp, Wallace J., and Mark L. Spearman. *Factory Physics.* New York: Irwin/McGraw-Hill, 2007.

Monden, Yasuhiro. *Toyota Production System: An Integrated Approach to Just-in-Time.* Engineering & Management Press, 1998.

Ohno, Taiichi. *The Toyota Production System: Beyond Large-Scale Production.* Cambridge, MA: Productivity Press, 1988.

Shingo, Shigeo. *A Study of the Toyota Production System.* Cambridge, MA: Productivity Press, 1989.

Operations Research

Conway, Richard W., William L. Maxwell, and Louis W. Miller. *Theory of Scheduling.* Mineola, NY: Dover, 1967.

Hillier, Frederick S., and Gerald J. Lieberman. *Introduction to Operations Research.* New York: McGraw-Hill, 2007.

Taha, Hamdy A. *Operations Research: An Introduction.* New York: Macmillan Publishing Co., 2006.

Probability and Statistics

Allen, Arnold O. *Probability, Statistics and Queueing Theory: With Computer Science Applications.* New York: Academic Press, 1978.

Feller, William. *An Introduction to Probability Theory and Its Applications: Volume I.* New York: John Wiley & Sons, 1968.

Hogg, Robert V., and Elliot A. Tanis. *Probability and Statistical Inference.* New York: Macmillan Publishing Co., 1983.

Larsen, Richard J., and Morris L. Marx. *An Introduction to Mathematical Statistics and Its Applications.* Upper Saddle River, NJ: Prentice Hall, 2005.

Pfeiffer, Paul E. *Concepts of Probability Theory.* New York: Dover, 1978.

Ross, Sheldon M. *Introduction to Probability Models.* New York: Elsevier, 2007.

Trivedi, Kishor S. *Probability & Statistics with Reliability, Queuing, and Computer Science Applications.* New Dehli: Prentice-Hall of India, 2001.

Walpole, Ronald E., Raymond H. Myers, Sharon L. Myers, and Keying Ye. *Probability & Statistics for Engineers and Scientists.* Upper Saddle River, NJ: Prentice Hall, 2002.

Queueing Theory

Gross, Donald, John F. Shortle, James M. Thompson, and Carl M. Harris. *Fundamentals of Queueing Theory.* New York: John Wiley & Sons, 2008.

Hall, Randolph W. *Queueing Methods for Services and Manufacturing.* Englewood Cliffs, NJ: Prentice Hall, 1991.

Kleinrock, Leonard. *Queueing Systems Volume I: Theory.* New York: John Wiley & Sons, 1975.

Kleinrock, Leonard. *Queueing Systems Volume II: Computer Applications.* New York: John Wiley & Sons, 1976.

Morse, Philip M. *Queues, Inventories, and Maintenance: The Analysis of Operational Systems with Variable Demand and Supply.* New York: John Wiley & Sons, 1958.

Saaty, Thomas L. *Elements of Queueing Theory with Applications.* New York: Dover, 1983.

The Principles of Flow

Variability Principles

Batch Size Principles

WIP Constraint Principles

Decentralization Principles

Index

277

and local WIP constraints, 148–150
predictable and permanent, 147–148
process before, 208
and TOC, 17
variability before, 208
WIP constraints and, 147–150, 226
Boundaries, Principle of, 253–254
Boyd, Colonel John, 255–256
Buffer Principle, 101–102
buffers, time, 101-102, *102f*
Buying Information, Principle of, 47–48

Cadence Batch Size Enabling Principle,
    179–180
Cadence Capacity Margin Principle,
    178–179
cadence, examples
    bus system, 178–179
    coffee breaks, 185–186
    design reviews, 184–185
    meetings, 180–181
    portfolio screening, 182–183
    product introduction, 182
    program status, 183
    project meetings, 184
    prototype part production, 185
    prototyping, 182
    resource access, 183–184
    supplier visits, 185
    testing, 182
cadence, management
    See also synchronization
    about, 18, 176
    effect on batch size, 180
    effect on waiting time, 179
    metrics for, 239
    need for capacity margin, 178–179
    nesting of, 190–191
    synchronous vs. asynchronous
        process, 179
    underutilization of, 10–11
    and variance accumulation, 177–178
Cadence Reliability Principle, 179
Cadenced Meetings, Principle of,
    180–181
CAD, queues in, 81
capacity utilization
    and batch size, 126

vs. batch size reduction, 133–134
effect on performance measures,
    59–61, *60f*
effect on queues, 59–62, *59f*
effect on variability, 62–64, *65f*
metrics for, 239–240
and optimum queue size, 68–69,
    69f
and WIP constraints, 145–146,
    146f, 147f
causality, 117, 231–232, 234–235
centralized control
    about, 14
    and alignment, 257–258
    balanced with decentralization, 246
    and opportunism, 249–250
    and problem scale, 247–248
    and response time, 246–247
    virtual centralization, 250–251
CFD. *See* cumulative flow diagram
change, implementing, 25–26
COD. *See* cost of delay (COD)
coefficient of variation
    and granularity, 11
    and late binding, *203n*
    and queue length, 62–64, *63f*
    and signal to noise ratio, 224
    and small experiments, 98–99
    and variability pooling, 95–96, *97f*
cognitive dissonance, 118
Colocation Principle, 230–231
Commander's Intent, 253
communication
    face-to-face, 263–264
    fast feedback and, 230–231
    peer-to-peer, 257–258
    planning, 258
computer operating systems
    as idea source, 23
    and priority queueing, 159–160,
        248–249
    and round-robin scheduling,
        196–197
    and timing out jobs, 164
conformance
    vs. dynamic goals, 218–219
    vs. opportunism, 249–250
    worship of, 8–9

congestion
about, 170–172
collapse, 172–174, *173f*
making it visible, 175–176
on highways, 170–172, *171f*
on Internet, 172–173, *173f*
vs. peak throughput, 174–175
and queueing, 175
routing around, 201–202
Congestion Collapse, Principle of,
172–174
Congestion Pricing, Principle of, 176
Continuous Economic Trade-offs,
Principle of, 37–38
control
See also centralized control;
decentralized control; flow control
choosing control parameters, 215
of decision timing, 44
of early actions, 40
economic view of, 213–219
by using decision rules, 41–42, *41f*
by using market forces, 42–44,
262–263
variables, 214–216
control engineering as idea source 23
Controlled Excursions, Principle of, 229
control loops and fast feedback,
228–229
control system design
about, 222
fast feedback and, 212
cost of delay (COD)
and control set points, 216–217, *217f*
and differential service, 161–162
and early harvesting, 40
and optimum queue size, 68–69, *69f*
quantifying, 31–32
and queueing discipline, 69–71
and queues, 34, 70, *239f*
and scheduling, 192–195
and time buffers, 101–102
and WIP constraints, 146, *147f*
covariance. *See* negative covariance
Critical Chain , 14, 195
critical fractile, 50
Critical Queue, Principle of, 164–165
Cross-Functional Synchronization,

Principle of, 188–189
cross-training
at adjacent processes, 156
in Navy, 250
of software programmers, 156
at Toyota, 150
cumulative flow diagram (CFD)
about, 71-72
to monitor batch size, 112, *113f*
to monitor queues, 76, *76f*
showing slow intervention, 79, *80f*
with synchronized batches, 189–190,
191f
with unsynchronized batches,
189–190, *190f*
Cumulative Flow Principle, 71–72
Cumulative Reduction Principle,
165–166
customers as judge of value-added, 32
cycle time
authority limits for buying, 40, *41f*
and batch size, 9–10, 112
economic value of, 31–32
effect of WIP constraints on,
145–146, *146f, 147f*
in Little's Formula, 73–75, *73f*
management vs. queue management,
145–147, *145f*
and queues, 56
queue size vs., 76
in traditional factory, 37

decentralized control
about, 21
balanced with centralized, 246,
248–249
and bandwidth, 261
with decentralized information,
260–261
with decision rules, 41–42, 225
and efficiency, 251
human side of, 263–265
and initiative, 263
and layered control, 248–249
with local priorities, 196
with markets, 43–44, 262–263.
and misalignment, 251
and mission, 252–253

Going Further

Companion Web Site

This book has a companion Web site to provide updates, user tips, case histories, and supplementary materials. You can find it at:

www.LPD2.com

The Planned Second Edition

The compelling logic of small batch size does not just apply to product development; it also applies to books. Valuable new ideas can be delivered in one large batch when they have fully matured, or they can be communicated in smaller batches when they have progressed far enough to be useful. This book uses the small batch size approach.

This means that the principles in this book are still evolving quite rapidly. This book only documents a stage in their evolution. Skillful practitioners will continue to advance these ideas in clever and useful ways. I hope some of you will be willing to share your insights and experiences so that they can be incorporated in a second edition of this book. To this end, I welcome hearing about your experiences and answering your questions at:

Donald Reinertsen
Reinertsen & Associates
600 Via Monte Doro
Redondo Beach, CA 90277
+1-310-373-5332
Email: don@ReinertsenAssociates.com

About the Author

For 30 years, Don Reinertsen has been a thought leader in the field of product development. In 1983, while a consultant at McKinsey & Co., he wrote the landmark article in *Electronic Business* magazine that first quantified the financial value of development speed. This article is believed by some observers to have triggered the movement to shorten development cycles in American industry. It is frequently cited as the McKinsey study that reported "six months' delay can be worth 33 percent of life cycle profits."

In 1985, he coined the term *Fuzzy Front End* to describe the earliest stage of product development. In 1991, he wrote the first article showing how queueing theory could be practically applied to product development.

His 1991 book, *Developing Products in Half the Time,* coauthored with Preston Smith, has become a product development classic. It has been translated into seven languages. His 1997 book, *Managing the Design Factory,* was the first book to describe how the principles of Just-in-Time manufacturing could be applied to product development. In the 12 years since this book appeared, this approach has become known as lean product development.

For 15 years, Don taught executive courses at California Institute of Technology, and he currently teaches public seminars throughout the world. He has a B.S. in electrical engineering from Cornell, and an M.B.A. with distinction from Harvard Business School.

His company, Reinertsen & Associates, has helped leading companies throughout the world improve their product development processes for over 20 years.